Gram Panchayat Leadership

Gram Panchayat Leadership

The Grassroots Realities of Select Districts of Madhya Pradesh

Nalini Rewadikar

Rawat Publications

Jaipur • New Delhi • Bangalore • Hyderabad • Guwahati

ISBN 81-316-0356-3

The publication of this book was financially supported by ICSSR and the responsibility for the facts stated, opinions expressed, or conclusions reached, are entirely that of the author. ICSSR accepts no responsibility for them.

ICSSR Consultant: Professor S.N. Mishra, IIPA, New Delhi.

Published by
Prem Rawat for **Rawat Publications**
Satyam Apts, Sector 3, Jawahar Nagar, Jaipur 302 004 (India)
Phone: 0141 265 1748 / 7006 Fax: 0141 265 1748
E-mail: info@rawatbooks.com
Website: www.rawatbooks.com

New Delhi Office
4858/24, Ansari Road, Daryaganj, New Delhi 110 002
Phone: 011 2326 3290

Also at *Bangalore, Hyderabad* and *Guwahati*

Typeset by Rawat Computers, Jaipur
Printed at Nice Printing Press, New Delhi

Contents

Preface

Village was the basic unit of administration since ancient times. References are found in ancient scriptures and later literature about villages, their clusters and officials. Village headman and village council of elders were the prominent institutions performing executive and specially judicial functions in villages. Village communities were also in charge of the defence of villages and for the protection of life and property, for carrying out public utility works, for arranging village festivals etc. Tax collection in cash and kind and managing the village funds were the two important activities discharged within villages.

Thus, villages worked as active units for centuries with well established administrative structures. However, with the change in social, economic and political circumstances the corresponding alterations were not effected resulting in the stagnation of villages life.

Indian National Congress under the leadership of Mahatma Gandhi promised a vibrant system of village self-government after independence. Heated debates over the issue in Constituent

Assembly could just incorporate Panchayat Raj system under the Directive Principles of State Policy to be actualized by the states. Activization of villages through community development programmes failed to evoke either people's initiative or rural upliftment at the grassroots. Review committees to enquire into the state of affairs in countryside ultimately culminated in the 73rd Constitutional Amendment Act, 1993.

Decentralization of powers at the third stratum of government was effected on the keynote of power to the people and development by the people. Reservation for the weaker sections of people and women so far the excluded ones, within the mainstream of political power structure is a unique feature of the Act. Economic development and social justice are the declared objectives. To a large extent all this depends on the leaders who have to play the role of skilful community opinion makers and also of dynamic implementors.

Accordingly the Madhya Pradesh Panchayat Raj and Gram Swaraj Act, 1994 devolved certain specific powers and responsibilities to Panchayat Raj Institutions along with some funds to operationalize the system. Gram Panchayat being the basic unit of self-governance in the system, this study is undertaken to understand the role played by the emerging Gram Panchayat leadership in the fulfilment of the declared objectives of the 73rd Constitutional Amendment Act, 1993.

Three districts of Jhabua, Ujjain and Indore of Malwa plateau situated in western Madhya Pradesh are specifically selected as each of these districts has a distinct socio-cultural background. Jhabua has the largest Scheduled Tribe population, Ujjain has the largest Scheduled Caste population and Indore has the largest General category population in Madhya Pradesh.

Leadership in the universe of this study is basically assessed on the bases of SES characteristics of the Panchayat Raj Representatives, their awareness of the structure and of the powers and responsibilities devolved, and their performance in the actualization of self-governance with peoples participation.

Two major groups using the powers and discharging the responsibilities devolved at the grassroots are the elected Panchayat Raj representatives and the members of Gram Sabha. In Madhya Pradesh Gram Sabha has been declared as the supreme repository of all the powers devolved. Awareness of the members of Gram Sabha, their constant vigilance and active participation in decision-making for the community welfare are the most significant indices in keeping democratic development on track. Hence, two interview schedules were structured separately for interviewing the two groups. A few specific questions for women were added to the schedule for Panchayat Raj Representatives to assess their position as leaders vis-à-vis the male Panchayat Raj Representatives and the community at large.

I would like to express my gratitude to Professor R.S. Gautam, the president of Madhya Pradesh Institute of Social Science Research (MPISSR), Ujjain for his encouragement since the formulation of the project till its completion. I am grateful to Dr B.R. Purohit, Professor Emeritus, MPISSR for his skilful guidance. He has taken pains to go through the entire text enriching it with his valuable suggestions. I accord special thanks to Dr Y.G. Joshi of Babasaheb Ambedkar National Institute of Social Science for his very valuable assistance in structuring the interview schedules. I express my immense gratitude to Dr D.C. Sah, Director, MPISSR, without whose insistent persuasion it would not have been possible to finalize the work.

I acknowledge with thanks the Indian Council of Social Science Research, New Delhi for the financial support to the Project and its publication.

I thank all the Research Associates, for their painstaking and exhaustive field investigations along with all other assistance with computer and library work.

I am thankful to the Administrative Officer of MPISSR Mr L.P. Gautam and all the faculty members of the Institute, Dr Sandeep Joshi, Dr Yatindra Singh Sisodia, Dr Ashish Bhatt, Dr

Sunil Singh Chandel and Dr Manu Gautam, for their unfailing assistance in various ways. Mr Sudeep Mishra deserves special mention for the artistic get up of the work. Office assistants of MPISSR, Ujjain also deserve my thanks.

I am thankful to all the tehsil and district officials of Jhabua, Ujjain and Indore for providing the requisite information and to all my friends at different centres of the field, who saw to it that the survey and my stay in the field was comfortable. My thanks are due to all the 465 respondents who spared time from their busy schedule to answer queries of the field investigators.

Last but not the least, my thanks are due to my brother-in-law Mr V.B. Tilwankar, for procuring rare primary source material to help the investigation.

Nalini Rewadikar

1

Introduction

The Indian Scene

India, a traditional agricultural society with stratification based on class, caste, religion, region, sex, poverty, lack of opportunities and many other impedements, needed a drastic change for a vibrant nation to be built on the foundations of democratic principles. Initially, it was tried from above with a constitution ensuring adult franchise and fundamental rights to all its citizens. Widespread programmes of poverty alleviation and rural upliftment were undertaken by central and state governments enthusiastically but the exercise yielded minimum results; mixed economy with state planning plus free market did not yield the expected economic growth.

The vast geographical expanse of India, its population crossing one billion mark with multiple socio-cultural spectrum constituting the richness of Indian culture and heritage, needed an infrastructure to keep these varied identities secured, make them a part of the development process and ensure social equity. This could be achieved only if they were given an effective voice in deciding matters that concerned them. Hence, a multi-level third stratum of Panchayat Raj Institutions (PRIs) for grassroots participation was thought to be in tune with Indian society. Villages, which were looked down with disdain in the initial stages of framing the Constitution came to the centre stage again.[1] A further decentralization at the third stratum constitutionally ordained, was thus the measure to facilitate the socio-political economic process to trickle down to the grassroots through multiple centres of governance.

In India village was the pivot of administration since ancient times. References are found in ancient scriptures and later literature about villages, their clusters and officials. Village headman and village council of elders were the prominent institutions performing executive and specially judicial functions. Village communities were also responsible for the security of villages and for protection of life and property, for carrying out public utility works, for arranging village festivals etc. Tax collection in cash and kind and managing village funds were the two important activities undertaken within villages. Basically, through an informal practice of dispute resolution firmly rooted in village ethos, villages worked as active units of self-government within their own administrative structures. Largely this prevented disputes from disturbing village amity and unity. These were not the local planning or local development units; however, they managed their communities in their own way. Their remoteness from legal epicentres of power enabled them to enjoy a substantial degree of autonomy as well. With the change in social, economic and political circumstances the corresponding alterations were not incorporated in those informal structures resulting in the stagnation of village life.

Indian National Congress under the leadership of Mahatma Gandhi promised a vibrant system of village self-government after independence. Heated debates over the issue in Constituent Assembly could only incorporate Panchayat Raj system under the Directive Principles of State Policy. Some arrangements of local self-governance in the form of Municipal Corporations, Improvement Trusts, District Boards and Village Panchayats etc., were already there in force. Administration of these bodies was assigned to the states. Accordingly states established a network of Village Panchayats, but the pattern of their organization and jurisdiction varied from state to state. On the slightest pretext these local bodies were kept in abeyance and their strings handed over to bureaucratic control.

The Planning Commission also felt the need to introduce a scheme of Community Development Project and National Extension Service for rural upliftment, in fulfilment of the principal object of the Directive Principles of State Policy. The Review Committees starting with Balwant Rai Mehta Committee (1957), Ashok Mehta Committee (1977), G.V.K. Rao Committee (1985), L.M. Singhvi's Concept Paper (1986), Thungan Committee (1988) tried to assess the shortcomings of the various efforts to develop villages as units of self-government. V.T. Krishnamachari, who was Deputy Chairman of Planning Commission for a long time, realized in the early fifties that "the villagers should feel that it is only by their efforts that they can get all that is needed .... We should give up the idea that we are here to force our programmes and plans on the villagers. It is for the villagers to tell us what they want and for us to assist them".[2] Nurturing rural leadership was considered essential for this process.

In the course of various persistent efforts to uplift villages and extend the benefits of development to rural people, the 73rd Constitutional Amendment Act came into force in April 1993. An effort was, thus, undertaken to drive development not through representative but through participatory democracy.[3] The Act provided a constitutional power base to the then existing formal structures of PRIs. States were directed to enact Conformity Acts and devolve authority to the PRIs on the twenty nine subjects from State List as per the Eleventh Schedule appended to the Constitution.

A three-tier set-up of Panchayati Raj, legal status to Gram Sabha, reservation of seats for SCs/STs and women, State Election and Finance Commissions and most importantly, regular elections constitute the salient features of the 73rd Constitutional Amendment Act. The entire scheme being mandatory, states have limited choice either for variations or for dissolving the institutions at their whim and will, as was the practice earlier.[4]

Thus, power to the people and development by the people is the keynote of the new system. It is a constitutional statement of decentralization, political and economic decision-making and their implementation by the people, thus building up self-governing institutions at the grassroots. To a large extent this depends on leaders who have to play the role of efficient community opinion makers and also of dynamic implementers.

Theoretical Concepts

Democracy and Development

In the larger context, the world witnessed conflicting ideologies of centralized and monolithic types of governance, where state was an end and individuals its means. Opposed to such totalitarian systems stands democratic and decentralized governance where individual's dignity, his freedom, his free and full development along with equal opportunities of moral and material development are assured. After experimenting with various types of polities like monarchy, aristocracy and dictatorship, mankind has learnt the great lesson that it is only the democratic governance which is conducive to individual's free and full development. Great efforts have been made at political and civil society levels to strengthen egalitarian and participatory democracy. A broader view of development also insists on its sustainability which depends to a great extent on the benefits of development extended to all, "including even those who suffer, the sick, the wretched, the exploited ... those that had never truly lived".[5] Mahatma Gandhi with his deep insight into the Indian way of life visualized long back in 1925, "True democracy cannot be worked by twenty men sitting at the centre but it has to be worked from below by the people of every village ... . Real Swaraj will come not by the acquisition of authority by a few but by the acquisition of the capacity by all to resist the authority when it is abused. Swaraj is to be obtained by educating the masses to a sense of their capacity to regulate and control authority."[6] He was of the view that to develop India is to develop its villages, and developing a village is to make it self-sustaining and capable of managing its affairs. This calls for dynamic leadership at rural level.

Strengthening institutions of local self-government is thus considered significant for democratic values. Representative institutions and a set of rules and procedures constitute the structural part of democracy, but the "liberal" aspects of equality, freedom, tolerance, accountability; responsiveness, transparency, etc., stand neglected.[7] As such political equality gets restricted due to many being denied truly equal opportunities to influence decisions that affect their lives. Substantive democracy, it is held, should be directed to a search for freedom, dignity and sustainable living standards for masses, and essence of development democracy and change should be seen in those unfolding strivings.[8]

The concept of Swaraj as enunciated by Mahatma Gandhi has a reference to an ideal model of democratic governance. Conceded that no one model of democracy can lay claim to superiority or infallibility, certain common characteristic features of democratic societies have been ascertained by thinkers as well as activists for democratic governance. These are enumerated as equality and non-discrimination, freedom of choice, adherence to rule of law, tolerance of differences and no excluvism. The values and virtues of democracy, development and social inclusion to be widely spread need an additional concept of "good governance". The Secretary General of United Nations, Kofi Annan considers good governance as the single most important factor in eradicating poverty and promoting development. As early as 1944 M.N. Roy pleaded that democracy to be effective, power must always remain vested in the people even in day-to-day affairs, for this people need to remember precisely their "critical faculty" so that they can develop their capacity to "regulate and control authority".[9] The key concept may be described as democratizing development through empowerment of the people at the grassroots level. Thus development has to be a bottom-up process and basically participatory, equitable and all-inclusive.

Decentralization

Decentralization is considered as the major tool in the process of bringing government closer to the people and make them participate in decision-making about programmes and activities that concern them. Laski talked of advantages of democracy only when local problems are locally solved.[10] This alone can give people a feeling of freedom. Hence, Mahatma Gandhi kept on insisting that self-sufficient villages alone could ensure democracy and development in India. This needed a constitutional power base. Decentralization is the key concept for this support base for sharing the decision-making power with the lower levels of governance. Thus, democracy as a widely accepted mode of modern governance needs decentralization for its actualization.[11]

Howard Zinn, Professor of History and political activist points to the crisis of democracy in United States as due to "centralization of power, defying public opinion". However, he views the possibility of a progressive change "with the creation of strong infrastructure of democracy at the grassroots, without which even national democracy cannot survive".[12] Democracy with decentralization is supposed to provide "greater transparency, accountability, responsiveness, efficiency, equity and opportunities of mass participation".[13] Participation, thus, has a wider perspective to include administrative, socio-economic, political and structural ramifications. Since the grassroots unit of governance has to play an equally significant role in the participation process along with the national unit, the concept of decentralization assumes a prominent place as it involves a wider society in the use of community power.

Leadership

Leadership is a central concept related to the theoretical as also the practical forces that set institutions in motion. Many a sound constitutional power structure has been nullified in the absence of sound leadership.[14] It is leadership that transforms the visualized theoretical perspective into real achievements. The success of democracy and development depends on the quality of leadership and the style of their functioning. Decentralization being the major tool in promoting participatory development process, leadership at grassroots level acquires added significance not only politically but also for socio-economic upliftment and equity. Leaders are consequential for the functions they perform a propos of their position in the power structure. Leaders are thus expected to mobilize, direct, guide and control their groups, i.e., their local communities. In this role leaders are expected to have the capability to encourage their community for voluntarily cooperating in the venture of identified common goals. Leadership in this sense refers to specific qualities of leaders and their performance in development.[15]

Democratizing development, being accepted as *sine qua non* of sustainability, equity, human dignity, social justice, peace and people's participation, it dominates all development studies. Leadership as a driving force of development in concrete situations, relates to the influence one has in community decision-making and in extracting people's voluntary cooperation in implementing those decisions.

For this leadership is expected to be intelligent, vibrant, responsive, convincing and likable. David Camron, the young

British leader, gave a bold call for a change to the conservative party for such a dynamic leadership "change the way we look, the way we feel, the way we think, and the way we behave". No doubt, society begets a leader in its image, but a dynamic leader can transform a society he intends to lead.[16] Leaders may follow varied methods of mustering people's cooperation, but one thing is certain that the attitude of domination or headship does not yield the required result. Hence, in their activity of organizing people's participation, leaders have to assume the roles of key communicators, catalyst, and development agents for constructive change. Voluntary cooperation flows spontaneously as a result of such a role. Lippman holds that the final test of a leader is that he leaves behind him in other men the conviction and the will to carry on.

For achieving development goals people also have to be taught to help themselves and at the same time hold them accountable for the results of the use of power and responsibilities devolved on them. In rural context it is the Herculean task of awakening the docile rural masses which the leadership has to perform.

As the 73rd Constitutional Amendment Act 1993 intends sowing democratic seeds at the grassroots, Gram Panchayat leadership has a key role in attaining the objectives on ground realities by directing it to specific development goals of need based planning, local resource mobilization and striving for local peace and social justice. Thus, the practice of democracy in its significant dimensions of government 'by' the people and government 'for' the people, in this context, rests on local leadership to mobilize local people for the identified goals of development. Hence, Panchayat leadership has attracted the due attention of academicians as also politicians since long. Constitutional status bestowed on PRIs has laid added stress on grassroots leadership emerging at Gram Panchayat level.[17]

Madhya Pradesh Scenario

Madhya Pradesh geographically located in the middle of India and surrounded by five different states of diverse socio-cultural shades, reflects the diversity of Indian society to a great extent. It also faces the problems arising out of these diversities, similar to those that the Indian polity is coping with. Malwa plateau of Madhya Pradesh locates the categorywise areas that represent the reservation provisions of the 73rd Constitutional Amendment Act, 1993. The three districts of the plateau, viz., Jhabua, Ujjain and Indore represent the ST, SC and General category respectively, and give glimpses of the diversities and inadequacies in social, economic, political, cultural, educational and infrastructural domains.

Madhya Pradesh was the first state to formulate Conformity Act in accordance with the 73rd Constitutional Amendment Act, 1993. It provided for a three tier system, viz., Gram Panchayats in villages, Janpad Panchayats in blocks and District Panchayats in districts. Their tenure was fixed for five years unless earlier dissolved.

A State Election Commission was provided for the conduct of elections and a State Finance Commission for the distribution of funds to the Panchayats at all levels. Gram Panchayats are to be constituted of elected panch from wards with an elected Sarpanch as its head. Gram Sabha of all the adults of Panchayat jurisdiction is provided for as an apex body. Reservation of seats for SCs/STs according to their proportion in the total population of the Village/Janpad/District constitute the salient features of the Act. Reservation for Other Backward Classes is also included when SC/ST reservation amounts to just 50 per cent or less of the total seats of a Gram Panchayat. Thirty-three per cent reservations for women in each category, provisions for no confidence motion and recall of Panchayat post holders constitute the other special features of the Act. Panchayats are endowed with powers to administer the subjects transferred from the State List. They can collect funds of various types, besides the State Government grant and Central Government grants for the sponsored schemes. They can also impose taxes within their jurisdiction.[18]

Accordingly, the first Panchayat election was conducted in May–June 1994. Constitutional Panchayats started their second term with the election of January–February 2000. With this, more educated, more aware and more dynamic second generation leaders were expected to emerge on the scene. However, experience of Panchayat Raj in Madhya Pradesh indicates that the State Act has been amended from time to time to make it more effective in establishing Panchayat Raj system as genuine structure of grassroots democracy, the level of participation of people at grassroots is very low and Gram Sabha is almost a formal institution with no role in various assigned works related to rural development. This situation thus facilitated a solid ground for the introduction of Gram Swaraj in Madhya Pradesh from 26 January 2001. The state government transferred nearly all the powers to Gram Sabha which were earlier assigned to Gram Panchayat. It has thus, gone from representative democracy to direct democracy at the grassroots.[19] Empowerment of Gram Sabha calls for a more dynamic grassroots leadership for the success of direct democracy.

The socio-cultural structure of a community extensively affects its thought-process and social behaviour. People are set to think and act within those parameters and assume their social roles accordingly. It is very difficult to break these and come out of the structural set-up they are used to, for many a generation. Political behaviour too, is largely a result of their socio-cultural milieu. Constitutional and legal efforts to provide something different in the name of democracy, development, social justice or anything else have a limited appeal and the expected transformation is a very slow process. Leadership roles also emerge from the socio-cultural environment and the ethos of a community. Differences in these bring forth differences in various types of leaders as well. Besides, the capability of each community to reap the fruits of educational and economic benefits extended by the state also differs, resulting in differences of economic and educational levels to understand and assume the roles of power and responsibilities for self-governance.

Grassroots Realities

Dynamics of grassroots leadership in the power structure and of ground realities, however, pose multiple challenges that need to be discerned so as to enable them to assume the role of navigators of the vast experiment of Panchayat Raj.

The state legislations have made provisions for the reservation of the marginalized social groups and women. The emergent Scheduled Caste leadership is confronted with greater discrimination and receives much less cooperation from the administration and other groups. Acute poverty, illiteracy and predominant position of the traditional rural elite have further incapacitated them in discharging their duties effectively. Tribal participation in the Panchayat Raj system also points out that much needs to be done to equip them for facing the challenges of the new task. The remaining rural leadership of the General category is also encumbered with problems due to traditional rural leaders, mainly landlords and moneylenders, who consider the Constitutional Amendment Act, 1993 as a challenge to their power positions in villages. Position of women of all strata is much pitiable due to socio-cultural, economic, educational and rural milieu. Patriarchal society is also an obstacle in their attempt to assume leadership role. Many reasons can be pointed out for this situation: illiteracy, poverty, lack of awareness, socio-cultural deprivations, lack of experience and training, etc.

A careful review of decentralization of power in India reveals that after a period of more than a decade one cannot say that Panchayats have become institutions of self-governance. Devolution of power has been half-hearted. An important aspect of devolution package was to empower the Gram Sabha so that it may act as a vibrant institution to provide the elements of transparency, responsiveness and accountability which were hitherto missing. Gram Sabha, the basic institution where leadership was supposed to emerge is most ineffective. Gram Sabha meetings are a formality in majority of cases. Scheduled Tribes/Scheduled Castes participation is minimal, women folk are usually absent. Meetings are attended only when beneficiaries are to be identified. Vested interests of different groups create hindrances in the way. Bureaucracy believes in maintaining the status quo. Majority of Panchayats depend on funding from the state and avoid generating their own funds by levying local taxes. At grassroots level, there is clear lack of understanding of the new system among the masses. Decentralized planning is an issue yet to be understood. Social audit is not a familiar term for grassroots people. In a nutshell, the problems are basically associated with lack of understanding and awareness and socio-cultural economic milieu of those who are expected to play the role of an active leadership in the entire process.[20]

The Study Plan

Since, leadership is the central concept interrelated to the issue of democracy at all levels, the study is planned to comprehend this key notion in its operative dimensions. Development in democracy has to be participatory, hence, the ground level of people's participation is considered to be the grassroots level of governance, i.e., the Gram Panchayat level. The 73rd Constitutional Amendment Act, 1993 dug deep to reach this grassroots level and structured it as the basic operative unit of self-governance, a vision long nurtured by Mahatma Gandhi. With the acquisition of the constitutional base, Gram Panchayat leadership assumed a key role in the implementation of the Panchayat Raj system for the specific goal of decentralized governance through need based planning, material and human resource mobilization and striving for social justice with the object of development and peace. Since it is the local leadership which is supposed to mobilize local people for the powers and responsibilities devolved, an analysis of their operative behaviour is of immense practical import. Reservation component of the Act being its special feature, it was necessary to investigate it in a broader perspective.

The study is therefore planned to assess the various types of leadership in accordance with the constitutional provisions of reservation. This would help in highlighting the variety of leadership roles and the impact of such leadership on overall development of the stratified society that they represent.

A considerable number of studies have centred round social and political leaderships in world communities. Initially these were basically an enumeration of ideal qualities that leaders should possess. It was a field mainly for sociologists and psychologists. The advent of democratic governments brought the study of leadership in political domain as well.[21] Immediately after Indian independence, researchers were attracted towards leadership studies with reference to the Members of Parliament and Legislative Assemblies. Since Panchayat Raj system also existed in various forms in different states in response to Article 40 of the Indian Constitution, Panchayat leadership also attracted the attention of many scholars. These studies were about overall Panchayat leadership, area specific or Panchayat specific. The institution of Panchayat Raj in its rejuvenated form after the 73rd Constitutional Amendment Act, 1993 brought the issue of Panchayat leadership to the forefront. As a result, a number of studies about roles and patterns of Panchayat leadership came up. These also related to specific states. Studies have been made on Scheduled Tribes, Scheduled Castes, General and Women categories of leadership independently.[22] Comparative studies relating to various categories of local leadership are still very few. The present study is intended to assessing and comparing the various categories of leadership as per the reservation provisions of the Act.

Malwa plateau of Madhya Pradesh has numerical predominance of ST, SC and General category of rural majority districts. It was therefore, felt that the region should provide a compact field of research to investigate the leadership roles of all the three categories. This would help in understanding the types of emerging local leadership, the various challenges they face, the manifold efforts needed to overcome these at personal, administrative and policy levels for the success of the Panchayat Raj experiment.

Objectives

Against this backdrop the objectives of the study are:

- to investigate the various types of Panchayat leadership based on class, caste, sex, education, etc.;
- to investigate the SES characteristics of various categories of leaders and correlate them with their leadership roles;
- to investigate their awareness about the Constitutional Panchayat Raj system of 1993;
- to investigate their development perceptions;
- to investigate their capabilities of ushering in changes in rural scenario;
- to investigate their ability to mobilize rural masses to participate in the activity of self-governance; and
- to investigate the various challenges they face in the task of rural development and to find out pathways to overcome them.

Issues

1. One of the major suppositions is that the quality of emerging leadership would be different in character in tribal dominant, Scheduled Caste dominant and General category districts, hence the purposive selection of the universe of study, viz., Jhabua (ST), Ujjain (SC) and Indore (General) districts of Madhya Pradesh.

2. Economic affluence/deprivation is one of the major determinants of an effective/ineffective leadership role.
3. Illiteracy and lack of awareness are the major hurdles in the assumption of skilful leadership roles.
4. Variables like region, religion and party affiliations do not determine building up of leadership roles at the grassroots.
5. Sex variable brings forth differences in the working of Panchayat in being headed by either a male or a female leader. Female leaders with rare exceptions are proxy representatives.

Methodology

The present study is specifically designed as comparative; a comparison of various categories of leaders. Accordingly, the three districts Jhabua (ST), Ujjain (SC) and Indore (General) constitute the universe of discourse. On the basis of ground realities the study analyses the operative part of the scheme of democratic decentralization. An attempt is also made to evaluate the capabilities of Panchayat Raj representatives as grassroots leaders, to direct the experiment towards the desired goal, viz., of constructing Gram Panchayats as institutions of self-government working for development along with social justice and social harmony.

Ascertainment of leadership roles at grassroots units in the above perspective is considered to specify the overall rural leadership roles in the state. A proportionate sampling framework is designed accordingly. Individual Panchayat Raj representatives being the main source of information, they are identified so as to obtain a representative sample of the universe. Leader's performance has a frame of reference to the members of the community as a whole, whom they represent, i.e., the members of Gram Sabha. As such they also form a significant source of information. Hence, equal number of respondents were chosen from: (i) Panchayat Raj representatives; and (ii) randomly chosen other members of Gram Sabha.

The sample is made multistage, stratified and purposive. A mix of sampling procedures is adopted as per the need.

Stage One: Selection of Districts

The districts are purposively selected on the basis of their categories as reflected in their population and in the number of seats in Parliament and in state legislature.

Population Composition of the Districts

1. Jhabua has the highest percentage of Scheduled Tribes population vis-à-vis the total Scheduled Tribes population of Madhya Pradesh. Provisions of "Panchayat Extension of Scheduled Areas Act, 1996" (PESA) are applicable to Jhabua.
2. Ujjain has the highest percentage of Scheduled Caste population vis-à-vis the total percentage of Scheduled Castes population in Madhya Pradesh.
3. Indore, an adjacent district to the sample districts, is classified as a General category district.

Table 1.1

Categorywise Population Percentage and Districtwise Seats in Lok Sabha and Vidhan Sabha

	Categorywise population percentage			*Districtwise seats in Lok Sabha*				*Districtwise seats in Vidhan Sabha*			
State/ District	*ST*	*SC*	*General*	*No. of seats*	*ST*	*SC*	*General*	*No. of seats*	*ST*	*SC*	*General*
Madhya Pradesh	20.3	15.3	64.5	–	–	–	–	–	–	–	–
Jhabua	86.8	2.8	10.4	01	01	00	00	05	05	00	00
Ujjain	3.1	24.7	72.2	01	00	01	00	07	00	02	05
Indore	6.6	15.8	77.6	01	00	00	01	08	00	01	07

Source: Census, 2001, Area Profile, Madhya Pradesh Districts: Jhabua, Ujjain, Indore. Office of the Register General, India.

Stage Two: Selection of Tehsils

Tehsils were selected in a stratified manner. All tehsils of the three chosen districts are separately listed along with the percentage of the various specified categories in the total population. Three tehsils are selected from each district in the following manner:

(i) From Jhabua, one tehsil with highest percentage of ST population, another tehsil with middle percentage of ST population and a third tehsil with lowest percentage of ST population are selected. These are Bhabra, Ranapur and Petlawad.

(ii) From Ujjain, one tehsil with highest percentage of SC population, another tehsil with middle percentage of SC population and a third tehsil with lowest percentage of SC population are selected. These are Tarana, Mahidpur and Badnagar.

(iii) From Indore, one tehsil with next to highest percentage of General population (leaving Indore, having highest urban population), another tehsil with middle percentage of General population and a third tehsil with lowest percentage of General population are selected. These are Depalpur, Sanwer and Mhow.

Table 1.2
Tehsilwise Category Percentage of the Three Districts

District	*Tehsil*	*ST %*	*SC %*	*General %*	*Remark*
Jhabua	Bhabra	92.3	–	–	Highest
	Alirajpur	91.4	–	–	
	Jobat	91.0	–	–	
	Thandla	88.6	–	–	
	Ranapur	88.1	–	–	Middle
	Meghnagar	87.9	–	–	

Cont'd...

Cont'd...

	Jhabua	87.5	—	—	
	Petlawad	80.3	—	—	Lowest
Ujjain	Tarana	—	30.3	—	Highest
	Ghatia	—	30.2	—	
	Khachrod	—	27.8	—	
	Mahidpur	—	26.9	—	Middle
	Nagda	—	25.2	—	
	Ujjain	—	21.2	—	
	Badnagar	—	20.9	—	Lowest
Indore	Indore	—	—	81.0	Though highest, left being the highest urban tehsil
	Depalpur	—	—	76.1	Highest
	Sanwer	—	—	68.8	Middle
	Mhow	—	—	63.9	Lowest

Source: Census, 2001, Area Profile, Madhya Pradesh Tehsils. Office of the Registrar General, India.

Thus a total of nine tehsils are chosen from the three districts.

Stage Three: Selection of Gram Panchayats

Gram Panchayats with male and female Sarpanch are first listed separately and secondly, random sampling is made.

From each tehsil two separate lists of all Gram Panchayats are prepared. List one is of Gram Panchayats with male Sarpanch and list two is of Gram Panchayats with female Sarpanch. Three Gram Panchayats from list one and two Gram Panchayats from list two are randomly selected.

Thus five Gram Panchayats are selected from each tehsil. 9 Tehsils × 5 Gram Panchayats = 45.

List of 45 chosen Gram Panchayats is thus prepared. Districtwise, tehsilwise, male and female Gram Panchayats are as depicted below.

Table 1.3
45 Chosen Gram Panchayats

District	*Tehsil*	*Gram Panchayat*	*M/F*
(1) Jhabua	1. Bhabra	1. Jheran	M
		2. Roligaon	M
		3. Aman Kuan	M
		4. Kakadbari	F
		5. Badi Pol	F
	2. Ranapur	6. Matasula	M
		7. Dholyavad	M
		8. Lambela	M
		9. Ban	F
		10. Bhut Barda	F
	3. Petlawad	11. Khoriya	M
		12. Kachbi	M
		13. Annant Khedi	M
		14. Panchpipla	F
		15. Kasarbardi	F
(2) Ujjain	4. Tarana	16. Makdon	M
		17. Khar Khedi	M
		18. Zalara	M
		19. Khajuriya	F
		20. Lasurdiya Bechar	F
	5. Mahidpur	21. Palwa	M
		22. Delchibuzurg	M
		23. Nalkheda	M
		24. Bansingh	F
		25. Dhanodiya	F
	6. Badnagar	26. Baledi	M
		27. Kharsodkhurd	M
		28. Gajnikhedi	M
		29. Bardiya	F
		30. Malpura	F

Cont'd...

Cont'd...

(3) Indore	7. Depalpur	31. Chirakhan	M
		32. Gokalpur (Kuti)	M
		33. Sanghvi	M
		34. Chander	F
		35. Birgoda	F
	8. Sanwer	36. Darjikaradia	M
		37. Barodiya Khan	M
		38. Ringnodiya	M
		39. Pirkaradiya	F
		40. Jamburdi Sarwar	F
	9. Mhow	41. Rajpura	M
		42. Simrol	M
		43. Harsola	M
		44. Sherpur	F
		45. Bhicholi	F

Stage Four: Selection of Respondents

Initially the respondents are purposively selected. In the second stage they are randomly selected.

Category (i) Panchayat Raj Representatives (PRR)

1 Sarpanch

1 Upsarpanch

3 Panch (at least one or two female Panch included in these three). Total 5

Category (ii) Members of Gram Sabha (GS)

A total number of five Gram Sabha members other than the Panchayat Raj representatives (PRRs) are selected from each Gram Panchayat. At least two female respondents are purposively selected. Random sampling from the voter's lists and the respondents available in the village during investigation are the bases for selection.

From each Gram Panchayat five PRRs and five members of Gram Sabha equalling to ten units are identified for investigation. Some significant persons from both the categories available in villages during field visit are also added as extra units.

Thus, the total sample size was 450 plus 15 as per the following table.

Table 1.4
Sample Size

<table>
<tr><th>Category and type</th><th>No. of panchayats</th><th></th><th>No. of units</th><th></th><th>Total</th><th></th><th>Extra units</th><th colspan="2">Grand total</th></tr>
<tr><td>PRRs</td><td>45</td><td>×</td><td>5</td><td>=</td><td>225</td><td>+</td><td>8</td><td>233</td><td rowspan="2">465</td></tr>
<tr><td>GS</td><td>45</td><td>×</td><td>5</td><td>=</td><td>225</td><td>+</td><td>7</td><td>232</td></tr>
</table>

Factual information is collected from Gram Sachiv and from the official records of Gram Panchayats.

Overall village profiles prepared by the field investigators constitute an important source of information.

All these constitute the junction points to collect and to cross-tally the field data from various sources.

Government Publications—Concerned Acts of Government of India and of Madhya Pradesh constitute the constitutional legal source. Books and articles on development, democracy, decentralization, self-governance, leadership and Panchayat Raj helped in building up a theoretical construct to assess and evaluate the grassroots leadership roles of various categories. Literature on the functioning of various Panchayats in different states, capability building programmes for Gram Panchayat Representatives, achievements/failures of specific Gram Panchayats and case studies are an important source of understanding the ground realities and to set the data in a proper frame.

Scope of Study

The scope of study is extended mainly to an assessment of various categories of leaders emerging after the implementation of 73rd Constitutional Amendment Act, 1993.

As the Act has the basis of democratic decentralization and aims at creating a third stratum of Indian federalism, the study, includes examining the various leadership roles on the touchstone of developing villages as institutions of self-governance at the grass-roots level. From the point of view of public and financial administration, the vertical and horizontal linkages of the PRIs also form an aspect of the study. Development with equity and peace are the declared goals of the 73rd Constitutional Amendment Act, 1993, hence, the capabilities of leaders to direct the experiment towards these desired goals go to form the core criterion to assess the leadership at the grassroots.

Tools of Research

Two detailed interview schedules are prepared, viz., questions pre-tested and revised where necessary.

Schedule One is for Panchayat Raj representatives and Schedule Two is for members of Gram Sabha other than the representatives. It is essential to cross-tally the information given by PRRs and by members of the Gram Sabha in order to guard against over self-estimation or distortions of actual situations. While investigating the operationalization of the system, theoretical issues like decentralization, participatory democracy, self-governance, development, social justice, peace etc., are also assessed. Leadership performance, is thus judged on these criteria, which required a qualitative analysis as well.

In addition to the two main interview schedules one more data collection schedule is prepared—the Village Data Schedule—to collect basic information about the village, its social composition and infrastructural facilities. This projected the Gram Panchayat profile in which the leadership operates.

The schedule administered to Gram Sabha members relates to corresponding questions that ascertain or negate the Panchayat representatives responses. Leaders are leaders because they are followed by others; hence, followers' responses are of immense value in the assessment of leaders. Traditional rivalries, party affiliations, personal equations, etc., have extracted extreme responses on either side. This has, however directed us in reaching for a balanced assessment of the situation in the field.

Record of Gram Panchayats and observations of field investigators have been useful aids of understanding ground realities vis-à-vis the responses of both the categories of respondents. Observation diaries and records of group discussion, where conducted, are maintained. A codebook is prepared as per the data thus collected, SPSS software is used for data entry and comparative tables of the three districts are generated.

As the study is basically factual and quantitative, the technique of percentage analysis is mainly followed. Theoretical issues and performance are assessed qualitywise.

Limitations of the Study

Illiteracy of the respondents has been a major impediment for the study. Ignorance of the Panchayat Raj system is another limiting factor in getting proper responses from such respondents. Poverty of villagers also limited their activities and responses. To an extent this was supplemented by group discussions and by minute observations of the milieu.

The discriminatory social practices, though apparently invisible, their subtle existence in social interactions and behaviour have also been a limitation of the study. 'Purdah' system and male members of the family managing the affairs on behalf of female representatives in Panchayats found to be generally in vogue. Most of the female respondents accepted that they were unaware of the system and its working and said that the questions be addressed to the male members who know and manage the entire show. Similarly, the influentials in the community though not in legal positions, were observed managing the show in many SC/ST Panchayats.

The introductory part of the study gives an overview of the Indian scene and the main theoretical concepts involved viz., democracy and development, decentralization and leadership. It includes Madhya Pradesh scenario and ground realities. It explains the study plan along with its objectives and issues. Methodology adopted, scope of the study, tools and limitations of the study are included in this chapter.

A profile of the universe of the study, i.e., the three selected districts as per the reservation provisions of 73rd Constitutional Amendment Act, 1993—Jhabua (ST), Ujjain (SC) and Indore (General)—seeks to project their geographical, historical, economic, political and cultural background. It helps in understanding the characteristics of the universe and the data collected during field investigations. This constitutes the chapter two.

Initial part of field investigations deals with SES characteristics of the respondents on the variables of caste, religion, education, status, family background, party affiliations, training, etc. The effort is made to assess as to how the SES characteristics and training of the respondents have moulded their attitudes and capabilities to run the system for the achievement of the declared goals. This forms the chapter three of the study.

The 73rd Constitutional Amendment Act, 1993 aims at structuring Gram Panchayats as institutions of self-governance through decentralization. As such it is expected that the grassroots units formulate their plans according to local needs. Community itself needs to be mobilized so that participatory democracy could take shape at grassroots level. The Act devolves this responsibility on Panchayat Raj representatives (PRRs), at the same time makes Gram Sabha the repository of all the powers. The extent of awareness and capabilities of PRRs in shouldering the responsibilities and of the community to 'regulate and control' their authority so as to direct them in achieving community goals creates the platform for dynamic leadership to emerge. How do the PRRs fare in navigating the ship of their community and how the members of Gram Sabha regulate and control them while evaluating their performance is the enquiry of the chapter four.

A study of the nature of gender equity particularly in the context of 33 per cent reservation for women within each category is also undertaken. Accordingly, the sample includes seventy nine women, equalling 33.9 per cent of the total of PRRs. In addition to the common questions, the women PRRs were addressed few specific questions so as to assess their problems and performance as leaders. An analysis of their responses vis-à-vis the ground realities observed during field investigations constitutes the chapter five of the study.

Implementation of the system at the grassroots is not quite smooth. Practically, a leader's skill lies in overcoming the challenges in the way of operationalization of the system. The challenges exist at structural level both vertically and horizontally. The Madhya Pradesh Panchayat Raj Act, 1994 has been amended from time to time keeping in view the practical difficulties during a decade or more of its implementation. More challenges arise from various corners on the forward march of the grassroots activity towards achievement of the declared goals. A part of the study tries to assess these challenges to the leaders in performing the Herculean task that determines the worth of their role performance. This is the subject of the chapter six.

Concluding chapter of the study elucidates the symmetries and asymmetries of the various categories of leaders. It tries to highlight the issues which need rethinking and reform so that the roadblocks in the way of emerging leadership could be cleared for smooth working of the new system.

Notes

1. Mahatma Gandhi was disturbed at the omission of constitutional status to villages. K. Santhanam moved a resolution to include it in Article 40 of the Constitution which was not a justiciable part.

Dr Ambedkar was very much against village panchayats. He was of the view, "What is a village but a sink of localism, a den of ignorance, narrow mindedness and communalism". He considered villages unworthy of entrusting with authority and responsibility to govern themselves. It would be ruination of India, he held. *Constituent Assembly Debates*, Vol. VII, No. 39, November 4, 1948.

2. V.T. Krishnamachari's Report on the Rationale of Community Development Programme, 1952. A detailed account of rural development efforts in India since independence is given by Carl. C. Taylor et al., *India's Roots in Democracy*, New Delhi, 1965.
3. For a detailed account of participation and development in India see Jean Dreze, and Amartya Sen, *India: Development and Participation*, New Delhi, 2002.
4. Prior to 73rd Constitutional Amendment Act, 1993 election to local bodies were not held in many states for a decade or two.
5. "Aldo capitini", *Gandhi Marg*, Vol. 24, April–June 2002, p. 12.
6. M.K. Gandhi, *Young India*, January 29, 1925.
7. Nirja Gopal Jayal, *Democracy in India*, New Delhi 2001. How could accountability and responsiveness the two major attributes of good democratic governance be achieved through the means of transparency has been discussed within a wider perspective by Yogendra Narayan, "Transparency and Accountability in Public Governance", *Mainstream*, Vol. XLIII, No. 6, January, 29, 2005, pp. 21–25.
8. G. Hargopal, "Limits of Amartya Sen's Three Rs of Reform", *Economic and Political Weekly*, Vol. XL, No. 24, June 11, 2005, pp. 2453–54.
9. M.N. Roy, *Draft Constitution 1944* and *New Humanism: A Manifesto*, 1947. Also see, *Mainstream* (New Delhi) Vol. XLIII, No.15, April 2, 2005, for M.N. Roy's views on "Organized Democracy".
10. H.J. Laski, *Democracy in Crisis*, London, 1933, and *Liberty in Modern State*, London, 1948. Laski vehemently pleads for decentralization for involving people in the governance. He also considers it essential for assuring liberty to the people.

12. Significance of decentralization for democracy and empowerment in a stratified class, caste, religious society of India has been discussed in details in S.N. Jha and P.C. Mathur, (ed.), *Decentralization and Local Politics*, London, 1999, pp. 13–35.
13. *Frontline* (Chennai), December 31, 2004, Vol. 21, No.26, pp. 48–51; Professor Zinn in an interview to Shellpy Walia.
14. R.C. Crook and James Manor (ed.) *Democracy and Decentralization in South Asia and West Africa*, Cambridge, 1998. Decentralization, its philosophy and principles along with the concept of decentralized planning has been brought with reference to local self-governance through Panchayat Raj Institutions by G. Palanithurai, ed., in *Dynamics of New Panchayat Raj System in India*, Vol. 1, New Delhi, 2002, pp. 148–53. Initially Panchayats were viewed as service institutions, by 70s it was recommended to organize these as political and constitutional power units. In this context, an effective decentralized governance was conceived to be all comprehensive to include functions, funds and functionaries: Meenakshi Sundaram, *Decentralization in Developing Countries*, New Delhi 1994.
15. The Weimer Constitution described as the best democracy visualized, was turned into a dangerous dictatorship by Hitler, is a well-known fact of modern history.
16. On the basis of analysis of some panchayats of Tripura, leadership is defined in terms of their performance in development; Bholanath Ghosh and Utpal Kumar De, "Leadership and the Performance of Panchayat in Rural Development: An Experience from Tripura", *Man and Development*, Vol. XXV, No. 4, December 2003, pp. 135–48.
17. Karan Thapar, "Looking for Leadership", *Hindustan Times*, New Delhi, December 18, 2005.
18. Even before the 73rd Constitutional Amendment Act 1993 came into force the significance of Panchayat leadership vis-à-vis the ones at state and national levels has been extensively studied. See e.g., N.R. Inamdar "Panchayati Raj Leadership: Emerging Dimensions", *Journal of Rural Development*, Vol. 10(5), NIRD, Hyderabad, 1991, pp. 561–73. West Bengal was the first to recognize the significance of grassroots leadership and developed it practically under the provi-

sions of Article 40 itself. This has contributed a great deal for the sustained communist rule in the state.

19. For details see Madhya Pradesh Gazette (Extraordinary) dated 25 January, 1994.
20. Madhya Pradesh Panchayat and Gram Swaraj (Amendment) Act 2001, M.P. Gazette (Extraordinary) dated 24.08.2001.

    For other important amendments to the Act see

    M.P. Gazette (Extraordinary) dated 27.09.94.

    M.P. Gazette (Extraordinary) dated 19.12.95.

    M.P. Gazette (Extraordinary) dated 05.12.97.

    M.P. Gazette (Extraordinary) dated 04.09.98.

    M.P. Gazette (Extraordinary) dated 16.06.2005.
20. Elucidating are the books by G. Palanithurai, et al. (ed.), *Major Issues in New Panchayat Raj System*, New Delhi, 1997. G. Palanithurai, *New Panchayat Raj System at Work: An Evaluation*, New Delhi, 1999 and *Dynamics of New Panchayati Raj System in India*, New Delhi, 2002.
21. There are a number of eminent studies on leadership theory and activity and specific studies on rural leadership. Some of these are landmarks in the field:

    H.H. Jennings, *Leadership and Isolation*, London, 1950.

    R.M. Stodgil, "Leadership, Membership and Organization", *Psychology Bulletin*, Vol. 47, No. 1, New York, 1956.

    Avatar Singh, *Leadership Pattern and Village Structures*, New Delhi, 1963.

    Arjun Rao Darshankar, *Leadership in Panchayat Raj: A Study of Beed District*, Jaipur, 1979.

    G.D. Bhatt, *Emerging Leadership Pattern in Rural India: An Empirical Study*, New Delhi, 1994.

    Sudha Pai, "Pradhans in the New Panchayats", *Economic and Political Weekly*, Vol. 33 (18), 1998.

    S.C. Jain, *Grass Without Roots: Rural Development under Government Auspices*, New Delhi, 1999.

    D. Bandyopadhyay and A. Mukherjee (eds.), *New Issues in Panchayat Raj*, New Delhi, 2004.

22. D.S. Choudhari, *Emerging Rural Leadership in Indian States*, New Delhi, 1981.

    K. Chakravarty, and S.K. Bhattacharya, *Leadership Factions and Panchayati Raj*, Jaipur, 1993 (Reference to West Bengal).

    Pravakar Das, *Emerging Pattern of Leadership in Tribal India*, Delhi, 1994 (Reference to Orissa).

    Kailashchandra Sharma, *Leadership in Panchayat Raj*, Jaipur, 1996 (Reference to Rajasthan).

    Poornima Vyasulu, and Vinod, "Women in Panchayati Raj: Grassroots Democracy in Malgudi", *Economic and Political Weekly*, Vol. XXXIV, No. 52, December 25–31, 1999, pp. 3667–86.

    Shyamlal, *Tribal Leadership in India*, Jaipur, 2000.

    Ashish Bhatt, *Democratic Decentralisation and Tribal Leadership* (Hindi), Jaipur, 2002 (Reference to Jhabua).

    Ajit Kumar, "Politics in Three Villages: A Study in Nagpur District", *Economic and Political Weekly*, Vol. XXXIX, No. 3, January 17–23, 2004, pp. 228–33.

2

Profile of the Study Area

The present study is primarily based on field investigation. Topography, socio-economic conditions, cultural traditions and infrastructural facilities determine the quality of emerging leadership to a considerable extent. Hence, a short profile of the three selected districts, viz., Jhabua, Ujjain and Indore, would be helpful for a clearer understanding of the universe of discourse.

Madhya Pradesh, located as it is in the middle of India, has predominantly rural population (73.5%) and is the home of nearly 46 Scheduled Tribes (STs). Conditioning factors like the unexploited natural resources and high rate of illiteracy (58%) have classed the state as one of the backward states of India. The Vindhyachal and the Satpura ranges almost cut across the state and obstruct smooth connections with neighbouring areas.

The three selected districts, Jhabua, Ujjain and Indore, are the categorywise distinct districts situated around the Malwa plateau to the south-western part of Madhya Pradesh. A profile of the three districts is presented in this chapter.

1. Jhabua District (ST)

Jhabua district, situated in the extreme south-western corner of Madhya Pradesh, forms the core of the western tribal belt of the country. The district has a population of nearly 14 lakh with an overwhelming ST population (86.8%) more than four times than that of the state.[1]

Topography

Lying on the western fringe of Malwa plateau between 21.30° and 22.55° to the north latitude and 73.30° and 75.1° to the east longitude,[2] Jhabua is marked with steep hilly terrain, heavily eroded slopes and devastated forests. The Vindhyachal and the Satpura ranges cover almost the entire area of the district. Few plains and small hillocks extend over the northern part and high ranges of the Vindhyachal with hard rocks and almost no plains form the southern part of the district. To the extreme south the river Narmada forms the boundary line between Jhabua, Maharashtra and Pashchim Nimar district of Madhya Pradesh. At the northern tip the river Mahi forms the boundary of Jhabua with Gujarat. Extreme climatic conditions mark very hot summers and mild winters.

Resources: Physical

Overexploited natural resources and population pressure put Jhabua in contrast to other tribal areas in the state. The result is a development lag despite huge amount of money being poured in the district by state, national and international agencies.

Average rainfall of 845 mm throughout Jhabua is most fluctuating and unevenly distributed. The district is classified as a drought prone area. Government efforts at water conservation and regeneration of forests under the project 'Green Beginnings' during 1980–90 did not last long.[3] Thus, scanty rainfall with large-scale deforestation has resulted in loss of water retention capacity of the soil hampering the agricultural work. Rajiv Gandhi Watershed Mission has slightly improved the situation. Maze and black grams are the two main kharif crops. Cotton and groundnut are also cultivated. Wheat and soyabean cultivation are the recent diversifications. Most of the produce is locally consumed. Rabi season being dry people migrate to nearby states of Gujarat and Rajasthan as agricultural labourers and construction workers. Total area cultivated and the total produce give the following picture:[4]

Table 2.1
Agricultural Produce: Jhabua

Year	*Total land cultivated in hectares*								
	Kharif	*Rabi*	*Maze*	*Black Gram*	*Other Grams*	*Cotton*	*Ground nut*	*Soyabean*	*Wheat*
2002–2003	2,67,694	29,236	1,10,585	72,075	19,207	31,085	15,391	30,078	15,748

Rock phosphate near Petlawad is the only mineral wealth worth mentioning. Some lime is mined near Alirajpur (declared as a separate district in 2008). Private and government efforts for industrial exploitation of these minerals have proved disadvantageous hampering the industrial prospect of the district. Only small scale industries totalling 72 exist in the entire district with a population exceeding 13 lakh.[5]

Jhabua reflects the economic situation prevalent on the national level with a wide gap between rich and poor. A few rich and many poor mark the tribal scene of Jhabua in a more pitiable condition. Pressure of population, devastation of forests, agriculture and industries not being a profitable activity in the district and a very high rate of illiteracy block any development activity in Jhabua.[6]

Human Resource

Jhabua, the district of highest tribal concentration in Madhya Pradesh has mainly three sub-groups—Bhils, Bhilalas and Patlyas—all tenacious and hard working people. Bhilalas trace their connections to Rajputs of Rajasthan and Patlyas to Gujarat. They have their own hierarchy in which the original tribe of 'Bhils' is the lowest. Migration from the district in search of work has brought them in touch with urban areas and the people there, causing slow change in their attitudes and lifestyles.[7]

However, practices of socio-cultural traditions are well preserved throughout Jhabua. The 'Jati Panchayat' and leadership system in the form of 'Tadwi' have a strong hold over their respective communities. Despite special provisions for the tribal areas in the form of Panchayat Extension to Scheduled Areas Act, 1996, the unique tribal traditions still play a powerful role in the lives of the communities. All civil and criminal offences are finally settled in 'Jati Panchayats'.

In a way they pose a challenge to the new Panchayat system and emerging new leadership. The control of administrative system after independence extending over tribal areas through Patwaris, Gram Sevaks, school teachers, bureaucrats, etc., have posed a counter challenge to the tribal socio-cultural traditions. Glimpses of urbanization and development, democratic elections and the new Panchayat system have forced a significant change in tribal thought process and their socio-political behaviour, and this is expected to change their leadership system. However, tribal society is still in a flux and the final shape of things to come is yet to go a long way.

In the initial wave of religious conversions during the advent of British rule, a sizeable number of tribals were converted to Christianity. Literacy rate is higher among these converted Christians as compared to the rest of the ST population. They have Christian names and follow Christian religion.[8] Some worship Hindu gods and follow Hindu religious traditions but almost all of them worship their ancestors as gods and follow their unique tribal traditions side by side. They primarily worship their ancestors on all occasions of festivities. The tribals mostly live in nuclear families, but they have a sign of their extended family in the form of 'totem' which they all revere. This has helped in building up a social structure of mutual cooperation and assistance within the totem clan. This strongly controls their political behaviour as a group.

They have a harmonious tradition of marriage ensuring the approval of brides and grooms and also of their parents without any religious ritual whatsoever. Marriages are equally harmoniously broken by repayment of the bride price to the previous husband. Females have an upper voice in both the cases. They have an upper hand in many a decision of economic import in the family. This, however, has not led to their social or political empowerment. They have almost no place in Jati Panchayat and are unable to assume de facto leadership role in the legally constituted Panchayats. This is the situation despite their better traditional position and also higher sex ratio.

Table 2.2
Jhabua District and its Three Chosen Tehsils[9]

Place/ district/ tehsils	*Area sq km*	*Population*	*No. of small scale industries*	*Agricultural Land in hectares*	*Roads in km*		
					Pakka	*Kachcha*	*Total*
Jhabua District	8,793	13,94,561	72	25,047	1,824.49	992.65	2,817.14
Tehsils							
1. Bhabra	338	8,747	01	732	144.6	51.6	196.2
2. Petlawad	957	1,70,412	11	3,851	287.1	94.6	381.7
3. Ranapur	400	90,995	05	1932	98.7	98.9	197.6

The tehsils of Bhabra and Ranapur situated in hilly terrains with less of rainfall, no irrigation facilities, no minerals and no rail track are in a position of comparative disadvantage. Petlawad tehsil houses a number of big landholders in the entire district. Despite rural electrification and widespread network of roads, only small-scale industries exist in the tehsils as also in the entire district. Tehsil Petlawad of course is at an advantageous position on this count.

Gram Panchayats

Jhabua has a total of 612 Gram Panchayats covering 1,322 villages. The randomly selected five Gram Panchayats from each of the three tehsils—three headed by males and two headed by females—are the sample tehsils of the study. These Gram Panchayats are basically rural with no urban population and with a very low percentage of Scheduled Caste population having a considerably high ratio of illiterates. More than half of the population are workers even though the fact that almost each household owns some land.

Two Gram Panchayats of Petlawad tehsil, Annantkhedi and Panchpipla, slightly differ from the rest of the 13 Gram Panchayats all of which have a lesser percentage of General population, and a higher percentage of ST population vis-à-vis the entire district. Annantkhedi and Panchapipla have a higher percentage of General population and a slightly lower percentage of ST population. However, quite significantly the percentage of illiterates is lower in 12 out of the 15 selected Gram Panchayats vis-à-vis the district. Lambela Gram Panchayat of Ranapur tehsil stands distinct in having a lower percentage of total workers with 50.2 per cent as against the district having 52.5 per cent of total workers. The rest of the 14 Gram Panchayats have a higher percentage of total workers varying from 55.3 per cent to as high as 69.1 per cent.

Sex ratio of eleven Gram Panchayats is higher than that of the district having 986 and the state having 919 females per thousand males. All of these Gram Panchayats cross the thousand mark. The four Gram Panchayats with a lower sex ratio to that of the district are Roligaon of Bhabra tehsil and Khoria, Kajbi and Panchpipla of Petlawad tehsil.

All the Gram Panchayats have a school each (primary/middle/high school). Except four Gram Panchayats all have electricity. Housing facilities exist in all the 15 Gram Panchayats of the district. Five Gram Panchayats have health facilities in their area. The residents of remaining 10 have to travel a distance of 2 to 14 kilometres for medical facilities. Police Stations are situated at a distance of 2 to 14 kilometres from the various Gram Panchayats. Except 3 Gram Panchayats all have their Panchayat Bhavans. Rationing facilities are available within the areas of 10 Gram Panchayats. The remaining five have this facility at a distance of 2 to 6 kilometres. Six Gram Panchayats have a direct access to pakka roads while the remaining 9 are situated at a distance of 2 to 15 kilometres away from the nearest *pakka* roads. However, all the Gram Panchayats are situated far away from the district headquarters. The nearest Gram Panchayat is at a distance of 14 kilometres and the farthest one is at a distance of 70 kilometres. Human resource features and insfrastructural facilities are depicted in the Tables 2.3 and 2.4.[10]

With this overall picture, Jhabua stands out as a unique ST district in the state, where emergence of grassroots leadership requires Herculean efforts on the part of the community, the government authorities and NGOs working in the area.

2. Ujjain District (SC)

Ujjain district, situated in the south-western part of Madhya Pradesh, is the centre of Malwa plateau. The Vindhyachal ranges. are spread towards the south-eastern direction of the district. The

Table 2.3
Human Resource Features: Jhabua Panchayats

Name of place		*Total population*	*Rural population*	*Urban population*	*SC population (%)*	*ST population (%)*	*General population (%)*	*Sex ratio females per 1000 males*	*Illiteracy rate (%)*	*Work partici-pation rate (%)*
0		*1*	*2*	*3*	*4*	*5*	*6*	*7*	*8*	*9*
Madhya Pradesh		6,03,48,023	4,43,80,878	1,59,67,145	15.2	20.3	64.5	919	58.0	42.7
Jhabua		13,94,561	12,73,530	1,21,031	2.8	86.8	10.4	986	92.8	52.5
Tehsil – Bhabra										
Panchayat (Male/Female)										
Jhiran	M	2,149	2,149	0	1.1	93.7	5.2	1037	95.1	55.3
Roligaon	M	1,852	1,852	0	—	99.8	0.2	979	83.7	56.0
Amankuan	M	2,681	2,681	0	0.5	98.8	0.7	992	89.8	58.7
Kakadbari	F	1,629	1,629	0	—	99.6	0.4	1039	97.3	60.1
Badipal	F	2,804	2,804	0	—	99.7	0.3	1044	85.7	58.1

Cont'd...

Cont'd...

Tehsil - Petlawad										
Khoriya	M	781	781	0	—	100.0	0.0	953	72.6	60.1
Kajbi	M	785	785	0	—	100.0	0.0	924	82.54	57.8
Annantkhedi	M	1,166	1,166	0	2.1	73.4	24.5	1046	78.3	59.4
Panch Pipla	F	1,045	1,045	0	2.1	81.5	16.4	942	72.1	64.7
Kasarbardi	F	1,611	1,611	0	0.0	91.6	8.4	1042	91.9	56.8
Tehsil - Ranapur										
Matasula	M	1,793	1,793	0	0.0	99.9	0.1	1063	98.5	56.6
Dholyabad	M	1,993	1,993	0	3.9	95.7	0.4	1009	77.11	63.9
Lambela	M	1,925	1,925	0	—	90.2	9.8	1016	82.75	50.2
Ban	F	2,491	2,491	0	4.5	93.4	2.1	1072	81.9	64.4
Bhutbarda	F	587	587	0	—	100.0	—	1031	76.49	69.1

Table 2.4

Infrastructural Facilities: Jhabua Panchayats

Name of panchayat	M/F headed	No. of Panch		Sarpanch and Up-sarpanch	Total	School H.M.P. No.	Hand-pump Y/N	Electri-city Y/N/P	Housing		Health facility Y/N distance in km	Police station distance in km	Pan-chayat bhawan Y/N	Ration shop Y/N distance in km	Access to pakka road distance in km	distance from district head-quarters in km
		M	F						K	P						
								Tehsil – Bhabra								
Jhiran	M	12	08	1+1	22	H-1	Y	P	K	P	Y	9 km	Y	Y	3 km	50 km
Roligaon	M	09	03	1+1	14	M-1	Y	P	K	P	Y	3 km	Y	N-3 km	Direct	60 km
Amankaun	M	13	07	1+1	22	M-1	Y	Y	K	P	N-4 km	4 km	N	Y	4 km	70 km
Kakdbadi	F	09	04	1+1	15	M-1, P-1	Y	Y	K	P	N-12 km	12 km	Y	N-4 km	Direct	65 km
Badipol	F	12	05	1+1	19	M-1	Y	N	K	P	N-7 km	10 km	N	Y	Direct	65 km
								Tehsil – Petlawad								
Khoria	M	08	04	1+1	14	P-1	Y	N	K		N-5 km	5 km	Y	N-4 km	Direct	58 km
Kajbi	M	09	04	1+1	15	P-1	Y	Y	K	P	N-6 km	6 km	Y	N-6 km	6 km	65 km

Cont'd...

Cont'd...

Annantkhedi	M	08	06	1+1	16	M-1	Y	Y	K	P	N-4 km	4 km	Y	Y	2 km	60 km
Panchpipla	F	06	03	1+1	11	M-1	Y	Y	K	P	N-14 km	14 km	Y	Y	15 km	60 km
Kasarbardi	F	11	04	1+1	15	P-1	Y	P	K		N-8 km	8 km	Y	Y	2 km	70 km
								Tehsil - Ranapur								
Matasula	M	14	06	1+1	22	M-1	Y	N	K	P	N-2 km	2 km	N	Y	12 km	18 km
Dholyabad	M	13	03	1+1	18	H-1	Y	Y	K	P	Y	7 km	Y	Y	10 km	30 km
Lambela	M	13	07	1+1	22	P-1	Y	N	K	P	N-2 km	14 km	Y	N-2 km	Direct	25 km
Ban	F	11	07	1+1	20	H-1	Y	P	K	P	Y	7 km	Y	Y	Direct	22 km
Bhutbarda	F	10	05	1+1	17	P-1	Y	P	K	P	Y	7 km	Y	Y	5 km	14 km

Note: M—Male; F—Female
H—High; M—Middle; P—Primary
Y—Yes; N—No; P—Partial
K—Kachcha; P—Pakka

district with the commissionary headquarters at Ujjain is an ancient and holy city of Madhya Pradesh. It is believed that the city existed from times immemorial around 'Mahakal', one of the twelve "Jyotirlingas" and the "Shaktipeeth, Harsiddhi". Many a mythological and scriptural reference is found about the city of Ujjain and its vicinity. The district has a population of nearly 17 lakh with a sizeable number of rural and Scheduled Caste population. The Scheduled Caste percentage in the district is more than one and a half times to that of the state. It has the highest percentage of the Scheduled Caste population among the four districts that have a Scheduled Caste seat reserved in Parliament from Madhya Pradesh.[11]

Table 2.5
Districts with SC Seats in Parliament

State/districts	*Total population*	*Rural population (%)*	*ST (%)*	*SC (%)*	*General (%)*
Madhya Pradesh	6,03,48,023	73.5	20.3	15.2	64.5
Districts having a SC seat in Parliament from M.P.					
Ujjain	17,10,982	61.2	3.1	24.8	72.1
Shajapur	12,90,685	81.46	2.73	22.0	75.27
Morena	15,92,714	78.44	6.81	21.1	78.09
Sagar	20,21,987	70.77	9.71	20.5	69.79

Topography

Lying at the heart of Malwa plateau between the latitudes 22.36° and 23.36° to the north and longitudes 75.00° and 76.30° to the east with no marked hill ranges at a height of 527 metre from sea level, Ujjain district is covered with black cotton soil and trap rocks. The slope of the plateau is from south to north with a number of small rivers joining the main river Chambal forming the feeders of the system of the river Ganga. As such the water divides are also from south to north direction. The river Sipra mainly flows in the district around Ujjain and Mahidpur tehsils. Average rainfall of 597 mm throughout the year is insufficient for the district mostly dependent on agriculture. Tanks and reservoirs abound in the district but are slowly degenerating due to overexploitation and dumping of garbage. However, a variety of flowers, fruits and vegetables is cultivated in the district. Trading in these commodities is a flourishing business.

An archaeological survey and excavations in Ujjain district have yielded early sites of protohistoric deposits in Malwa. Carbon dates of trenches at 'Kaytha', 24 kilometres east of Ujjain city, dates back to 2015 BC, the times around which Harappan tribes moved towards eastern and southern lands. Excavations at Ujjain reveal Ujjayini as one of the largest and the most celebrated ancient cities of India, probably of the earlier half of the first millennium BC.[12] A long history of rulers and their rule at Ujjain is traced back to seventh century BC to the present age. The most famous among these was the spiritual king Bhartrihari who handed over the reigns of his empire to his younger brother Vikramaditya for his spiritual pursuits. He started a time measurement schedule (Indian calendar) named after him as Vikram Samvat. The Tropic of Cancer once passed through Ujjain which has shifted over ages to Gram Dogla 45 kilometres away from Ujjain. Established in 1733 by Maharaja Jai Singh II of Jaipur, the observatory at Ujjain is one of the distinct ones. Thus, the present Ujjain district carved out of Badnagar, Khachrod and Ujjain tehsils of the erstwhile Gwalior state, and Mahidpur and Tarana tehsils of the erstwhile Holkar state, has a rich cultural, socio-religious and political history. Today its area covers 6,091 square kilometres.[13]

Resources: Physical

Agriculture is the main occupation of the bulk of the population of Ujjain district. A total of 61.2 per cent of the rural population constitutes either cultivators or agricultural labourers. Some urban population has also moved to agriculture during the last two-three decades.[14]

Almost all kinds of grains, grams, fruits, vegetables, cotton and other fibres and medicinal plants are cultivated in the district. Once famous for Malvi wheat and cotton, Ujjain district has taken over to soyabean cultivation. Cultivation of tobacco, an important product of trade of the district, and vegetables, fruits and species, etc., are on a receding scale. During the sixties and the seventies soyabean was not cultivated at all.[15] Starting in the late eighties, soyabean cultivation rose to the highest point in the late nineties and the trend still continues.[16]

Table 2.6
Cultivation in Hectares: Ujjain

Year	*Wheat*	*Cotton*	*Tobacco*	*Soyabean*	*Vegetable*
1998–1999	1,77,667	35	48	4,14,624	3,54,408
1999–2000	1,89,419	15	47	4,16,931	3,65,400
2000–2001	36,916	17	43	4,21,517	82,149
2001–2002	55,753	19	40	4,16,685	2,04,819
2002–2003	46,099	19	31	4,14,654	1,34,452

Livestock, forestry, fishing and orchards are the other occupations taken up by a few.

Since there are no important minerals like iron, coal, manganese ore, etc., in the district, it has no prospects of heavy industrial units. In the Deccan trap a number of quarries and mines of lime *kankri* are found. Agriculture-based industries flourished in the district. Cotton, groundnut and linseed oil seeds, and tobacco provides the base for the agricultural industries and trade. Textile industries and oil extraction plants flourished till the eighties of the twentieth century. Cotton ginning and pressing, textile mills, oil mills, rose water and distilleries of scents and tobacco trade at Ujjain, yarn and some chemicals at Nagda, sugar mills at Mahidpur, leather tanning and fine chemicals at Badnagar were the famous industrial activities. ISCO Stanton Pipes and synthetic yarn at Shri Synthetics, Ujjain, were industrial units of repute. During mid-eighties almost all these industrial activities receded towards their downfall. At present most of them are either liquidated or defunct.

A power generation unit with turbine and spray coolers established during early 1920s marked a unique feature of Ujjain district but the supply of hydel power from Gandhi Sagar on the river Chambal since the sixties led to its closure. Cottage industries of food processing and plastic goods are in operation in the district.[17] Present trade pattern in the district is of goods required for religious rituals in temples and social festivals in households.

Human Resource

Ujjain, the district of highest SC population in Madhya Pradesh, has unique socio-cultural traditions of Malwa. The SC population is concentrated in rural areas and follow the same Malwi traditions as the caste Hindus.

Consequent upon the partition in 1947, 5,448 displaced persons settled in urban areas of the district.[18]

A majority of these came from West Pakistan and were Sindhis and Punjabis. Protected by various statutory provisions, hard working and possessing a rare acumen of trade activity, they soon captured trade, commerce and transport. They partially assimilated the socio-cultural life of Malwa while maintaining their separate identity.[19]

Rural areas observe joint family structure of patriarchal type. Urban population has nuclear family structure. Sex ratio tilting to minus mark (938 per 1,000 males) and a high rate of illiteracy among women (61.6%) have reduced their status to inequality with almost no role in decision making process either in families or in communities.[20]

With a long history of rules of Rajputs, Muslims, Marathas and Britishers, Ujjain district reflects an amalgam of various peoples, cultures and religions.

The prominent SCs recorded in the district are Bagri, Balai, Chamar, Mehtar and Nat. Their highest concentration is in Tarana tehsil and lowest in Badnagar tehsil. Mahidpur tehsil stands in between. This trend is continuous since 1961 to date.[21]

Table 2.7
Trend of SC Population in the chosen Tehsils: Ujjain

Percentage

Year	*District Ujjain*	*Tehsil*		
		Tarana	*Mahidpur*	*Badnagar*
1961	23.28	29.80	27.12	19.57
2001	24.56	30.33	26.09	20.88

The Scheduled Caste people were agricultural labourers and bonded to the rural landlords for generations.

Concerted move for the abolition of bonded labour and liquidation of their debts resulted in a slight change in the master-servant relationship in villages. Though this has provided a viable space for SC leadership at the grassroots under the 73rd Constitutional Amendment Act, 1993 a positive/constructive environment is yet to emerge.

The city of Ujjain situated on the banks of the river Shipra had been a famous seat of learning, culture and religion for centuries. Numerous ancient temples have made it a holy place and a pilgrim centre. It is developing as a trade centre of articles for religious rituals and social festivities. Ujjain district appears to be entering the modern era on the basis of its spiritual/religious heritage of ancient times.

Abolition of Zamindari and Jagirdari systems has changed the actual farmers to the status of owners of lands and brought them in direct contact with district headquarters and other government authorities enhancing their socio-economic prestige and awareness. Panchayats, self-help groups, educational and social welfare activities in rural areas have made the rural mass politically conscious. Successive Gram Panchayat elections under the 73rd Constitutional Amendment Act 1993 reflect the increasing awareness of the rural people including the rural SC population. with 75 per cent of the SC people being beneficiaries of government schemes, the district seems to be a model of social transformation.

Tehsils

Out of the three selected tehsils, two, viz. Tarana and Mahidpur have a higher percentage of SC population vis-à-vis the district and the state. Only Badnagar tehsil has a lower percentage of SC population vis-à-vis the district but higher vis-à-vis the state. They cover the north-eastern, northern and south-western parts of the district respectively. The overall physical and human resources of the three tehsils do not record any specific differences vis-à-vis the district profile, except that they have a higher percentage of rural population and also of work participation than that of the district.[22]

Table 2.8
Population Features of Three Tehsils vis-à-vis State and District

State/District/ Tehsil	*SC (%)*	*ST (%)*	*Rural (%)*	*Work participation %*
Madhya Pradesh	15.2	20.3	73.5	42.7
Ujjain	24.8	3.1	61.26	36.31
Tehsils				
1. Tarana	30.3	3.3	89.66	37.67
2. Mahidpur	26.9	1.1	83.64	38.72
3. Badnagar	20.9	7.3	85.59	40.76

The district headquarters, Ujjain is a junction of broad and metre gauge lines of Western Railway and is well connected with other states. However, the selected tehsils do not have a broad based rail connectivity. A widespread network of pakka and kachcha roads covers the entire district including all the tehsils.

The selected tehsils being predominantly rural and agricultural, with no industrial possibility, only a few small-scale industries are located in the tehsils as is the situation in the district also.[23]

Table 2.9

Ujjain District and its Three Chosen Tehsils

Place District/ Tehsil	*Area sq km*	*Population*	*Agricultural land in hectares*	*No. of Small Scale Industries*	*Roads in km*		
					Pakka	*Kachcha*	*Total*
Ujjain	6,091	17,10,982	10,950	3,655	1,528.27	187.04	1,715.31
Tehsils							
1. Tarana	1,041.1	2,17,229	1,196	372	276.50	19.90	296.80
2. Mahidpur	1,137.3	2,17,426	1,426	706	210.08	21.60	231.68
3. Badnagar	1,229.5	2,36,640	957	614	201.60	39.21	240.81

Human Resource

Human resource of the tehsils corresponds more or less to the district scenario. However, the tehsils having a higher percentage of rural population, exhibit stronger family ties and have deep rooted socio-cultural practices in vogue. The SC population in tehsils is the largest beneficiary of development schemes of the state and central governments enhancing their social and political consciousness and overall condition.

Gram Panchayats

Ujjain district has 517 Gram Panchayats covering 1,135 villages. The randomly selected five Gram Panchayats from each of the three tehsils three are headed by males and two headed by females. All the 15 Gram Panchayats from the three tehsils have no urban population. Tarana tehsil selected as the tehsil of highest SC percentage in the population has a unique Gram Panchayat of Kharkhadi consisting of three villages, viz., Kharkhadi, Murdawan and Bordagujar. Kharkhadi village has no SC population. The entire village consists of Gujars, but it is the seat of SC Gram Panchayat. The other two villages have SC population to the tune of 14.6 per cent, lower than that of the district and also the state. Similarly, Gram Panchayats of Gajnikhedi of Badnagar tehsil and Bansing of Mahidpur tehsil have a comparatively very low percentage of SC population of 8.8 and 9.9 respectively with an SC Sarpanch. There is negligible ST population in 12 selected Gram Panchayats. Only three Gram Panchayats of Badnagar tehsil record ST population to the tune of 19.3, 13.6 and 17.9 per cent.

Four Gram Panchayats of Mahidpur tehsil and one of Tarana tehsil have a sex ratio lower to that of the district and the state. However, all the five Gram Panchayats of Badnagar tehsil cross the 950 mark reaching to 995 in Bardia Gram Panchayat. Tarana tehsil has exceptions of Zalara Gram Panchayat and of village Lasurdiabechar crossing the one thousand mark in sex ratio. Murarkhedi, a small village of Gram Panchayat Malpura of Badnagar tehsil, also crosses the one thousand mark in sex ratio. Though these Gram Panchayats, have a total rural population, they seem to be tolerant towards females, that attitude is, however, missing towards their socio-political empowerment.

The illiteracy rate is quite low in all the Gram Panchayats of Badnagar tehsil and three Gram Panchayats of Tarana tehsil.

Table 2.10

Human Resource Features: Ujjain Panchayats

Name of Place	*Total population*	*Rural population*	*Urban population*	*SC category (%)*	*ST category (%)*	*General category (%)*	*Sex ratio females per 1000 Males*	*Illiterates (%)*	*Total work participation (%)*
Madhya Pradesh	6,03,48,023	4,43,80,878	1,59,67,145	15.2	20.3	64.5	919	58.0	42.7
Ujjain	17,10,982	10,48,195	6,62,787	24.7	3.1	72.1	938	48.6	44.1
Tehsil—Tarana									
Panchayat (Male/Female)									
Makdon (M)	5,990	5,990	0	26.3	9.2	64.5	964	41.8	48.1
Kharkhadi (M)	638	638	0	0.0	1.4	98.6	839	56.8	57.8
+ Murdawan	413	413	0	22.0	0.0	78.0	976	82.5	55.4
+ Bordagujar	595	595	0	21.8	0.0	78.2	871	82.3	61.0
	1,646	**1,646**	0	**14.6**	0.46	**84.09**	**895**	**73.86**	**58.06**

Cont'd...

Cont'd...

Zalara (M)	938	938	0	30.9	0.0	69.1	891	32.4	41.8
+ Bhatkhedi	208	208	0	6.3	0.0	93.7	1,059	57.5	63.9
+ Jhalari	419	419	0	59.2	0.0	40.8	1,116	41.2	53.0
	1,565	**1,565**	0	**32.13**	0.0	**67.86**	**1022**	**43.7**	**52.9**
Khajuriya (F)	1,255	1,255	0	41.5	0.0	58.5	958	33.3	48.2
Lasurdiyabechar (F)	1,180	1,180	0	24.7	0.0	75.3	1024	98.0	57.1
+ Kharpa	1,358	1,358	0	6.3	0.0	93.7	980	79.93	56.46
+ Guradiyadongar	173	173	0	47.4	0.0	52.6	989	64.7	53.2
	2,711	**2,711**	0	**26.13**	0.0	**73.86**	**980**	**79.93**	**56.46**
Tehsil—Mahidpur									
Palwa (M)	1,332	1,332	0	22.7	2.1	75.2	936	67.3	49.5
+ Belakheda	1,205	1,205	0	34.9	0.0	65.1	950	73.5	57.0
	2,537	**2,537**	0	**40.15**	**1.05**	**70.15**	**943**	70.4	**53.25**
Delchibuzurg (M)	1,774	1,774	0	32.1	0.5	67.4	897	65.9	53.5

Nalkheda (M)	1,225	1,225	0	19.3	0.0	80.7	899	83.9	65.4
Bansing (F)	1,314	1,314	0	9.9	0.0	90.1	930	97.2	59.4
Dhanodiya (F) + Nayakhedi	1,140	1,140	0	14.0	0.0	86.0	929	96.0	58.2
+ Marukheda	440	440	0	27.3	0.0	72.7	930	91.9	55.0
+ Padikheda	622	622	0	8.7	0.0	91.3	879	93.1	60.1
	2,202	**2,202**	0	**16.66**	**0.0**	**93.33**	**913**	**93.66**	**57.76**
				Tehsil—Badnagar					
Baledi (M)	3,962	3,962	0	24.5	4.6	70.9	959	32.0	47.6
Kharsodkhurd (M)	4,389	4,389	0	24.0	19.3	56.7	951	40.9	49.5
Gajnikhedi (M)	1,660	1,660	0	8.8	13.6	77.6	958	32.7	52.2
Bardiya (F)	1,861	1,861	0	14.3	4.1	81.6	995	38.2	52.3
Malpura (F)	987	987	0	19.1	17.9	63.0	962	36.6	56.8
+ Murarkhedi	534	534	0	16.7	0.2	83.1	1008	36.4	53.4
	1,521	**1,521**	0	**17.9**	**9.05**	**73.05**	**985**	**36.5**	**55.1**

However, all the Gram Panchayats of Mahidpur tehsil and two of Tarana tehsil have a very high percentage of illiteracy. The percentage of work participation in all the selected Gram Panchayats comes about 50 per cent and above.[24]

As regards infrastructural facilities, all the selected Gram Panchayats have primary, middle or a high schools located in the Panchayat area. All of these have hand pumps in each village, adequate housing facilities and Panchayat Bhavans. Except Bansing, a Gram Panchayat of Mahidpur tehsil, all other selected Gram Panchayats of Ujjain district have electricity. Bansing is located in a hilly area encircled by the river Chhoti Kalisindh. People of Bansing have to cross the river for health, ration and police station facilities. Gram Panchayat Makdon is the only one having a police station in its Panchayat area, while people from all other Gram Panchayats have to travel 2 to 22 kilometres to have an access to the nearest police station. However, pakka roads run at a distance of 1 to 7 kilometres from the Gram Panchayats. Distance from Gram Panchayats to district headquarters varies from 24 to 90 kilometres. The Table 2.11 depicts the infrastructural facilities of the selected Gram Panchayats of Ujjain district.

With the human resource and infrastructural situation presented in the Tables 2.10 and 2.11, the chosen Gram Panchayats of Ujjain district have a significantly different projection. With a total rural background and Scheduled Caste preponderance the Panchayat Raj representatives of Ujjain (SC) district face some specific problematic situations in assuming leadership roles at the grassroots level. However, a sizeable number of general category population inhabits the Gram Panchayats of Ujjain district giving the SC Panchayat Raj representatives a better socio-political exposure vis-à-vis the rural (ST) district of Jhabua.

Table 2.11

Infrastructural Facilities: Ujjain Panchayats

Name of Panchayat	M/F headed	No. of panch		Sarpanch and Up-sarpanch	Total	School H.M.P. No.	Hand-pump Y/N	Elec-tricity Y/N/P	Housing		Health Facility Y/N Distance in km	Police Station Distance in km	Pancha-yat Bhawan Y/N	Ration Shop Y/N Distance in km	Access to Pakka Road Distance in km	Distance from District Head-quarters in km
		M	F						K	P						
Tehsil – Tarana																
Makdon	M	14	7	1+1	23	H-1	Y	Y	K	P	Y	Y	Y	Y	Y	65 km
Kherkhedi	M	11	5	1+1	18	P-1	Y	P		P	N-5 km	N-22 km	Y	Y	N-5 km	55 km
Zalara	M	9	4	1+1	15	M-1	Y	Y	K	P	Y	N-3 km	Y	Y	Y	39 km
Khajuriya	F	6	1	1+1	9	M-1	Y	Y	K	P	N-5 km	N-18 km	Y	Y	N-7 km	50 km
Lasurdiyabechar	F	8	4	1+1	14	P-1	Y	Y	K	P	N-4 km	N-7 km	Y	Y	N-4 km	44 km
Tehsil – Mahidpur																
Palwa	M	13	6	1+1	21	M-1	Y	Y	K	P	N-5 km	N-6 km	Y	N-3 km	N-1 km	28 km
Delchibuzurg	M	14	3	1+1	19	M-1	Y	Y	K	P	Y	N-9 km	Y	Y	Y	56 km
Nalkheda	M	7	4	1+1	13	P-1	Y	Y	K	P	N-5 km	N-5 km	Y	Y	N-5 km	65 km

Cont'd...

Cont'd...

Bansing	F	2	2	1+1	6	M-1	Y	N	K	P	N-5 km	N-5 km	Y	N-5 km	N-5 km	40 km
Dhanodia*	F	6	13	1+0	20	M-1	Y	Y	K	P	N-5 km	N-10 km	Y	Y	N-5 km	45 km
Tehsil – Badnagar																
Baledi	M	15	5	1+1	22	P-1 M-1 H-1	Y	Y	K	P	Y	N-2 km	Y	Y	Y	24 km
Kharsodkhurd	M	16	4	1+1	22	H-1	Y	Y	K	P	Y	N-14 km	Y	Y	N-1 km	35 km
Gajnikhedi	M	13	5	1+1	20	P-1	Y	Y	K	P	N-2 km	N-12 km	Y	Y	N-2 km	65 km
Bardiya	F	9	5	1+1	16	M-1	Y	Y	K	P	Y	N-7 km	Y	N-7 km	Y	90 km
Malpura	F	8	4	1+1	14	P-1	Y	P	K	P	N-15 km	N-6 km	Y	N-5 km	N-4 km	40 km

Note: M—Male, F—Female; H—High, M—Middle, P—Primary; Y—Yes, N—No, P–Partial; K—Kachcha, P—Pakka

*Dhanodia: The Upsarpanch died after being elected; another Upsarpanch could not be elected for the rest of the term.

3. Indore District

Indore district is situated in the south-western part of Madhya Pradesh and is the southernmost part of Malwa plateau. The Vindhyachal ranges to the south of the district are at their highest. Indore district is the most populated district of the three districts of Jhabua, Ujjain and Indore, which constitute the universe of this study; it is also the most populated of all the districts of 'Rajbhogi' towns of Madhya Pradesh, viz., Jabalpur, Bhopal, Gwalior and Indore.[25] Besides being the next most densely populated district of Madhya Pradesh, Indore has the highest percentage of urban and General category population, next only to the district of Bhopal. The literacy rate is also next to highest in the state. Areawise Indore district goes much below in the list of 48 districts of the state; the only other three districts having lesser area are Bhopal, Datia and Harda.[26]

Table 2.12
Comparative Position of Indore District

State/District	*Population total*	*Urban %*	*General category %**	*Literacy rate %*	*Area sq. km*	*Density of population per sq km*
Madhya Pradesh	6,03,48,023	26.5	64.5	63.7	3,08,245	158
District						
Indore	25,85,321	70.2	77.6	75.2	3,898	471
Ujjain	17,10,982	38.7	72.2	70.9	6,031	227
Jhabua	13,94,561	8.7	10.4	36.9	6,782	167
Jabalpur	21,51,203	57.1	72.3	75.7	65,534	261
Bhopal	18,43,510	80.4	82.7	74.6	2,772	488
Gwalior	16,32,109	60.2	77.5	69.4	5,214	271

*The General category includes all others than Scheduled Castes and Scheduled Tribes.

Most of the present Indore district was a part of the erstwhile Holkar state. The Holkar dynasty was known as the promoter of commercial, educational, sports and developmental activities. Ahilyabai Holkar, the woman ruler of the dynasty was famous for her bravery, religious charity and dispensation of justice to her subjects.

Military Headquarters of War (MHOW) at a distance of 22 kilometres from district headquarters, is the oldest and largest military cantonment of the state, and also a tehsil headquarters. Army transit camps attracted many landlords to settle in the nearby area for commerce and also for agriculture. These activities flourish in the district even today. Border Security Force also has its centre at Bijasan, a township ten kilometres away from Indore city.

Topography

Lying in the southernmost part of Malwa plateau between latitudes 22.02°–23.05° to the north and longitudes 75.25° and 76.16° to the east, most of the Indore district is covered with black cotton soil and trap rocks. The climate of the district is moderately cool with 656.7 mm. of average rainfall throughout the year. Agra-Bombay National Highway passes diagonally across the district cutting the high Vindhyachal ranges towards the south. It is an important trade route of north-west India. Besides the national highway the district headquarters is well connected by rail, road and airways with all important cities not only of Madhya Pradesh but the entire country.

The river Narmada evades the district to flow into the neighbouring southern district of Paschim Nimar. The river Chambal flows through the north-western tehsil of Depalpur in south-north direction at the westernmost tip of the tehsil to enter the northern district of Ujjain. Thus the two main rivers of the region are not of direct benefit to the district. The flow of the Narmada has been slightly diverted for lifting drinking water in the district.

Resources: Physical

Devoid of mineral resources worth the name, red soil, quarry and stone are mined in a very small quantity in the district and is used as plinth material for construction of buildings. Surprisingly enough, Indore district is the major industrial centre of Madhya Pradesh with concentration of vehicle, engineering, paper and textile industries of small scale. Mostly located at Pithampur 32 kilometres away from Indore city, these industries have a major contribution to the prosperity of the district. Silk, readymade garments and food processing constitute the major portion of cottage industries numbering nearly two thousand.

The city of Indore is the oldest trade centre of cloth and readymade garments. The cloth market at Indore is known for its variety and cheap rates in the state. Hatod, a township, 30 kilometres away from Indore, is a centre of sericulture. Silk thread and silk cloth weaving are the major occupation of local people of nearby villages.

Industries are located mostly in the vicinity of Indore city. Agriculture is the main occupation in the rest of the district. Recently the Patidars of Mhow tehsil have taken up potato plantation on a large scale. Chips making and export of raw chips for further processing is a flourishing household industry in the tehsil.[27]

Almost all kinds of grains, grams, fruits, vegetables and oilseeds are cultivated in the district.[28]

Raja Ramanna Centre for Advanced Technology established at Indore in the year 1984 is conducting major research in laser and information technology. It is an added facility for research in medical, agricultural and other scientific fields. A software technology park is proposed to be established in Indore city with a view to making it an IT city of Madhya Pradesh.

Institutions of higher learning of various faculties are located in Indore city and its vicinity. Colleges of Nursing and Social Work and Institutes of Management are of special significance attracting students from all over the country. The college of Combat and the Veterinary college of Mhow are well known for the training of Armed Forces of India and catering to the veterinary needs of animals used for army purposes.

With numerous medical facilities, government and private, Indore is also the largest centre for medical treatment in the State. Promotion of sports by Holkar dynasty has given rise to well equipped sports stadia inculcating sports culture among the youth.

Thus the variety of physical resources has given a distinct place to Indore district not only in Malwa region but also in the State.

Human Resource

A very high percentage of General category population settled in urban area and having a high percentage of literacy rate, human resource of Indore district stands qualitatively different from the other two districts of this study, viz., Jhabua and Ujjain.[29] The SC population in the district nearly equals to that of the state but is lower than that of Ujjain district. The percentage of ST population is, however, double than that of Ujjain district. Jhabua stands distinct an ST district.[30]

ST population has its closed pockets in rural areas toward south and west of Indore district. Their largest concentration is in Mhow tehsil. They are akin to the tribals of Paschim Nimar and Dhar districts and are mostly Bhils and Bhilalas. SC population is spread over all the tehsils and is intermingled with the General category population of urban areas. However, their concentration is in rural areas of Sanwer tehsil. They are akin to the SCs of Ujjain district and are mostly Bagri, Balai and Chamar. They follow Malwi traditions and also have their specific geo-cultural identity along with the General category people as “Indorians”. After independence the district had played a leadership role in socio-economic and political fields in the earlier state of Madhya Bharat which still continues in the present Madhya Pradesh.[31]

Table 2.13
SC, ST Pockets in the Tehsils of Indore

State/Districts/Tehsils	*SC %*	*ST %*
Depalpur	17.84	06.00
Indore	14.81	04.12
Mhow	13.60	22.44
Sanwer	25.70	05.41

Like Ujjain district, Indore too had its share of Sindhi and Punjabi displaced persons settling in urban areas of Indore tehsil. In course of time they have captured the key industries and the business of the district. The Holkars basically followed Maharashtrian traditions and the district still has strong links with Maharashtra. People of Indore district are known for their liking of rich food of different variety. Indore sweets and namkeens constitute a significant trade of the district. A new culture of yearly trade fares lasting for three to four days has recently come up which caters to carrier information, eatables, clothes, home appliances, books, machinery, ornaments, banking and many more items under one roof. Besides this, huge department stores and malls are setting a different trend of trading/shopping at one place.

Tourism is also an expanding business in Indore with a number of historical/religious places and natural beauty spots in and around Indore district. People visiting these places prefer to stay and do shopping in Indore city.

Malwi dialect is spoken in rural areas while Hindi is spoken by most of the urban population. Once an area of largest Marathi-speaking people with predominant Maharashtrian culture, Indore has slowly acquired a multi-lingual cosmopolitan culture.

With almost highest literacy rate in the state, even of females, Indore district has the lowest sex ratio among the districts chosen for this study. This scenario reflects a strong sex-biased attitude of the people which in turn poses problems for women to assume leadership roles at grassroots level.[32]

Table 2.14
Male and Female Literacy and Sex Ratio of the Three Districts

State/District	*Male literacy rate (%)*	*Female literacy rate (%)*	*Sex ratio per 1000 males*
Madhya Pradesh	76.1	50.3	919
Districts			
Indore	84.6	64.8	912
Ujjain	83.0	57.9	938
Jhabua	48.0	25.7	986

A district with dominant urban population, Indore observes patriarchal nuclear family structure of very small size. In rural areas people prefer joint family system but it is slowly disintegrating as the youngsters shift towards urban areas for better opportunities of education, jobs, trade and business. Urban women are coming forward in socio-economic and political fields but their continued active participation depends to a great extent on the support of the male members of their families. The ultimate decision-making power still reflects a strong patriarchal hold, more so at the grassroots level.

Tehsils

Indore district consists of only four tehsils. It is a district with largest General category population of Malwa plateau. Indore tehsil, though, with highest percentage of General category population has been excluded from the sample as it has the highest urban concentration. Out of the remaining three tehsils, Depalpur with 76.1 per cent is the tehsil next to highest percentage of General category population; Mhow with 63.9 has the lowest percentage of General category population and Sanwer with 67.9 per cent stands in between in the district. They cover the northern (Sanwer), western (Depalpur) and the southern (Mhow) parts of the district. Sanwer and Depalpur tehsils are the plains of the district. Western and southern parts of Mhow tehsil are situated in the high Vindhyachal ranges. This area is also covered with reserved forest spread over 22,236 hectares. The river Choral, flowing towards the southern part of Mhow tehsil through the high mountain ranges with beautiful water-falls, has created natural spots of tourist interest in the district. The river Chambal flowing in the westernmost part of Depalpur tehsil has given it an advantageous agricultural potential in the district.

Areawise, Depalpur is the largest tehsil in the district and population-wise it has a third place in the district; it has the lowest density of population and lowest literacy rate; but it has the highest rate of work participation. All this has placed Depalpur tehsil in a unique position in terms of total cultivated land and total agricultural items (grains, grams, oilseeds fruits vegetables, etc.) produced.[33]

Table 2.15
Infrastructure of the Tehsils: Indore

Name of Tehsils	*Area sq. km*	*Population*	*Density of Population per sq. km*	*Literacy rate %*	*Work participation rate %*	*In Hectares*				
						Total land	*Cultivated Total*	*Grains Grams*	*Oil-seeds*	*Vegetables/ fruits*
Depalpur	987.91	2,11,585	174	55.53	43.03	1,18,127	25,029	8,859	35,857	76,430
Mhow	884.23	3,02,046	248	67.99	38.73	64,078	11,813	4,005	24,165	33,141
Sanwer	745.95	1,88,028	227	60.68	39.57	97,008	22,635	8,139	33,932	58,845
Indore	948.77	18,83,662	265	79.32	31.85	9,113	18,865	8,726	33,727	51,756

All the tehsils have only small-scale industries. Some of these are established by District Industries Centre and by Khadi Gramodyog Board. These are concentrated in Indore tehsil. The other three tehsils have very few small-scale industries. The entire district records no medium-large-scale industry.[34]

Table 2.16
Industries in the Tehsils: Indore

Tehsils	*Smallscale*	*Mediumscale*	*Largescale*
Depalpur	31	Nil	Nil
Mhow	41	Nil	Nil
Sanwer	30	Nil	Nil
Indore	81	Nil	Nil

All these tehsils have a strong network of kachha and pakka roads that promote trade inside and outside the district by roadways. Metre gauge rail track touches all the tehsils in small areas but is of little commercial use. It carries local traffic mostly of commuters for their jobs and of village traders in nearby areas.

Human Resource

Human resource of the three selected tehsils is different from that of Indore tehsil.

Mhow tehsil, locating army headquarters with its supporting institutional infrastructure, has cosmopolitan population with people coming from all over the country. The cantonment area of the tehsil exhibits a disciplined military culture and a distinct market. Mhow cantonment had an SC, Mahar regiment, stationed during British rule, but the tehsil today has the lowest percentage of SC population in the district (Table 2.13) despite the National Research Institute for rural,

SC and ST population in the name of Dr Ambedkar. The south-western part of Mhow tehsil has the highest concentration of ST population in the district (Table 2.13).

Sanwer tehsil has a pocket of SC population to the tune of 25.70 per cent (Table 2.13), bordering Ujjain district. They follow the same rituals and socio-cultural traditions as the General category people in the area. In villages their localities are separated from the people of other castes and at times they suffer the wrath of these castes at the slightest violation of the unwritten caste rules prevalent in the community. They are mostly agricultural labourers.

Depalpur tehsil being totally agricultural, people have predominantly rural socio-cultural character. The tehsil locates a sizeable pocket of scheduled caste population (Table 2.13) who have similar life conditions as those of Sanwer tehsil. Animal husbandry and poultry are the main occupations in both the tehsils, catering milk and eggs to hotels and households at Indore.

Thus, Indore district has a unique physical and human resource character, which distinguishes it from the other two districts chosen for this study, viz., Jhabua (ST) and Ujjain (SC).

Gram Panchayats

Indore district has 646 villages and 304 Gram Panchayats. Out of the randomly selected five Gram Panchayats from each of the three tehsils, three are headed by male and two headed by female Sarpanch. All the fifteen Gram Panchayats from the three tehsils have no urban population.

Though all the Gram Panchayats are chosen on the basis of their higher General category population, they have a sizeable number of SC and ST population. Only three Gram Panchayats of Mhow tehsil, viz., Rajpura, Sherpur and Bhicholi and one Gram Panchayat of Depalpur tehsil, viz. Birgoda, have very low percentage of SC population ranging from 0.9 to 7.3 per cent. Rest of the 12 Gram Panchayats have SC population higher than that of the district and the state, ranging from 17.3 to 39.0 per cent.

In six Gram Panchayats, one of Mhow, two of Sanwer and three of Depalpur, percentage of ST population is lower than that of the district. Remaining nine Gram Panchayats have percentage of ST population ranging from 7.7 to 85.8 per cent; higher than that of the district. Three Gram Panchayats of Mhow tehsil ranging from 42.5 per cent to 85.8 per cent ST population clearly show the concentrated pockets of Scheduled Tribes population in those areas. Gram Panchayats of Rajpura Kuti and Bhicholi of Mhow tehsil have villages, viz., Biram and Ahilyapur with hundred per cent ST population and villages Ambada and Anwaliya with 99.7 and 85.9 per cent of Scheduled Tribes population respectively.

This clearly shows the pockets of SCs and STs concentrated in some Gram Panchayats and almost none in others.

Almost all Gram Panchayats of Depalpur and Sanwer tehsils have General category population nearing to the state percentage of 64.5, but lower than that of the district. Birgoda Gram Panchayat of Depalpur tehsil has General category population to the tune of 83.53 per cent. Gram Panchayats Darji Karadia and Barodia Khan of Sanwer tehsil with 74.4 and 75.4 per cent of General category population respectively are higher in percentage than that of the state.

Mhow tehsil is unique in the categorywise population distribution. Rajpura and Bhicholi Gram Panchayats of the tehsil record a very high percentage of ST population with 85.86 and 74.03 respectively. Consequently, they have a very low percentage of General category population. Gram Panchayat Harsola has the highest percentage of General category population with 78.1 per cent. Simrol and Sherpur Gram Panchayats stand in between with 61.1 and 47.5 per cent respectively of General category population. Village Sherpur, the seat of the Gram Panchayat along with two other villages, has the highest percentage of General category population with 83.5.

Table 2.17

Human Resource Features of Indore Panchayats

Name of place	*Population total*	*Population rural*	*Population urban*	*SC Population (%)*	*ST Population (%)*	*GEN Population(%)*	*Sex Ratio: females per 1000 males*	*Illiterates (%)*	*Work participation rate (%)*
Madhya Pradesh	6,03,48,023	4,43,80,878	1,59,67,145	15.2	20.3	64.5	919	58.0	42.7
Indore	24,65,827	7,35,464	17,30,363	15.8	6.6	77.6	912	42.5	36.2
Tehsil—Depalpur 76.1% General Category Population									
Chirakhan (M)	1,431	1,431	0	21.9	20.8	57.3	960	72.5	49.5
Gokalpur(Kuti) (M)	2,361	2,361	0	35.7	0.5	63.8	1,030	65.2	52.1
Sanghvi (M)	708	708	0	37.3	0.0	62.7	1076	57.9	52.3
Chander (F)	2,367	2,367	0	22.0	3.8	74.2	935	71.9	55.1
Birgoda (F)	1,444	1,444	0	14.9	9.4	75.7	973	61.7	58.5
Keer Kheda	361	361	0	4.4	0.0	95.6	984	54.9	31.3
Mundipur	232	232	0	2.6	18.1	79.3	902	64.5	34.5
	2037	**2,037**	0	**7.3**	**9.16**	**83.53**	**953**	**60.36**	**41.43**

Cont'd...

Cont'd...

Tehsil—Sanwer 67.9% General Category Population									
Darjikaradiaya (M)	1,992	1,992	0	19.8	5.8	74.4	938	59.0	42.2
Barodiaykhan (M)	1,651	1,651		7.5	4.0	88.5	952	70.2	47.5
Kithoda	816	816	0	59.4	4.7	35.9	962	79.2	46.4
Shahda	693	693	0	8.7	0.6	90.7	952	70.6	41.3
Lohagal	405	405	0	13.3	0.0	86.7	901	80.9	54.6
	3565	**3,565**	**0**	**22.22**	**3.32**	**75.45**	**942**	**75.22**	**47.45**
Ringnodiya (M)	942	942	0	33.2	2.0	64.8	1035	64.7	41.8
Barodiya	967	967	0	42.5	1.1	56.4	645	46.2	45.6
Amli Kheda	625	625	0	41.3	20.2	38.5	806	80.9	55.2
	2,534	**2,534**	**0**	**39.0**	**7.76**	**53.23**	**828**	**63.93**	**47.53**
Pirkaradiya (F)	2,247	2,247	0	15.5	6.9	77.6	879	44.5	42.2
Baroda Arjun	1,120	1,120	0	31.5	16.2	52.3	972	49.0	49.0
	3,367	**3,367**	**0**	**23.5**	**11.55**	**64.95**	**925**	**54.15**	**66.9**
Jamburdi Sarwar (F)	980	980	0	22.9	11.2	65.9	1,068	68.2	47.1

Cont'd...

Cont'd...

Tehsil – Mhow 63.9% General Category Population									
Rajpura Kuti (M)	1,825	1,825	0	2.7	57.9	39.4	956	73.4	57.2
Biram	331	331	0	0.0	100.0	0.0	1,082	79.4	35.6
Ambada	360	360	0	0.0	99.7	0.3	895	99.3	42.8
	2,516	**2,516**	**0**	**0.9**	**85.86**	**13.23**	**978**	**84.03**	**45.2**
Simrol (M)	7,309	7,309	0	17.9	21.0	61.1	936	63.6	49.2
Harsola (M)	7,818	7,818	0	16.9	5.0	78.1	919	48.9	48.9
Sherpur (F)	709	709	0	3.8	12.7	83.5	881	44.0	50.1
Malipura	444	444	0	25.9	43.7	30.4	922	62.7	50.9
Kodiya	459	459	0	0.0	71.2	28.8	937	56.1	71.5
	1612	**1,612**	**0**	**9.9**	**42.53**	**47.56**	**913**	**54.26**	**57.5**
Bhicholi (F)	1,036	1,036	0	6.9	36.2	56.9	873	62.9	50.7
Ahilyapur	174	174	0	0.0	100.0	0.0	1,203	91.8	52.3
Anwaliya	99	99	0	0.0	85.9	14.1	707	83.3	57.6
	1,309	**1,309**	**0**	**2.3**	**74.03**	**23.66**	**928**	**79.33**	**53.5**

All the selected Gram Panchayats except two have sex ratio higher than that of the district and also of the state. Some villages of these Gram Panchayats cross even the thousand mark. Only one Gram Panchayat, Ringnodia of Sanwer tehsil, record sex ratio of 828 per thousand males, lower than that of the district and the State. This situation is surprising in view of the proximity of the Panchayat to the district headquarters Indore, which is just 16 kilometres from Ringnodia. The Panchayat is also situated on the state highway.

So far as the percentage of illiterates is concerned, all the 15 Gram Panchayats have more illiterates than that of the district and 11 of these have higher percentage of illiterates than that of the state ranging from 70 to 84.

However, all the 15 Gram Panchayats have higher percentage of work participation than that of the district and the state.[35]

It is surprising to note that Indore district with highest percentage of urban and General category population in the state with best facilities for education, sports, health, business, trade and other developmental activities, has Gram Panchayats with very high percentage of illiterates.

As regards infrastructural facilities, all the selected Gram Panchayats have primary and/or middle schools located in their areas. Two Gram Panchayats of Gokalpura and Simrol have a high school each. All the Gram Panchayats have hand pumps, electricity and housing facilities of *kachcha/pakka* types. Six Gram Panchayats have health facilities within their area and the people of the remaining nine have to travel between 3 to 9 kilometres to reach their nearest health centres. Simrol is the only Gram Panchayat having a police station in its area; the rest have this facility at a distance ranging from 3 to 15 kilometres. Only one Gram Panchayat, Jamburdi Sarvar does not have a Panchayat Bhavan of its own; the rest of course have their own Panchayat Bhawans. Ten Gram Panchayats have ration shops

Table 2.18

Infrastructural Facilities of Indore Panchayats

Name of Panchayat	M/F Headed	No. of Panch		Sar-panch and Up-sarpanch	Total	School H.M.P. No.	Hand-pump Y/N	Elec-tricity Y/N/P	Housing		Health Facility Y/N Distance in km	Police Station Distance in km	Pancha-yat Bhawan Y/N	Ration Shop Y/N Distance in km	Access to Pakka Road Distance in km	Distance from District Head-quarters in km
		M	F						K	P						
Tehsil—Depalpur																
Chirakhan	M	6	4	1+1	12	P-1	Y	P	K	P	N-5	N-16	Y	N-5	7	28
Gokalpur	M	13	3	1+1	18	P-1, H-1	Y	Y	K	P	Y	N-11	Y	Y	2	50
Sanghvi	M	3	2	1+1	7	P-1	Y	Y	K	P	N-9	N-15	Y	N-5	4	45
Chander	F	9	3	1+1	14	P-1, M-1	Y	Y	K	P	N-9	N-9	Y	Y	5	30
Birgoda	F	8	4	1+1	14	P-1, M-1	Y	Y	K	P	N-3	N-3	Y	N-3	1	43
Tehsil—Sanwer																
Dargi-karadiya	M	9	4	1+1	15	M-1	Y	Y	K	P	N-9	N-9	Y	N-2	0	26
Badodia Khan	M	13	5	1+1	20	M-1	Y	Y	K	P	Y	N-4	Y	Y	0	35

Cont'd...

Cont'd...

Ringnodiya	M	8	5	1+1	15	P-1,										
M-1	Y	Y	K	P	N-3	N-14	Y	Y	0	14						
Pirkaradiya	F	10	6	1+1	18	H-1	Y	Y	K	P	Y	N-4	Y	Y	0	24
Jamburdi Sarvar	F	9	7	1+1	18	M-1	Y	Y	K	P	N-8	N-8	N	Y	5	23
Tehsil – MHOW																
Rajpura(Kuti)	M	7	4	1+1	13	M-1	Y	Y	K	P	N-5	N-5	Y	N-7	8	40
Simrol	M	12	6	1+1	20	P-1, M-1, H-1	Y	Y	K	P	Y	Y	Y	Y	0	30
Harsola	M	12	4	1+1	18	H-1	Y	Y	K	P	Y	N-7	Y	Y	0	22
Sherpur	F	8	3	1+1	13	M-1	Y	Y	K	P	N-3	N-3	Y	Y	0	45
Bhicholi	F	6	3	1+1	11	M-1	Y	Y	K	P	Y	N-10	Y	Y	1	35

Note:

M—Male, F—Female

H—High, M—Middle, P—Primary

Y—Yes, N—No, P—Partial

within their areas; the remaining five have this facility at a distance between 2 to 7 kilometres. Seven Gram Panchayats have direct access to pakka roads; two are 1 kilometre away from such road and people from six Gram Panchayats have to travel between 2 to 8 kilometres to reach the roads. District headquarters is at a distance between 14 to 50 kilometres from the Gram Panchayat seat.[36]

Indore district stands at a significantly better position than the other two districts of Jhabua (ST) and Ujjain (SC). Physical and human resources and infrastructural facilities of Jhabua and Ujjain are no match to the ones available in Indore district. However, the Gram Panchayats of Indore district do not exhibit much difference from the Gram Panchayats of Ujjain district and to an extent even from those of Jhabua district. One of the reasons for this situation seems to be the concentration of all the facilities in Indore tehsil and much more in the vicinity of Indore city.

Figure 2.1

Madhya Pradesh: District Map

Figure 2.2
Map of Jhabua District

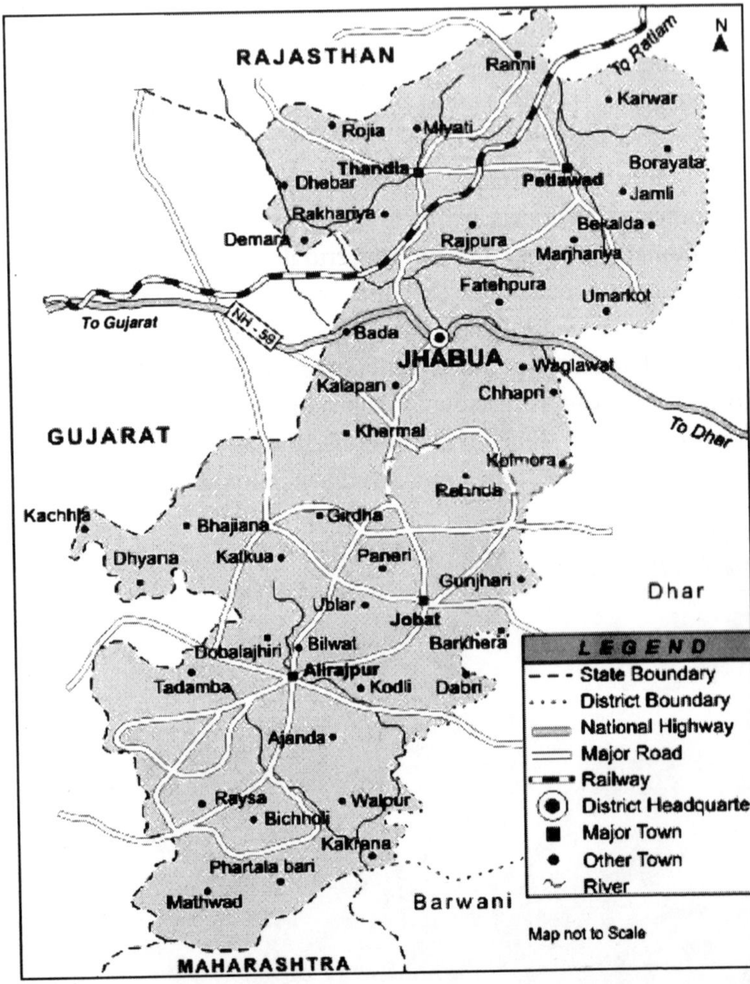

Figure 2.3
Map of Bhabra Tehsil (District Jhabua)

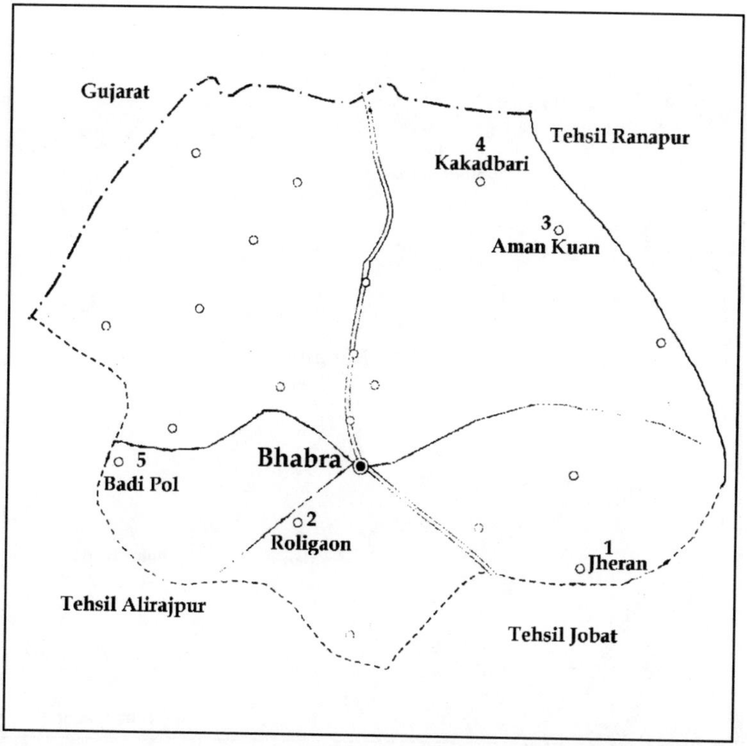

Figure 2.4
Map of Ranapura Tehsil (District Jhabua)

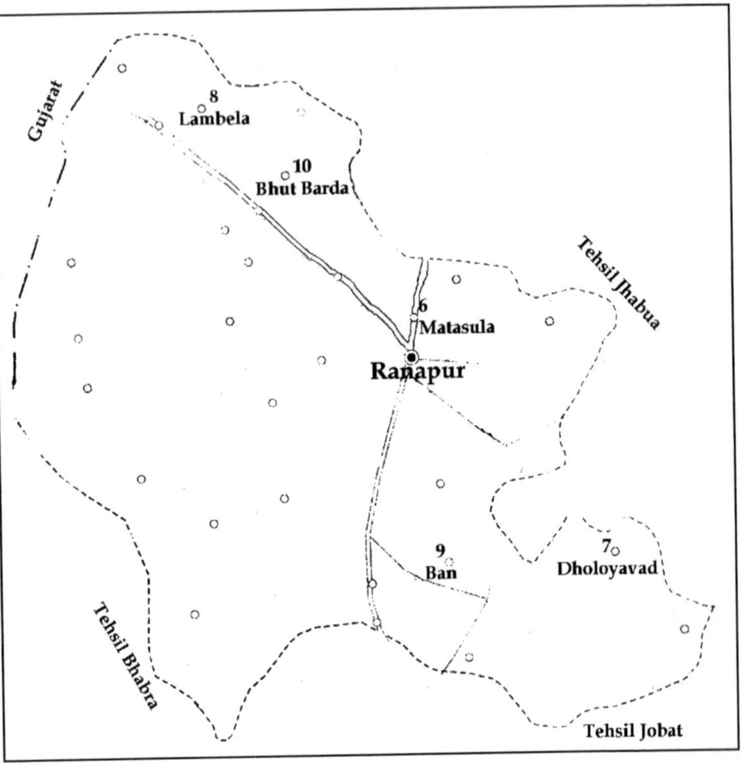

Figure 2.5
Map of Petlawad Tehsil (District Jhabua)

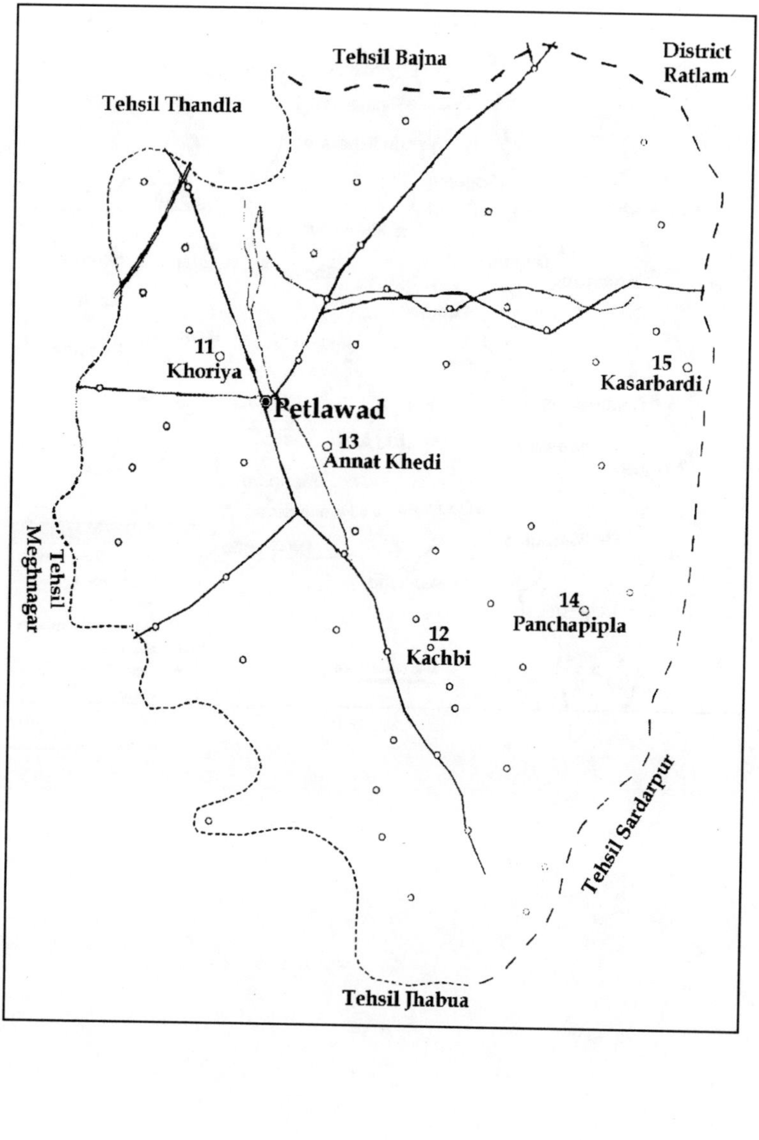

Figure 2.6
Map of Ujjain District

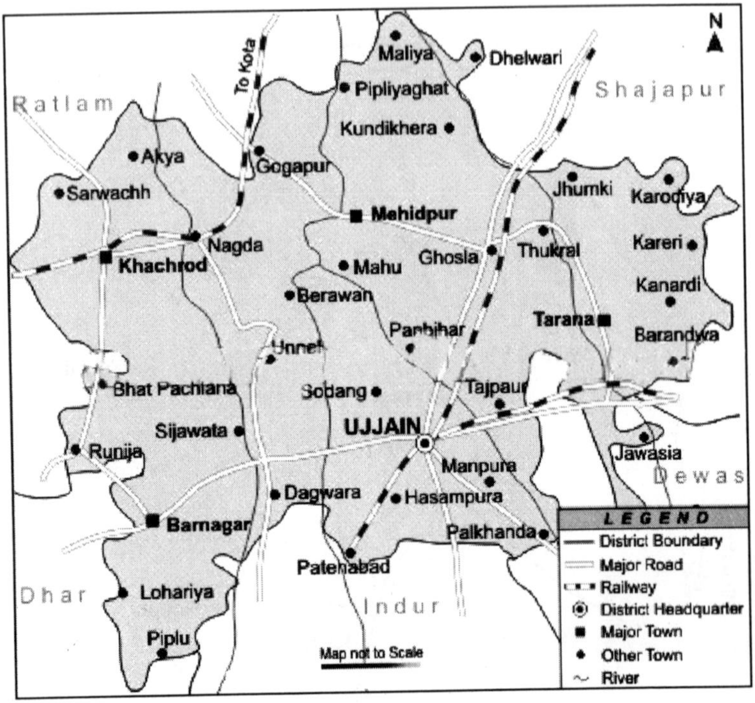

Figure 2.7
Map of Tarana Tehsil (District Ujjain)

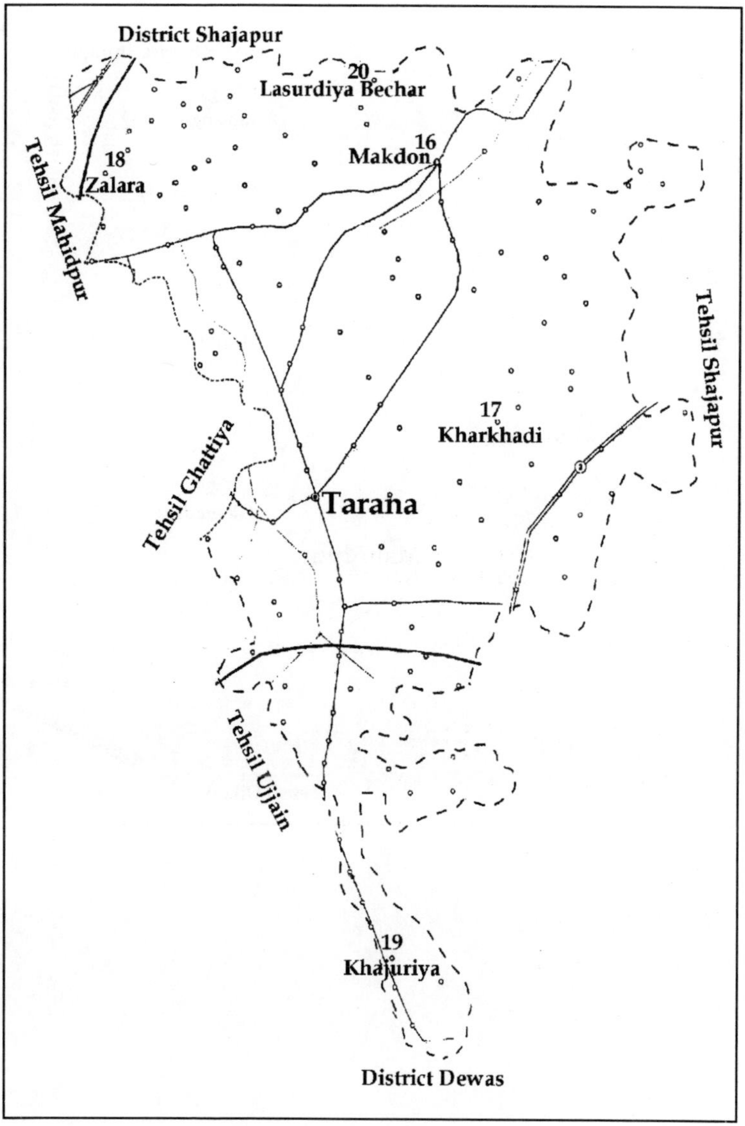

Figure 2.8
Map of Mahidpur Tehsil (District Ujjain)

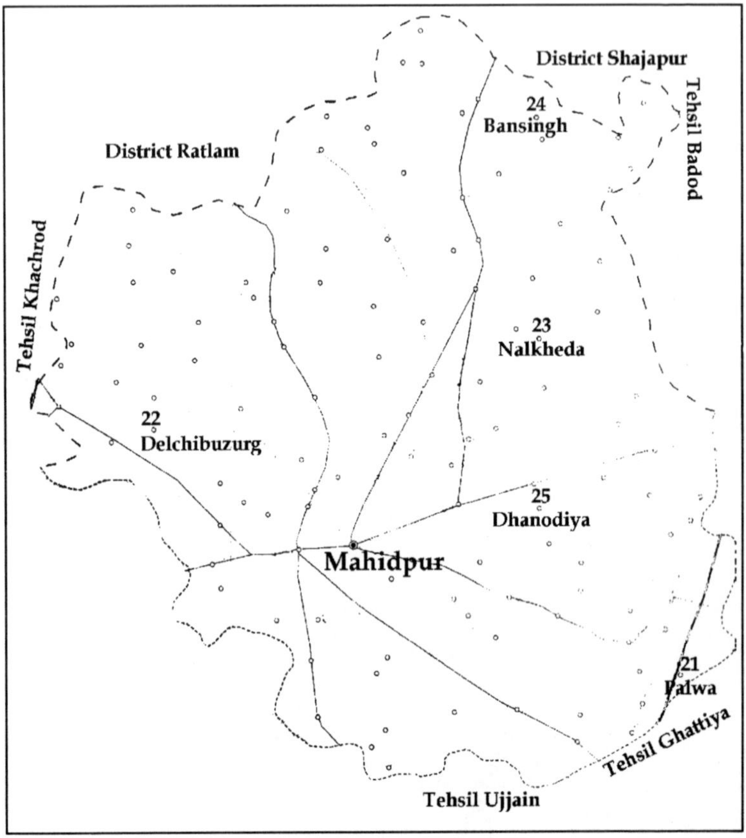

Figure 2.9
Map of Badnagar Tehsil (District Ujjain)

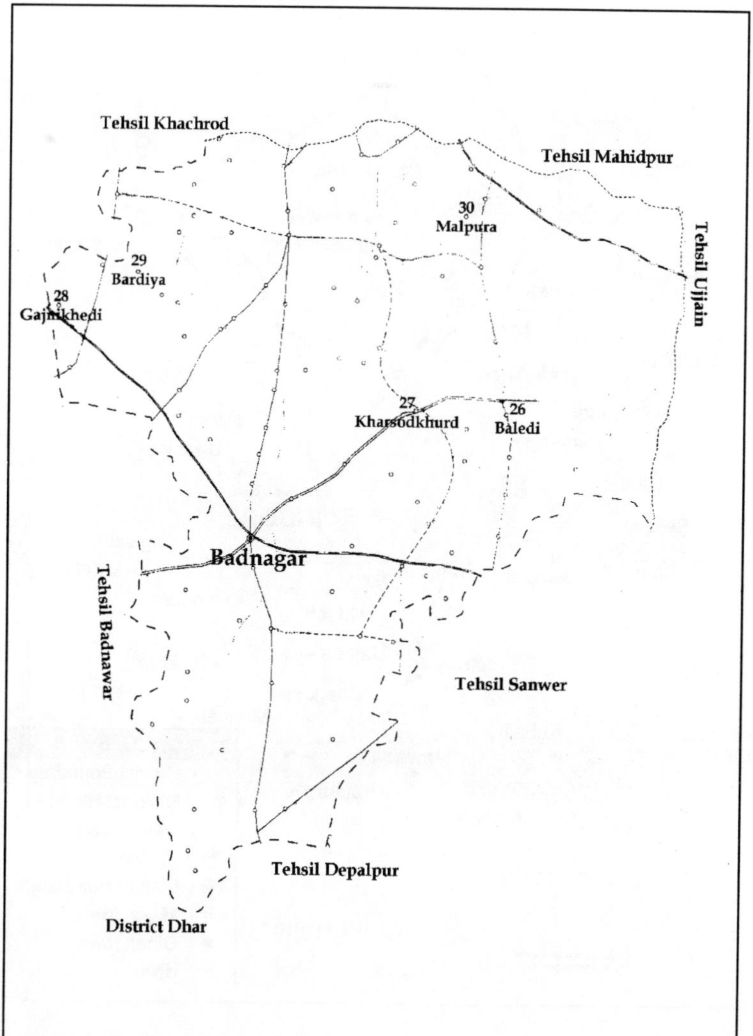

Figure 2.10
Map of Indore District

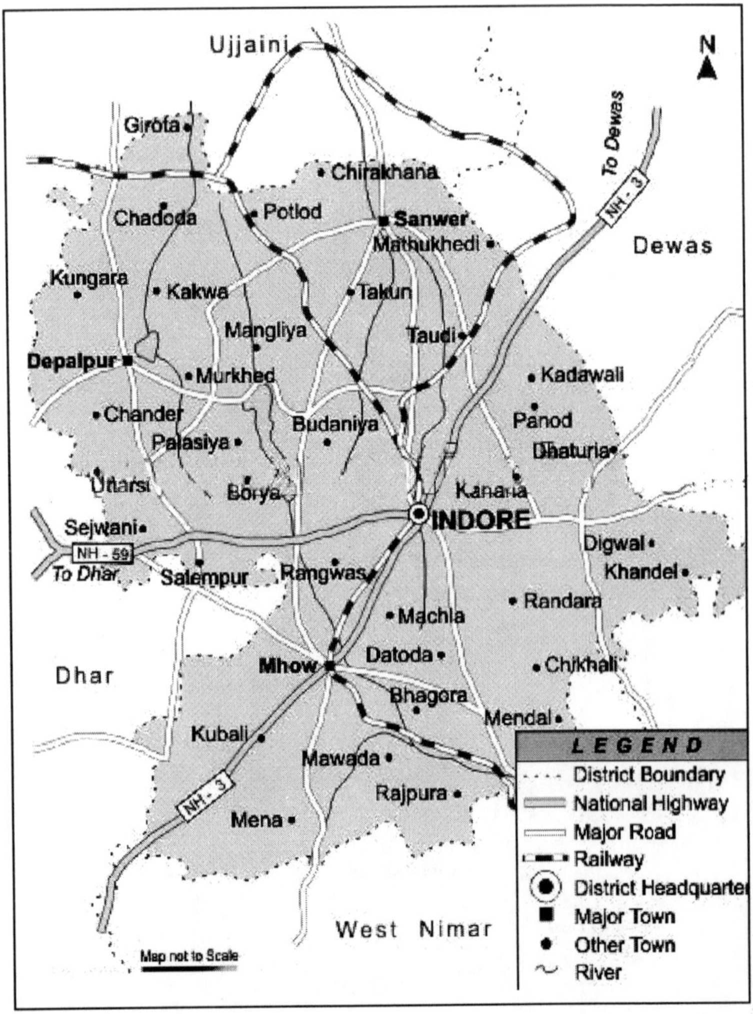

Figure 2.11
Map of Depalpur Tehsil (District Indore)

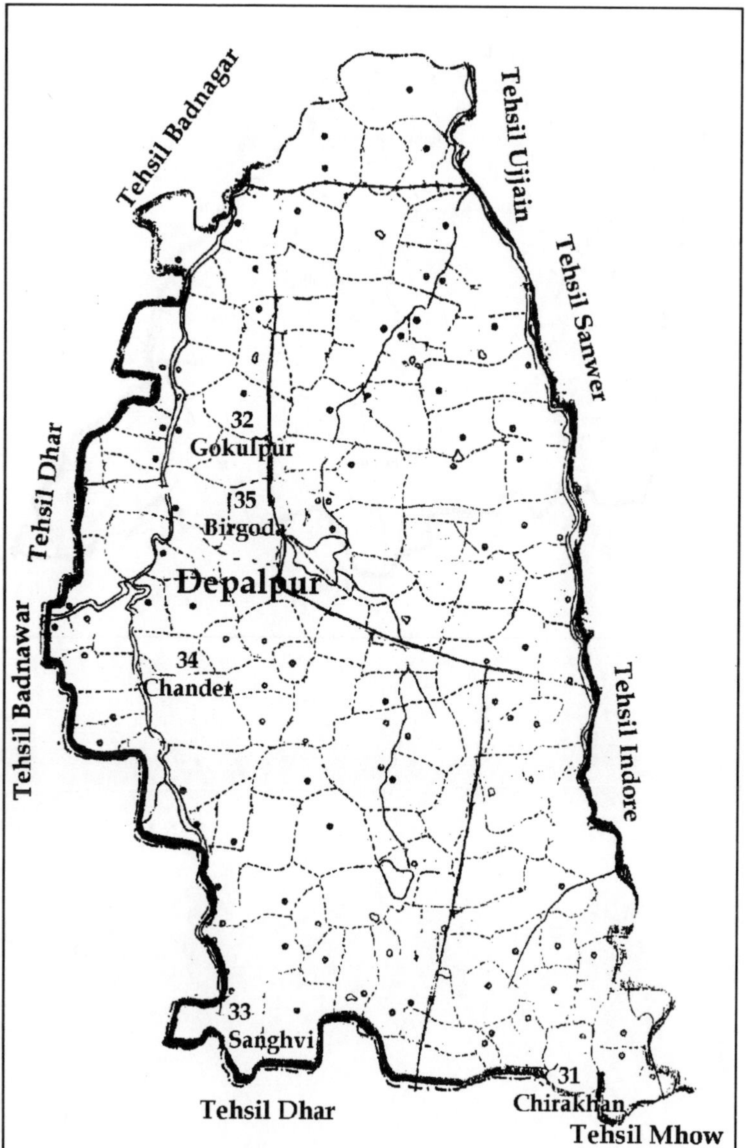

Figure 2.12
Map of Sanwer Tehsil (District Indore)

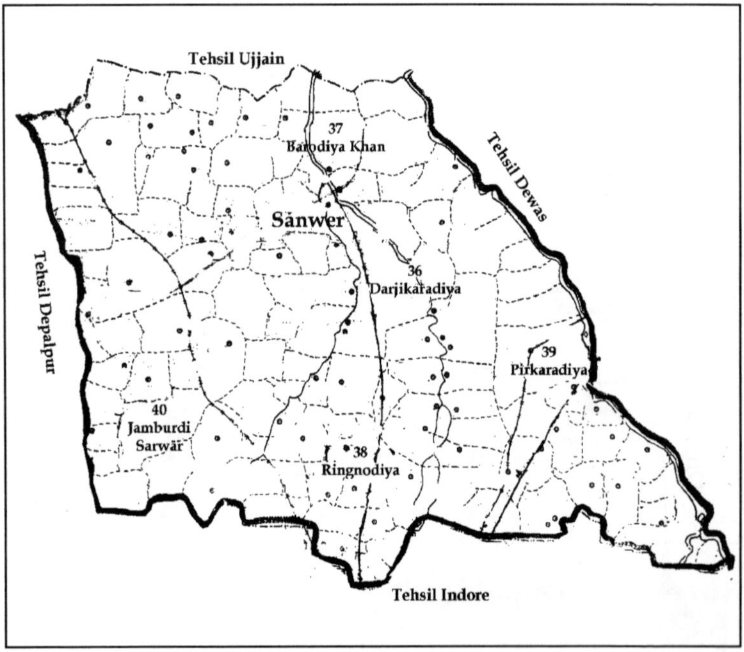

Figure 2.13
Map of MHOW Tehsil (District Indore)

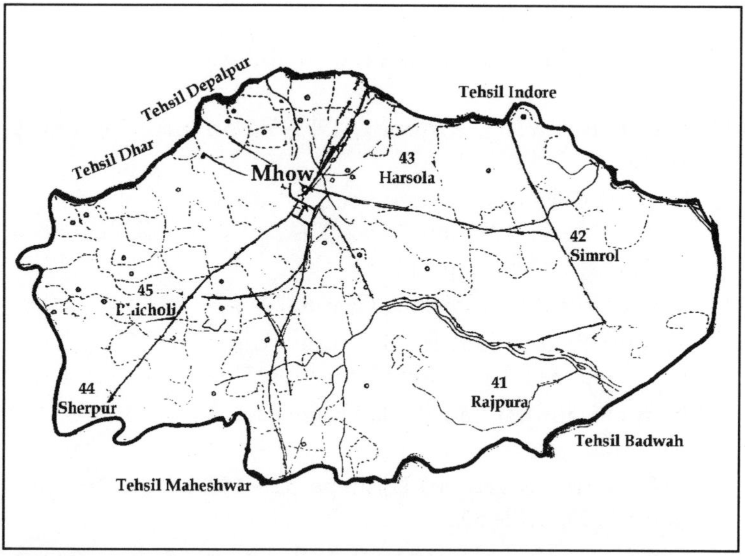

Notes

1. Office of the Registrar General India, Area Profile Madhya Pradesh and Area Profile District Jhabua, see Table 1.1.
2. District Statistical Year Book, Jhabua, 2003.
3. Report of the Centre of Water Resource Development and Management and Department of Forest, Government of Madhya Pradesh, 1980–1990.
4. Directorate of Land Records, District Statistical Year Book, Jhabua 2003, p. 31 and pp. 26–29.
5. District Statistical Year Book, Jhabua, 2003, p.47.
6. Office of the Registrar General of India, Census of India 2001, Area Profile, Jhabua.
7. Cases of loot and murder for food have been considerably reduced. Their dress code has assumed an urban look. However, most of their settlements are scattered in 'phalias' as earlier. They prefer to reside by their fields for protection and practice of their cultural traditions within their close group.

8. Recently they have started retaining their tribal names.
9. District Statistical Book, Jhabua, 2003, pp. 1, 2, 24, 47, 50.
10. Ibid., pp. 79, 80, 120, 139.
11 Office of the Registrar General, India, Area Profile Madhya Pradesh.
12. *Indian Archaeology, A Review*, 1955–56, p.1 and 1964–65, pp. 18–19.
13. District Gazetteers Department, Madhya Pradesh, Bhopal, District Ujjain, 1982, pp. 15–62. District Statistical Year Book, 2003, District Ujjain, p. 2.
14. Area Profile, Ujjain District, Census, 2001.
15. Madhya Pradesh District Gazetteers, Ujjain, pp. 107–111, the main crops and the cultivated area till 1977 shows no soyabeans.
16. District Statistical Year Book, Ujjain, 2003, Table 26, 28, 29, 30, pp. 18–20.
17. M.P. District Gazetteers, Ujjain pp. 123–148. District Statistical Book, 2003, Table 50.
18. District Gazetteers Department, M.P., Bhopal, Madhya Pradesh, District Ujjain, 1982, p. 69.
19. Ibid., p. 66. District Statistical Year Book 2003, District Ujjain Table 2.3 and 2.5, pp. 11–12.
20. Registrar General of India, New Delhi, Census 2001, Area Profile, District Ujjain.
21. Ibid., Gazetteer of India, Madhya Pradesh, Ujjain, 1982, p. 77, See Table 1.2.
22. Census 2001, District Ujjain.
23. District Statistical Year Book, Ujjain, 2003, Tables 24, 49, 55. Census of India 2001, Area Profile District Ujjain.
24. Census 2001, Area Profile of District Ujjain.
25. Rajbhogi towns have a special status in view of their development and expensiveness, hence, government pays special House Rent Allowance and Dearness Allowance to those in government service/duty in those towns (Ra: Raipur, J: Jabalpur, Bho: Bhopal, G: Gwalior, I: Indore), Raipur is now a part of Chhattisgarh.
26. Registrar General, India, New Delhi, Census 2001.

27. Census 2001 Area Profile Indore District.
28. District Statistical Year Book, Indore, 2003, pp. 21–24.
29. See Table 2.12.
30. See Table 1.1.
31. Census of India 2001. Area Profile, Madhya Pradesh, Tehsils of Indore district.
32. Ibid.
33. District Statistical Year Book, 2003 Indore, pp. 1, 2, 3, 16, 22, 25 and 70. Indore tehsil, though excluded from the sample, the tehsil is included in the tables to show its position vis-à-vis the other tehsils.
34. Ibid., p. 42.
35. Census 2001, Area Profile, District Indore.
36. Ibid.

3

The Moulding Factors

National freedom in India brought in its wake the opportunity of democratic system of governance to be adopted for the development of the Indian people. Self-government was the keynote of the struggle for independence. Decentralization was considered as the major tool of self-governance, hence federal form of government was the constitutionally accepted structure to bring more and more people closer to the activity of governance. Initially this was confined to national and states levels. It took nearly half a century to constitutionally bring local units—villages—to the centre stage in this process of decentralization.

In response to Article 40—Directive Principles of State Policy—of the Constitution, Panchayat Raj Institutions (PRIs) did exist much before the constitutional status was bestowed on these by the 73rd Constitutional Amendment Act, 1993. However, the decision-making and its implementation in these Panchayats vested mostly with the elected national or state leaders and government officials. It was also an act of power devolved from above, not emanating from the grassroots. Still leadership in PRIs has remained a widely discussed phenomenon in Indian polity even before the 73rd Constitutional Amendment Act, 1993 became operative.

Introduction of Gram Swaraj in Madhya Pradesh on January 26, 2001 converted the representative democracy of PRIs into direct democracy at rural level. The primary objective of the entire endeavour was to directly transfer power to the people, thus pushing forward the process of democratic decentralization to its ultimate end. As its corollary, it called for a vibrant and dynamic leadership at the grassroots level.

The hierarchical social order and the class, caste, wealth, religion, sex, family type and such other factors that structure the rural society, resulted in inequitable distribution of power at grass-roots level, thus marginalizing many groups from the mainstream of political life. Economically too, the rural structures were manipulated by the traditional wielders of power in villages, viz., the landlords, the moneylenders, the priests and the otherwise influential persons. To correct the resulting imbalance, the marginalized groups were required to be drawn into the process of decision-making and its implementation for an equitable socio-political structure, with the object of sustainable development. This is supposed to provide a sound base for national democracy to proceed forward towards its declared goals of liberty, equality and social justice. The reservation of seats to the marginalized ones in the 73rd Constitutional Amendment Act 1993, is an effort to bring these groups in the mainstream, with a view to ensuring the participation of the entire village community in the political process.

Scheduled Tribes, Scheduled Castes and Women were the prominently selected groups for whom seats were reserved in Gram Panchayats. Their differing socio-cultural identities, educational level, economic status, etc., posed different problems for these groups of leaders as they arrived at the threshold of the new power structure as Panchayat Raj representatives (PRRs). Besides their education and training, it was necessary to make them aware of the Panchayat processes in order to develop their confidence and capability to shoulder the power and responsibilities devolved on them. Sex discrimination being a significant factor in the patriarchal Indian society, leadership role of female PRRs posed a yet different dimension which needed special attention.

Against this backdrop the study is designed to investigate the emerging Gram Panchayat leadership of various socio-cultural groups and their women representatives. A structured interview schedule was administered to the selected PRRs. In order to verify their information/views another schedule was administered to Gram Sabha members of the same Gram Panchayat. A few questions in the main schedule were specifically addressed to women PRRs to clearly understand their position vis-à-vis their male counterparts. Help was taken of informal discussions and field observations for analysing the data collected from these schedules.

The present chapter analyses the SES characteristics of the PRRs, particularly their education, family background, their political and official level contacts, party affiliations and training, as these are the moulding factors in their assumption of leadership roles. Cross tables of the three districts depict their comparative positions.

The 73rd Constitutional Amendment Act, 1993 provides for the representation of Scheduled Tribes, Schedules Castes and General category in proportion to their percentage in the population of the concerned district. The Panchayat Extension to Scheduled Areas Act, 1996 provides for special status to tribal area Panchayats. Most significant among these is that each Panchayat in tribal area would be headed only by a tribal Sarpanch. Other PRRs could be of other categories. OBCs are opted only if the SC plus ST representatives in a Gram Panchayat are 50 per cent or below.

Table 3.1
Caste

District	*General (%)*	*SC (%)*	*ST (%)*	*OBC (%)*	*Total (%)*
Jhabua	2 (2.9)	1 (1.4)	64 (91.4)	3 (4.3)	70 (100)
Ujjain	22 (25.9)	21 (24.7)	07 (8.2)	35 (41.2)	85 (100)
Indore	14 (17.9)	8 (10.3)	03 (3.8)	53 (67.9)	78 (100)
Total	38 (16.3)	30 (12.9)	74 (31.8)	91 (39.1)	233 (100)

Castewise distribution of PRRs of the three districts reflects that Jhabua (ST) district has an overwhelming 91.4 percentage of ST PRRs as against 1.4 per cent of SC. Such an overwhelming percentage of SC PRRs in Ujjain (SC) or General category PRRs in Indore (General) is not found. However, Ujjain (SC) and Indore (General) reflect an exceptionally higher trend of OBC PRRs. The percentage of OBC PRRs is the highest in both Ujjain and Indore districts vis-à-vis the percentage of all the remaining categories. Indore, a General category district records nearly four times more of OBC PRRs vis-à-vis its General category PRRs. It seems as if General category people in Ujjain and Indore districts had left Gram Panchayat politics to OBCs.

Table 3.2
Religion

District	*Hindu (%)*	*Muslim (%)*	*Jain (%)*	*Total (%)*
Jhabua	69 (98.6)	–	01 (1.4)	70 (100)
Ujjain	85 (100)	–	–	85 (100)
Indore	75 (96.2)	03 (3.8)	–	78 (100)
Total	229 (98.3)	03 (1.3)	01 (1.4)	233 (100)

Religion as a moulding factor reveals an unexpected break-up of PRRs of the three districts. Maximum number of respondents claim to follow Hinduism. Jhabua has Jain PRRs to the tune of 1.4

per cent and Indore has Muslim PRRs to the tune of 3.8 per cent. No other religion is professed by the respondents. This is specially surprising in case of Jhabua, where a sizeable number of tribals were once converted to Christianity with Christian names. It is also astonishing in case of Ujjain where most of the SCs embraced Buddhism in response to Baba Saheb Ambedkar's call after independence. Hundred per cent respondents of Ujjain district claim to be Hindus. Informal discussions in the field in Jhabua as also in Ujjain districts revealed that the reservation provisions of the 73rd Constitutional Amendment Act, 1993 and other special benefits of national and state government schemes are extended to SCs and STs. If they declare themselves as Christians or Buddhists they become minority communities to whom these provisions do not apply. Consequently they are deprived of all such benefits and hence they prefer to declare themselves as Hindus so that their tribal or caste identities enable them to claim all such benefits. A few members of Gram Sabha in Ujjain district declared themselves as Buddhists but informed that they also write their caste—Mahar or Balai, etc.—along with their religion and enjoy all the benefits legally extended to those castes.

Figure 3.1
Education

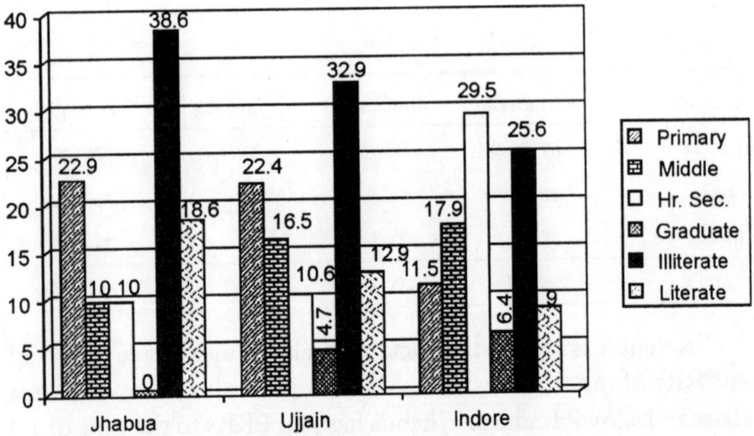

Table 3.3
Education

District	Primary (%) 1	Middle (%) 2	Hr.Sec. (%) 3	Graduate (%) 4	Illiterate (%) 5	Literate (%) 6	Total (%) 5+6	Gr. Total (%) 7
Jhabua	16 (22.9)	7 (10.0)	7 (10.0)	–	27 (38.6)	13 (18.6)	40 (57.2)	70 (100)
Ujjain	19 (22.4)	14 (16.5)	9 (10.6)	4 (4.7)	28 (32.9)	11 (12.9)	39 (45.8)	85 (100)
Indore	9 (11.5)	14 (17.9)	23 (29.5)	5 (6.4)	20 (25.6)	7 (9.0)	27 (34.6)	78 (100)
Total	44 (18.9)	35 (15.0)	39 (16.7)	9 (3.9)	75 (32.2)	31 (13.3)	106 (45.5)	233 (100)

Education is supposed to give a better understanding of the situation—legal and practical. It is supposed to enhance the capability to take decisions beneficial to the community and to properly implement them. It is also supposed to raise the level of awareness, specially required for dynamic leadership. All the selected Gram Panchayats have schools in their areas, at least of primary levels. However, the illiteracy rate of PRRs is very high in all the three districts. Field survey also reveals that the so called literates in all the three districts are those who can hardly read and can just sign; thus they are also very close to being illiterates. Together they constitute a very high percentage of the total respondents. In Jhabua (ST) it is 57.2 per cent followed by Ujjain (SC) with 45.8 per cent and in Indore (General) it is 34.6 per cent. Thus Jhabua stands at a position of disadvantage in comparison to Ujjain and Indore. Indore being a General category district with urban majority and better infrastructural facilities of education has more graduates, more higher secondary and high school passed PRRs as compared to Ujjain and Jhabua, still a total of 34.6 per cent of illiterates plus near illiterates is not a very hopeful scenario for leadership to emerge in a proper perspective. However, the rural/urban profile of the district affects the level of education of the PRRs to a considerable extent.

Table 3.4
Age

District	*25–34 (%)*	*35–44 (%)*	*45–54 (%)*	*>54 (%)*	*Total (%)*
Jhabua	9 (12.9)	23 (32.9)	29 (41.4)	9 (12.9)	70 (100)
Ujjain	11 (12.9)	31 (36.5)	30 (35.3)	13 (15.3)	85 (100)
Indore	14 (17.9)	34(43.6)	18 (23.1)	12 (15.4)	78 (100)
Total	34 (14.6)	88 (37.8)	77 (33.0)	34 (14.6)	233 (100)

Age is a factor depicting vibrancy, maturity and ability to take decisions from life experience for the benefit of the community. The PRRs of 35–44 age group have a highest percentage of 43.6 in Indore, followed by 36.5 in Ujjain and the lowest of 32.9 per cent in Jhabua. The 45–54 age group has a reverse trend of highest percentage of 41.4 in Jhabua receding to 35.3 in Ujjain and the lowest of 23.1 per cent in Indore. Thus the agewise break up shows a trend toward the matured ones. The urban and more literate district of Indore has a clear choice of mature leadership inclining towards the younger side of 35–44 age group. Group discussions clearly reflected the aspirations of the elders for the youth to come forward to shoulder the responsibilities of community development.

Table 3.5
Marital Status and Type of Family

District	*Marital Status*			*Type of Family*		
	Married (%)	*Unmarried (%)*	*Total (%)*	*Single (%)*	*Joint (%)*	*Total (%)*
Jhabua	70 (100)	–	70 (100)	43 (61.4)	27 (38.6)	70 (100)
Ujjain	85 (100)	–	85 (100)	43 (50.6)	42 (49.4)	85 (100)
Indore	78 (100)	–	78 (100)	47 (60.3)	31 (39.7)	78 (100)
Total	233 (100)	–	233 (100)	133 (57.1)	100 (42.9)	233 (100)

Hundred per cent married PRRs in all the three districts reflect a significant community choice. Marriage is associated with maturity, sense of responsibility and a reliable support of one's own kin, the conditions required for sound leadership in the discharge of its functions. As regards the type of family, Ujjain district has nearly an equal balance of single and joint families of the PRRs. Jhabua and Indore both have a ratio nearing 60:40. Jhabua's preference for nuclear families has a socio-cultural background, where newly weds build their separate huts apart from their parents; while Indore depicts economic reasons, where young couples move out of joint families for jobs/business away from their villages.

Table 3.6
Family Size

District	*1–3 (%)*	*4–6 (%)*	*7–9 (%)*	*> 9 (%)*	*Total (%)*
Jhabua	13 (18.6)	39 (55.7)	15 (21.4)	3 (4.3)	70 (100)
Ujjain	15 (17.6)	55 (64.7)	14 (16.5)	1 (1.2)	85 (100)
Indore	11 (14.1)	55 (70.5)	10 (12.8)	2 (2.6)	78 (100)
Total	39 (16.7)	149 (63.9)	39 (16.7)	6 (2.6)	233 (100)

All the three districts display the highest percentage of medium size families of 4–6 members followed by larger type of families of 7–9 members; small size of families also have a similar percentage. Families with 9 and above members are exceptions in all the three districts. This is surprising in view of rural traditions of large families considered essential for agricultural purposes just a decade or two ago. Legal prohibition is one reason. Informal discussions revealed that there was a widespread resistance to the two-child norm for the PRRs in all the three districts. People seem to be quite innovative in evading the two-child norm for the PRRs. Some record their own children as children of some other members of their families who are not PRRs. Some send the women to some remote village away from their own, in early stages of pregnancy so that no one knows that they have added a child to their family. In some cases women are deserted for ever, the male PRR marrying another woman with one child. Relatives of PRRs are at times forced to adopt the new-borns or take over the responsibility of nurturing the extra children of PRRs as their own on the decided cost which at times is quite high. Out of 2,122 total cases of disqualification, 1,140, i.e., 54 per cent were for the violation of two-child norm. Most of these were ST, SC and OBC, to the count of 72 per cent. Women overall formed 41 per cent disqualified vis-à-vis their total reservation of 33 per cent only. Foul practices and extreme pressures to amend the provision have forced the government to reconsider the situation. An ordinance has been promulgated by the state government on June 6, 2006 deleting the provision.[1]

Table 3.7
Residence Type

District	*Kachha (%)*	*Pakka (%)*	*Half Pakka (%)*	*Total (%)*
Jhabua	36 (51.4)	12 (17.1)	22 (31.4)	70 (100)
Ujjain	42 (49.4)	26 (30.6)	17 (20.0)	85 (100)
Indore	19 (24.4)	38 (48.7)	21 (26.9)	78 (100)
Total	97 (41.6)	76 (32.6)	60 (25.8)	233 (100)

The highest percentage of 51.4 of Jhabua PRRs have kachha houses made of mud walls and *kavelu* roof followed by 49.4 of Ujjain PRRs and the lowest of 24.4 of Indore PRRs. Pakka houses built up of bricks and cement have a reverse direction of highest in Indore receding in Ujjain and the lowest in Jhabua. Pakka portions added to kachha houses at a later stage depict an interesting trend, highest in Jhabua receding in Indore and the lowest in Ujjain. Pakka houses/portions are considered as marks of prosperity, status and influence of the PRRs in the community. A few villagers confided that the pakka houses or portions are mostly built after they became PRRs, thus indirectly pointing to the misuse of power for personal gains.

Table 3.8
Occupation

District	*Agriculture (%)*	*Business (%)*	*Labour (%)*	*Housewives (%)*	*Total (%)*
Jhabua	69 (98.6)	–	1 (1.4)	–	70 (100)
Ujjain	66 (77.6)	3 (3.5)	11 (12.9)	5 (6.0)	85 (100)
Indore	51 (65.4)	13 (16.7)	5 (6.4)	9 (11.5)	78 (100)
Total	186 (79.85)	16 (6.86)	17 (7.29)	14 (6.00)	233 (100)

Agriculture is the occupation of the highest percentage of PRRs in Jhabua 98.6 followed by Ujjain with 77.6 and Indore with 65.4. Business as occupation has the highest percentage of

Figure 3.2
Occupation

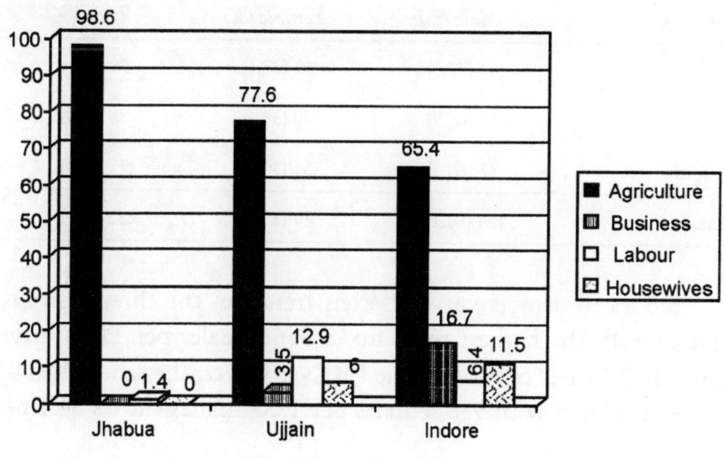

16.7 in Indore and very low of 3.5 in Ujjain. No PRR in Jhabua records business as his/her occupation. A few of PRRs record labour as their occupation. Their percentage is highest in Ujjain with 12.9, followed by Indore with 6.4. Jhabua has the lowest of 1.4 per cent who have labour as their main occupation. Female PRRs' response of being just housewives as an occupation is quite astonishing. None of the Jhabua PRRs records that she is just a housewife. It is the highest with 11.5 per cent in Indore followed by 5.9 per cent in Ujjain. This situation is again surprising in the General category urban district of Indore with the highest literacy rate and best infrastructural facilities for all types of general and professional education and also the best opportunities of service/business. In Jhabua, the rural ST district, female PRRs seem to be engaged in gainful economic activity on a larger scale. This, however, has not resulted in their empowerment in the socio-political field where they are just followers of their men folk. Neither have the female PRRs of Indore district been able to make a mark in assuming dynamic Gram Panchayat leadership.

Table 3.9
Sex

District	*Male (%)*	*Female (%)*	*Total (%)*
Jhabua	51 (72.9)	19 (27.1)	70 (100)
Ujjain	56 (65.9)	29 (34.1)	85 (100)
Indore	47 (60.3)	31 (39.7)	78 (100)
Total	154 (66.1)	79 (33.9)	233 (100)

Sex ratio depicts very different trends in the three districts. Jhabua with the highest sex ratio of 986 females per 1,000 males has only 27.1 per cent of female PRRs not even the sanctioned 33 per cent. Ujjain with 938 females per 1,000 males shows 34.1 per cent of women PRRs. Indore with the lowest sex ratio of 912 females per 1,000 males exhibits the highest percentage of 39.7 female PRRs. Leaving apart a few exceptions, however, no specific constructive leadership role by women representatives on an average is identified in the universe of this study.

Table 3.10
Income

District	*< 10,000 (%)*	*10,001–20,000 (%)*	*20,001–30,000 (%)*	*30,001–60,000 (%)*	*> 60,000 (%)*	*Total (%)*
Jhabua	41 (58.6)	13 (18.6)	5 (7.1)	8 (11.4)	3 (4.3)	70 (100)
Ujjain	30 (35.3)	19 (22.4)	6 (7.1)	11 (12.9)	19 (22.4)	85 (100)
Indore	9 (11.5)	10 (12.8)	10 (12.8)	14 (17.9)	35 (44.9)	78 (100)
Total	80 (34.3)	42 (18.0)	21 (9.0)	33 (14.2)	57 (24.5)	233 (100)

Sound economic background provides greater influence to PRRs in the discharge of their leadership role. Indore, the urban General category district has the highest percentage of 44.9 PRRs having yearly income of Rs 60,000 and above. Jhabua, the rural ST district has the lowest count of 4.3 per cent in this slab. Yearly income of Rupees 10,000 and below has the reverse trend of highest percentage of 58.6 in Jhabua and the lowest of 11.5 in Indore. Ujjain district has the middle position in both the slabs.[2] Thus Jhabua (ST) is a district with majority of PRRs of poor background vis-à-vis Ujjain (SC) and Indore (General).

Assets and landholding also show a similar tendency as is seen in income variable. The lesser the assets and landholding, the higher is the percentage in Jhabua, lower in Ujjain and the lowest in Indore. The more the assets and landholding, the higher is the percentage in Indore and lower in Ujjain, with Jhabua having the lowest count.

Table 3.11
Assets[3] and Landholding

District	*Assets*					*Land Holding*				
	0–4 (%)	*5–9 (%)*	*10–14 (%)*	*15–20 (%)*	*Total (%)*	*0–4 (%)*	*5–9 (%)*	*10–14 (%)*	*15–20 (%)*	*Total (%)*
Jhabua	58 (82.9)	6 (8.6)	1 (1.4)	5 (7.1)	70 (100)	61 (87.1)	6 (8.6)	2 (2.9)	1 (1.4)	70 (100)
Ujjain	54 (63.5)	15 (17.6)	3 (3.5)	13 (15.3)	85 (100)	66 (77.6)	9 (10.6)	4 (4.7)	6 (7.1)	85 (100)
Indore	29 (37.2)	15 (19.2)	10 (12.8)	24 (30.8)	78 (100)	54 (69.2)	11 (14.1)	10 (12.8)	3 (3.9)	78 (100)
Total	141 (60.5)	36 (15.5)	14 (6.0)	42 (18.0)	233 (100)	181 (77.7)	26 (11.2)	16 (6.8)	10 (4.3)	233 (100)

Income, assets and landholdings together show the economic strength or weakness of the PRRs. PRRs having sound economic position exhibit confidence and courage in decision-making and also its implementation. They have more influence in procuring grants from various sources. Jhabua PRRs stand at a disadvantage on this count as a majority of them have a weaker economic position. Though the central and state governments have a number of special development schemes for the ST district of Jhabua, the PRRs are not in a position to reap the fruits, as they lack confidence and courage. Their high rate of illiteracy is also one of the reasons for this situation (see Table 3.3). PRRs of Ujjain district are in a better position and PRRs of Indore district have the best footing, on these grounds.

However, exceptions are found in the field, when lower economic position and illiteracy have not deterred a PRR in assuming a confident and courageous leadership role and vice versa when an educated PRR with sound economic position was unable to do anything for the community.

Kamlabai

Makdon Gram Panchayat of Ujjain (SC) district has a female SC Sarpanch, Kamlabai, having very weak economic position with less than Rs 10,000 of annual income, no assets and just 2.4 hectares of unirrigated, almost barren land. She has a family of six members and is literate to the extent of just signing the papers. Kamlabai was elected Upsarpanch in the first Gram Panchayat elections. She seemed to be aware of the problems of the Panchayat and knew the contact points where these could be solved. She was able to procure grants from the central and also from the state government, from MP and MLA funds. With these funds she could get the village roads pitched, a connecting bridge built, a water ghat and funeral ghat constructed in the Gram Panchayat. She was bold enough to contact the concerned administrative officers and the political leaders of the area and was proud of meeting the then Chief Minister when the sanctioned grant for her Panchayat was not released. She had to face boycott by her jati panchayat for her activities of social upliftment of SC women. However, she is very vocal about the conservative traditions still followed by her caste people and lack of coordination between the SCs and the so-called upper castes. She considers the negative attitude of the upper caste people as the cause of Makdon Gram Panchayat not receiving full benefit of the Panchayat Raj system.

Sohanlal

On the other hand, Sohanlal, a General category male Sarpanch of Gram Panchayat Ringnodia of Indore district with extremely sound socio-economic position was handicapped to assume a bold leadership role due to politico-legal litigation concerning his own election which he had to fight upto the Supreme Court. Sohanlal with an yearly agricultural income of nearly 2 lakh, assets to the tune of 6 lakh and 12 hectares of irrigated land has a joint family of more than 10 members. He has a big pakka house on state highway, is educated up to higher secondary and has good contacts with administrative officials and political persons. An enthusiastic person for the development of the Gram Panchayat, Sohanlal fell victim to an 'administrative trick' as he calls it, during the counting of votes. He had to take resort to the court of law. The lower court though declared him elected as Sarpanch, the Panchayat was banned from any financial transactions till the final settlement of the dispute, which took almost the entire term for which he was elected. There was many an announcement for the development of the Gram Panchayat and also sanctioned funds, but no work could be undertaken with the result that people declared him as a corrupt person who used the funds for his personal gains.

However, both are exceptions that prove the rule.

Table 3.12
Personal Political Background and Post Held

District	*Personal Political Background*			*Post Held*			
	Yes (%)	*No (%)*	*Total (%)*	*Sarpanch (%)*	*Upsarpanch (%)*	*Panch (%)*	*Total (%)*
Jhabua	51 (21.4)	55 (78.6)	70 (100)	5 (33.3)	2 (13.3)	8 (53.3)	15 (17.9)
Ujjain	23 (27.1)	62 (72.9)	85 (100)	3 (13.0)	3 (13.0)	17 (73.9)	23 (10.7)
Indore	18 (23.1)	60 (76.9)	78 (100)	2 (11.1)	1 (5.6)	15 (83.3)	18 (71.4)
Total	56 (24.0)	177 (76.0)	233 (100)	10 (17.9)	6 (10.7)	40 (71.4)	56 (100)

The majority of PRRs in all the three districts deny having any personal political background, i.e., they were elected for the first time. A total of 24.0 per cent accept having personal political background. A majority of them (71.4%) were Panch. Amongst Jhabua PRRs 33.3 per cent had the earlier experience of being Sarpanch, while Ujjain had 13.0 per cent and Indore only 11.1 per cent of PRRs with previous experience of Sarpanch. They accept that their previous political experience has made them more matured to assume a better leadership role. However, their count is insignificant in all the three districts.

Table 3.13
Political Background of Family and Post Held

District	*Political background of family*			*Post held*		
	Yes (%)	*No (%)*	*Total (%)*	*Sarpanch (%)*	*Panch (%)*	*Total (%)*
Jhabua	26 (37.1)	44 (62.9)	70 (100)	11 (42.3)	15 (57.7)	26 (100)
Ujjain	21 (24.7)	64 (75.3)	85 (100)	7 (33.3)	14 (66.7)	21 (100)
Indore	25 (32.1)	53 (67.9)	78 (100)	13 (52.0)	12 (48.0)	25 (100)
Total	72 (30.9)	161 (69.1)	233 (100)	31 (43.1)	41 (56.9)	72 (100)

Figure 3.3
Party Affiliations

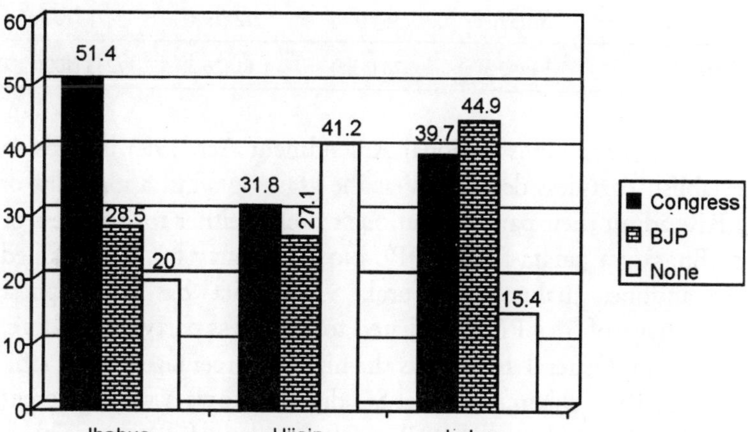

About 30.9 per cent of the total PRRs of the three districts have emerged from the families having political background. 56.9 per cent of the total count of such families were panch and 43.1 per cent were Sarpanch. Thus, these families had political background at grassroots level only. None of them personally and none from their families held a political post at district, state or national levels. A sole example of a female Sarpanch, Tola Bai of Gram Panchayat Ban of district Jhabua was identified whose maternal uncle was an MP She did display a high degree of political awareness as she had some formal education. She, however, accepted that ultimately her husband looks after her entire Panchayat work and she looks after the cultivation of the land and the family. As it was a seat reserved for ST women, she could get a chance to become a Sarpanch. Chapter 5 will have a discussion on women PRRs.

Table 3.14
Party Affiliations

District	*Congress (%)*	*BJP (%)*	*None (%)*	*Total (%)*
Jhabua	36 (51.4)	20 (28.5)	14 (20.0)	70 (100)
Ujjain	27 (31.8)	23 (27.1)	35 (41.2)	85 (100)
Indore	31 (39.7)	35 (44.9)	12 (15.4)	78 (100)
Total	94 (40.3)	78 (33.5)	61 (26.2)	233 (100)

The 73rd Constitutional Amendment Act, 1993 intends to establish partyless democracy at the grassroots but a majority of PRRs admit their party affiliations which is either to Congress or to Bharatiya Janata Party (BJP). No third party has been named by anyone. Jhabua, the rural, ST district has the highest percentage of 51.4 PRRs affiliated to Congress party and Indore, the urban, General district has the highest percentage of 44.9 affiliated to BJP. Ujjain, the rural SC district shows a very different trend of 41.2 per cent of PRRs with no party affiliations. This is the highest within the district vis-à-vis the Congress and BJP affiliations, and is also highest of no affiliations vis-à-vis Jhabua (ST) and Indore (General).

Table 3.15
Participation in Political Assemblies/Rallies

District	*Yes (%)*	*No (%)*	*Total (%)*
Jhabua	49 (70.0)	21 (30.0)	70 (100)
Ujjain	30 (35.3)	55 (64.7)	85 (100)
Indore	30 (38.5)	48 (61.5)	78 (100)
Total	109 (46.8)	124 (53.2)	233 (100)

PRRs participation in political assemblies/rallies shows highest percentage of 70.0 in Jhabua followed by Indore with 38.5 and lowest of 35.3 in Ujjain. 'No Participation' percentage is the highest of 64.7 in Ujjain followed by 61.5 in Indore and the lowest with 30.0 in Jhabua. The highest 'No' response of Ujjain and Indore PRRs clearly shows their apathy towards political activity. Those who participated in political activity did not in any way exhibit more political awareness or a higher level of understanding about the problems of their respective Gram Panchayats. Most of the PRRs could not name the party or the assembly or rally in whose activity they participated and for which purpose. Some of them were bold enough to accept that they were taken by party workers in a truck or tractor trolley, were nicely fed and transported back to their villages. This seemed to be a mob gathering exercise and not a constructive political activity through which the PRRs could be moulded for their leadership roles at grassroots level.

The PRRs contacts with political personalities and officials incharge at higher levels of governance could be of great help in expanding their horizon and moulding their attitudes towards constructive leadership. It was tried to assess how regularly the

PRRs maintain these contacts and get the benefits for their Panchayat work. The following Tables 3.16 and 3.17 depict a dismal picture as the PRRs maintain contacts at very restricted levels either with political persons or with officials.

Table 3.16
PRRs Contacts with Political Persons

Political Persons	*District*	*No (%)*	*Once (%)*	*2–4 times (%)*	*Often (%)*	*Total (%)*
Janpad Chairperson	Jhabua	38 (54.3)	6 (8.6)	7 (10.0)	19 (27.1)	70 (100)
	Ujjain	57 (67.1)	9 (10.6)	7 (8.2)	12 (14.1)	85 (100)
	Indore	53 (67.9)	6 (7.7)	6 (7.7)	13 (16.7)	78 (100)
	Total	148 (63.5)	21 (9.0)	20 (8.6)	44 (18.9)	233 (100)
Zila Panchayat Chairperson	Jhabua	49 (70.0)	8 (11.4)	4 (5.7)	9 (12.9)	70 (100)
	Ujjain	64 (75.2)	10 (11.8)	5 (5.9)	6 (7.1)	85 (100)
	Indore	55 (70.5)	6 (7.7)	6 (7.7)	11 (14.1)	78 (100)
	Total	168 (72.1)	24 (10.3)	15 (6.4)	26 (11.2)	233 (100)
Local MLA	Jhabua	44 (62.8)	13 (18.6)	3 (4.3)	10 (14.3)	70 (100)
	Ujjain	57 (67.1)	11 (12.9)	9 (10.6)	8 (9.4)	85 (100)
	Indore	51 (65.4)	7 (9.0)	2 (2.6)	18 (23.0)	78 (100)
	Total	152 (65.2)	31 (13.3)	14 (6.0)	36 (15.5)	233 (100)
Member of Parliament	Jhabua	49 (70.0)	9 (12.9)	3 (4.2)	9 (12.9)	70 (100)
	Ujjain	69 (81.2)	7 (8.2)	6 (7.1)	3 (3.5)	85 (100)
	Indore	62 (79.5)	3 (3.8)	5 (6.4)	8 (10.3)	78 (100)
	Total	180 (77.2)	19 (8.2)	14 (6.0)	20 (8.6)	233 (100)
Chief Minister	Jhabua	60 (85.7)	7 (10.0)	1 (1.4)	2 (2.9)	70 (100)
	Ujjain	78 (91.8)	6 (7.1)	1 (1.2)	—	85 (100)
	Indore	74 (94.9)	1 (1.3)	—	3 (3.8)	78 (100)
	Total	212 (91.0)	14 (6.0)	2 (0.9)	5 (2.1)	233 (100)

Table 3.17
PRRs Contacts with Government Officials

Officials	*District*	*No (%)*	*Once (%)*	*2–4 times (%)*	*Often (%)*	*Total (%)*
Janpad CEO	Jhabua	41 (58.6)	8 (11.4)	3 (4.3)	18 (25.7)	70 (100)
	Ujjain	57 (67.0)	6 (7.1)	10 (11.8)	12 (14.1)	85 (100)
	Indore	53 (67.9)	6 (7.7)	7 (9.0)	12 (15.4)	78 (100)
	Total	151 (64.8)	20 (8.6)	20 (8.6)	42 (18.0)	233 (100)
Zila Panchayat CEO	Jhabua	56 (80.0)	10 (14.3)	–	4 (5.7)	70 (100)
	Ujjain	71 (83.5)	6 (7.1)	7 (8.2)	1 (1.2)	85 (100)
	Indore	66 (84.6)	2 (2.6)	5 (6.4)	5 (6.4)	78 (100)
	Total	193 (82.8)	18 (7.7)	12 (5.2)	10 (4.3)	233 (100)
BDO	Jhabua	48 (68.6)	15 (21.4)	2 (2.9)	5 (7.1)	70 (100)
	Ujjain	71 (83.5)	6 (7.1)	5 (5.9)	3 (3.5)	85 (100)
	Indore	69 (88.5)	3 (3.8)	2 (2.6)	4 (5.1)	78 (100)
	Total	188 (80.7)	24 (10.3)	9 (3.9)	12 (5.1)	233 (100)
Collector	Jhabua	53 (75.7)	11 (15.7)	3 (4.3)	3 (4.3)	70 (100)
	Ujjain	71 (83.5)	10 (11.8)	3 (3.5)	1 (1.2)	85 (100)
	Indore	70 (89.7)	3 (3.8)	2 (2.7)	3 (3.8)	78 (100)
	Total	194 (83.3)	24 (10.3)	8 (3.4)	7 (3.0)	233 (100)

As regards PRRs contacts with political persons, their negative response is the highest in all the three districts. The next, in all the three districts, comes the percentage of contacts with MLAs. It is due to the MLA fund which they easily sanction for development works in Gram Panchayats and thus nurture their constituency. MPs too have such funds but the PRRs inform that they find it difficult to contact MPs, and more difficult to get a share out of their funds as their constituencies cover a larger area of the three-tier Panchayat Raj system. The PRRs do contact chairpersons of Janpad Panchayats; Janpad being the immediate fund releasing agency but not quite often the chairpersons of Zila Panchayats. Other social/political persons or traditional village heads do not attract them at all.

Regular contacts with political persons could be of help to PRRs in raising their political awareness and moulding them into dynamic leadership role in the community but the PRRs view these contacts from financial point only. This results in their short term vision of community development and has a clear impact on their restricted leadership vis-à-vis a broader horizon of the 73rd Constitutional Amendment Act, 1993. PRRs development vision revolves round beneficiaries selection, construction of a few kilometres of road, hand pumps, a bridge, a ration shop, a primary health centre and a school within the village area. This might be due to their deprivation of basic amenities for a long time and these need to be fulfilled before they could be pushed towards the spectrum.

The PRRs contacting government officials at higher levels also exhibit a similar trend.

PRRs contacting government officials of all the higher levels have a maximum percentage of 'No' count in all the three districts. Next in count is their contacts with Janpad CEO which is 25.7, 14.1 and 15.4 in Jhabua, Ujjain and Indore respectively. This is the highest of their positive response in all the three districts. This clearly shows that the majority of PRRs in all the three districts do not regularly contact even the government officials concerned with Panchayat work.

Thus the PRRs normally confine their contacts to Janpad CEO, Janpad chairperson and local MLA, the immediate upper level either at political or bureaucratic strata. The emerging leadership seems to be unaware of the benefits of maintaining regular contacts with political persons and with government officials which might enlighten them for a better leadership role. Nonetheless this has limited their activity to a narrower field and to very limited persons, not congenial to the evolution of dynamic leadership at the grassroots. More consistent efforts are required for their exposure and understanding in order to mould them into dynamic leaders.

Besides the SES characteristics, caste, religion, education, wealth, family background, political and bureaucratic contacts, training is a significant moulding factor. PRRs need to be trained for the responsibilities devolved on them. Many government agencies and NGOs are engaged in the training process for PRRs. However, the field situation indicates that these efforts fall short of the required need.

Table 3.18
Training and Subject of Training Received

District	*PRRs training*			*Subject of training total Yes—24 (10.3)*			
	Yes (%)	*No (%)*	*Total (%)*	*Panchayat process (%)*	*Agric-ulture (%)*	*Enviro. Conser. (%)*	*Total (%)*
Jhabua	11 (15.7)	59 (84.3)	70 (100)	8 (72.7)	1 (9.1)	2 (18.2)	11 (100)
Ujjain	2 (2.4)	83 (97.6)	85 (100)	2 (100)	—	—	2 (100)
Indore	11 (14.1)	67 (85.9)	78 (100)	9 (81.8)	2 (18.2)	—	11 (100)
Total	24 (10.3)	209 (100)	233 (100)	19 (79.2)	3 (12.5)	2 (8.3)	24 (100)

A vast majority of PRRs have not received any training. The highest percentage of those who have received training is in Jhabua and that too to the count of 15.7 only, followed by Indore,

14.1 and the lowest in Ujjain, just 2.4. The total count of such PRRs is just 10.3 per cent. The types of training they named are the ones of Panchayat Process, Agriculture and Environment Conservation. The highest percentage is that of Panchayat Process, 72.7, 100 and 81.8 in Jhabua, Ujjain and Indore respectively. 9.1 per cent of Jhabua PRRs and 18.2 per cent of Indore PRRs accept having received training in Agriculture, while 18.2 per cent of Jhabua PRRs respond that they received training in environment conservation also.

Thus, training which could edify the PRRs for a better leadership role has not been imparted on a wider scale. Majority of PRRs do feel the necessity of training but a sizeable percentage of them also respond in negative about the need for training as is clear by the following table:

Table 3.19
Need for Training

District	*Yes (%)*	*No (%)*	*Total (%)*
Jhabua	39 (55.7)	31 (44.3)	70 (100)
Ujjain	61 (71.8)	24 (28.2)	85 (100)
Indore	46 (59.0)	32 (41.0)	78 (100)
Total	146 (62.7)	87 (37.3)	233 (100)

It is not the case that the PRRs who have recorded negative response have the knowledge of the subjects in which they need training, specially the Panchayat process and its objectives, but they are not aware of the vast horizon with which the power is devolved at the grassroots level. Empowerment of the marginalized, equity, social justice and peace with participatory democracy are the novice terminologies for them. Those who respond positively, opt for training in the following subjects:

Table 3.20
Subject of Training Needed

District	*Panchayat Processes (%)*	*Watershed (%)*	*Agriculture (%)*	*Total (%)*
Jhabua	38 (97.4)	1 (2.6)	–	39 (100)
Ujjain	54 (88.5)	–	7 (11.5)	61 (100)
Indore	40 (87.0)	1 (2.2)	5 (10.9)	46 (100)
Total	132 (90.4)	2 (1.4)	12 (8.2)	146 (100)

Besides the highest count for training in Panchayat system, agriculture is the subject recorded for training and a very few PRRs have thought of watershed training. The total count of all the three districts is just 1.4 per cent for watershed, when non-availability of drinking water for humans and cattle and for irrigation is the most severe problem in rural areas. Training in agriculture is the demand of a total of 8.2 per cent in all the three districts.

In a specific way leadership at grassroots, i.e., the Gram Panchayat level covers the persons who occupy the position of members—the Panch—and officials—Upsarpanch and Sarpanch who are supposed to exercise authority at Gram Panchayat level. The actual realization of the tasks and functions allotted to Gram Panchayats depends to a great extent on the complexities arising out of caste, class, kinship, religion, educational and economic levels and other social and physical variables. These variables mould the character and personality of leaders and also shape their attitudes. Though it is difficult to change their personality thus built, it may be possible to improve their performance by raising their educational and information levels, making them more knowledgeable about the system, inculcating in them the values and norms of the new socio-political order, thus preparing them to take wise decisions about developmental problems of the community in their charge. In short, they need to be made aware of the system, its goals and objectives. Training in Panchayat system and other important aspects affecting the rural community like agriculture, water, forest and environment conservation, local resource mobilisation of men and material can be of great use and help in evolving grassroots leadership.

A general view of the three districts of Malwa plateau, the universe of this study, does not depict a very widely varied scenario on the parameters of moulding factors, though they have a vivid caste, class, rural/urban, educational, economic, socio-cultural, kinship and other such variables. Leaders' contacts at political and official levels is so meagre that it limits their fruitful exposure to the political processes on a wider horizon. Though there is a vast difference of infrastructural facilities between the urban district of Indore (General) on one hand, and rural district of Jhabua (ST) and Ujjain (SC) on the other, the grassroots leadership of Indore does not depict the dynamism expected in a comparatively developed urban district.

To an extent this is due to their lack of awareness of the powers and responsibilities devolved on them and of their role for self-governance, i.e., planning for development and mobilizing community participation which is the crux of their leadership role. Their exclusion from the power structure so far, has also resulted in their restricted leadership activity. An assessment of their awareness of the system and its working and their role for self-governance will be the focus of the next chapter.

Notes

1. Nirmala Buch, "Law of Two-Child Norm in Panchayats: Implications, Consequences and Experiences", *Economic and Political Weekly*, Vol. XL, No. 24, June 11–17, 2005, pp. 2421–29. The author holds that the law is discriminatory as it is applied only to grassroots bodies; it is distracting representatives from development work and is adversely affecting women with serious personal and social consequences.

2. Income has been calculated as per the market price of the yearly agricultural produce according to 1 bag = 1 Qtl. yearly earning from business and labour done for others is added. Investments like seeds, pesticides, diesel for irrigation pumps, electricity bills and labour charges, if paid have been deducted. Thus:

   Income = Agricultural earnings + Business earnings + Labour earnings – All investment expenses

3. Assets have been roughly calculated in the following way:

Item	*Value (in Rs)*
Well	2,00,000
Tube well	15,000
Ox	3,000
Cow	1,500
Buffalo	6,000
Colour TV	8,000
Irrigation Pump	10,000
Tractor Trolly	30,000
Motorcycle	30,000
Telephone	1,000
Car	2,00,000

Rupees 10,000 = 1 Unit

4

Perceptions about the Awareness of Powers and Responsibilities

Leadership of Panchayat Raj Institutions (PRIs) being the most crucial in determining the quality and level of realization of the tasks and functions vested in them by 73rd Constitutional Amendment Act, 1993 and the conformity State Acts, the grass-roots Panchayat leaders are expected to play a significant role in shaping the process of rural development. The complexities arising out of ground realities of caste, class, kinship, education, economic status and a number of other societal and physical variables in the Indian rural society generally cast a fixed mould of leadership at grassroots level. However, leadership, conceptualized as an activity of influencing people to strive willingly for group objectives or to persue in achieving common goals, considerably depends on the elements of knowledge, skill and attitudes of the leaders themselves, reason being that primarily leaders have to organize development works, allocate funds and coordinate different programmes at community level to ensure welfare of the people. This is a challenging task for the rural community as a whole, either for getting willing cooperation for group objectives on the part of leaders, or to follow in the achievements of common goals on the part of the rural community as a whole. Just a decade of constitutional devolution of powers is insufficient a period either to impart to them the knowledge of the legal structure and the processes/system of the Panchayat Raj and make them fully aware of the powers and responsibilities devolved on them, or to inculcate in them the requisite skills for handling those responsibilities.

Training of PRRs has to some extent created awareness of the system but the required skill and change in their attitude to absorb the powers and handle the responsibilities is not perceptible on a wider scale. Representative cases are identified where even in challenging situations PRRs have been able to create their own pathways. These are sizeable in numbers in states with comparatively better infrastructural facilities in rural areas of Kerala, Karnataka, Tamil Nadu, Gujarat, West Bengal and the like.[1] However, in Madhya Pradesh, classed as a "BIMARU"—backward state, such cases are expectedly rare.

Awareness emanates from the knowledge of the structure, the system, the staff, the work strategy and such other factors. To an extent skills and style of work could be evolved on the basis of knowledge thus acquired. The traditional attitudes of rural society could be transformed to suit the liberal goals of the 73rd Constitutional Amendment Act, 1993 provided the leaders come to know the processes and objectives of the new system and their own significant role to adapt it to their specific rural milieu.

Not only that the leaders should be aware of the processes, the system, the needs and demands of the community, but the people should also be harnessed in the process for their own safe, secure, healthy and harmonious livelihood. People's empowerment and their participatory involvement in community development can be ensured only with such an overall awareness of the larger community and the leaders concerned. Devolution of powers from above can create a support system, which can be used fruitfully only if the leaders along with the community are aware of and are vigilant about the entire endeavour, and are ready to play their respective roles. The exercise of influence and authority for common objectives, the crux of leadership, could yield results only in such a broader perspective.[2]

This is all the more significant in view of Madhya Pradesh Panchayat Raj and Gram Swaraj Amendment Act, 2001 which made Gram Sabha the repository of all the powers devolved. Decision-making power is vested with the Gram Sabha and Panchayat has to see to it that these are properly implemented with transparency for the betterment of the community.

How far the village community as a whole has the knowledge of various provisions of the Act and is ready to handle the responsibilities assigned, decides the level of self-governance in the community. Hence, respondents, both PRRs and Gram Sabha members, were asked questions that would reflect their awareness of the system of powers and of responsibilities. An evaluation of the situation is attempted here on the basis of responses of both the categories of respondents. Here, abbreviation PRR is used for Panchayat Raj representatives and GS for members of Gram Sabha.

Table 4.1
Base of Candidature

District	*Caste (%)*	*Villagers' support (%)*	*Self inspiration (%)*	*Family support (%)*	*Political affiliation (%)*	*Total (%)*
Jhabua	1 (1.4)	68 (97.2)	1 (1.4)	—	—	70 (100)
Ujjain	1 (1.2)	59 (69.4)	18 (21.2)	6 (7.0)	1 (1.2)	85 (100)
Indore	4 (5.1)	41 (52.6)	21 (26.9)	10 (12.8)	2 (2.6)	78 (100)
Total	6 (2.6)	168 (72.1)	40 (17.2)	16 (6.9)	3 (1.3)	233 (100)

The highest percentage of PRRs in all the three districts profess that their candidature was decided by the villagers. Next count is of those who accept that they were self-inspired. In Jhabua the self-inspired candidature is just 1.4 per cent, while Ujjain and Indore record self-inspired candidature to the count of 21.2 and 26.9 per cent respectively.

Family support and political affiliations have been totally denied by the Jhabua PRRs, while the PRRs of Ujjain and Indore districts accept these factors as the bases of their candidature, however, to a very low percentage. Caste as a basis of their candidature has been accepted by a very low percentage of PRRs of all the three districts. Group discussions with villagers, however, highlight that caste and sub-caste is a strong base right at the starting point, that is, while deciding the candidature. They also point out that the PRRs nurture their sub-caste wards by way of giving priorities in matters like constructing roads or bridges, installing hand pumps, opening a school or a ration shop and so on. This was also confirmed during field observations.[3] Denial of family support for candidature in Jhabua district reflects the deep-rooted nuclear pattern of their families. PRRs of Ujjain and Indore districts accept family support to the count of 7 and 12.8 per cent respectively. This is maximum in case of women candidates. None of the women candidates accepted that they were self-inspired. Almost all of them accepted that without family support they could not have moved into the quagmire of political field.[4]

Our field responses indicate that none of the Jhabua PRRs has any political affiliations; in Ujjain district 1.2 per cent and in Indore district 2.6 per cent of PRRs profess their political affiliations. However, the field situation is quite different. In almost all the Gram Panchayats, Congress and BJP groups of villagers could be distinctly identified.

Gram Panchayat Baledi of Ujjain district has a Congress Sarpanch and a majority of Congress Panch. The previous Gram Panchayat of Baledi had a BJP Sarpanch and a majority of BJP Panch. In course of a field visit when discussions were being held with the Congress Sarpanch and his associates, the BJP Panch did not join. After the Congress Sarpanch left with his associates another group of PRRs, who professed BJP affiliations, came up and started disclosing that the Congress Sarpanch was telling lies about his achievements. When asked as to why they did not join the discussions earlier, while the congress affiliates were sitting around, they confessed that due to their political differences they do not want to be with the Congress Sarpanch; however, they did admit that this was not congenial for the development of the Panchayat.

Similarly, Gram Panchayat Chander of Depalpur tehsil with a woman Sarpanch of a rich family in the village has Congress affiliations. Gram Panchayat has a majority of Congress Panch. The BJP PRRs of Chander too did not join the discussions with the Sarpanch and other Congress Panch. Later they came up separately and complained about the Congress PRRs. They were quite frank in admitting that, "when they (Congress) are in majority we do not go to the Panchayat and, when we are in majority, they do not come to the Panchayat".

Thus, sharp political differences of the two national parties at grassroots level have hampered the objectives and goals of the 73rd Constitutional Amendment Act, 1993.[5] Though indirect political affiliations do play a significant role in deciding candidates for Panchayats and even in the functioning of the Panchayats, the vocal non-acceptance of political affiliations by the PRRs on a large scale seems to reflect their awareness of the constitutional non-recognition of political parties in Panchayat elections.

Table 4.2
Issues Raised During Contest

District	*Development issues (%)*	*Don't know (%)*	*No issues (%)*	*Total (%)*
Jhabua	21 (30.00)	6 (8.6)	43 (61.4)	70 (100)
Ujjain	18 (21.02)	5 (5.9)	62 (72.9)	85 (100)
Indore	15 (19.2)	3 (3.8)	60 (76.9)	78 (100)
Total	54 (23.2)	14 (6)	165 (70.8)	233 (100)

As regards the issues raised by the PRRs during their contest the highest response in all the three districts was for no issues, while a few talked of development issues. A few recorded their ignorance also. Thus, the grassroots leadership seems to be unaware of the basic socio-economic and political issues of their Panchayats.

Table 4.3
Number of Panchayat Meetings during the Previous Year

District	*0–2 (%)*	*3–5 (%)*	*6–8 (%)*	*> 8 (%)*	*Total (%)*
Jhabua	14 (20.0)	27 (38.5)	9 (12.9)	20 (28.6)	70 (100)
Ujjain	26 (30.5)	30 (35.3)	6 (7.1)	23 (27.1)	85 (100)
Indore	17 (21.8)	20 (25.6)	15 (19.3)	26 (33.3)	78 (100)
Total	57 (24.5)	77 (33)	30 (12.9)	69 (29.6)	233 (100)

When it comes to PRRs knowledge about the number of Panchayat meetings held during the previous year, majority of respondents tread a middle path. However, the official records of Panchayat Sachivalayas are at variance with their responses.[6]

Table 4.4
Number of Gram Sabha Meetings during the Previous Year

District	PRR response				Gram Sabha response			
	0–2 (%)	3–5 (%)	>5 (%)	Total (%)	0–2 (%)	3–5 (%)	>5 (%)	Total (%)
Jhabua	27 (38.6)	34 (48.6)	9 (12.9)	70 (100)	22 (30.5)	40 (55.5)	10 (14.0)	72 (100)
Ujjain	40 (47.1)	42 (49.4)	3 (3.5)	85 (100)	31 (37.4)	46 (55.4)	6 (7.2)	83 (100)
Indore	44 (56.4)	32 (41.0)	2 (2.6)	78 (100)	30 (39.0)	38 (49.3)	9 (11.7)	77 (100)
Total	111 (47.6)	108 (46.4)	14 (6)	233 (100)	83 (100)	124 (100)	25 (100)	232 (100)

The response of PRRs and of Gram Sabha members about the Gram Sabha meetings during the previous year has the highest count in Jhabua and Ujjain for 3–5 meetings. PRRs of Indore, however, record the highest count for 0–2 meetings, and Gram Sabha members record the highest count for 3–5 meetings in all the three districts. Thus, in all the three districts, PRRs and Gram Sabha members seem to agree on the number of meetings held, Indore PRRs are the only exception.

Table 4.5
Information of Gram Sabha Meetings: PRR Response

District	Peon (%)	Panchayat Secretary (%)	Villagers (%)	Notice in Gram Panchayat (%)	No information (%)	Total (%)
Jhabua	41 (58.6)	15 (21.4)	3 (4.3)	5 (7.1)	6 (8.6)	70 (100)
Ujjain	44 (51.8)	10 (11.8)	5 (5.8)	20 (23.5)	6 (7.1)	85 (100)
Indore	49 (62.8)	11 (14.1)	3 (3.8)	7 (9.0)	8 (10.3)	78 (100)
Total	134 (57.5)	36 (15.5)	11 (4.7)	32 (13.7)	20 (8.6)	233 (100)

The Madhya Pradesh Panchayat Raj and Gram Swaraj Act, 2001 has made Gram Sabha all powerful, as such PRRs receiving the information of Gram Sabha meetings and attending them is an important activity for the members of the community and more so as elected representatives.

Table 4.6
PRRs Attending Gram Sabha: PRR Response

District	*0–1 (%)*	*2–4 (%)*	*5 and Above (%)*	*Total (%)*
Jhabua	20 (28.6)	41 (58.5)	09 (12.9)	70 (100)
Ujjain	30 (35.3)	51 (60.0)	04 (4.7)	85 (100)
Indore	30 (38.5)	45 (57.7)	03 (3.8)	78 (100)
Total	80 (34.3)	137 (58.8)	16 (6.9)	233 (100)

The PRRs admit that they do get information of Gram Sabha meetings through various sources. The 'No Information' response is just 8.6 per cent in Jhabua, 7.1 per cent in Ujjain and 10.3 per cent in Indore. However, the percentage of PRRs attending the Gram Sabha meetings between 2 and 4 is just 58.5, 60 and 57.7 in Jhabua, Ujjain and Indore respectively, that means nearly 40 per cent of them are absent. A sizeable percentage of PRRs, viz., 28.6 in Jhabua, 35.3 in Ujjain and 38.5 in Indore records that they have attended 0 to 1 meeting only. A 12.9 per cent in Jhabua and 4.7 per cent in Ujjain and 3.8 per cent in Indore respond that they have attended five or more meetings. The Gram Panchayat record does not verify this. Thus, PRRs absence from Gram Sabha meetings despite getting prior information, reflects their unconcern and non-serious attitude towards the basic institution empowered for decision-making at the grassroots.

Table 4.7
Role in Gram Sabha: PRR Response

District	*Suggestion for development (%)*	*Discussion (%)*	*Chairmanship of Gram Sabha (%)*	*No Role (%)*	*Total (%)*
Jhabua	58 (83.0)	4 (5.7)	7 (10.0)	1 (1.3)	70 (100)
Ujjain	50 (58.8)	6 (7.0)	10 (11.8)	19 (22.4)	85 (100)
Indore	58 (74.3)	4 (5.1)	8 (10.3)	8 (10.3)	78 (100)
Total	166 (71.4)	14 (6.1)	25 (10.2)	28 (12.3)	233 (100)

As to their own role in Gram Sabha the PRRs of all the three districts record their highest count for suggestion for development. Their next lower response in Jhabua and Indore is that they chair the Gram Sabha meetings, while Ujjain PRRs admit that they play 'No Role' in Gram Sabha (22.4%). PRRs of Indore district also admit to the count of 10.3 per cent that they play 'No Role' in Gram Sabha. Surprisingly enough, the PRRs of Jhabua district record the lowest response to the count of just 1.3 per cent for 'No Role' in Gram Sabha. A very low percentage of 5.7 in Jhabua, 7 in Ujjain and 5.1 in Indore say that they take part in discussions. 'Suggestion for development' and 'chairmanship' of Gram Sabha do not reflect any active leadership role of the PRRs as the Gram Sabha meetings are few, and when held nearly 40 per cent of PRRs do not attend these. Discussion which can be directed to constructive decision making has evoked a very low response. In fact Gram Sabha meetings if taken seriously, can be of great popular support for powerful leadership to emerge.[7]

Members of Gram Sabha also respond in a similar way to those of PRRs regarding their getting 'information of Gram Sabha meetings' through various sources, but not attending the same. More than 70 per cent of them get the information but the percentage of those not attending a single meeting is the highest within each district.

Table 4.8
Information of Gram Sabha Meetings: GS Response

District	*Peon (%)*	*Panchayat Secretary (%)*	*PRRs (%)*	*Villagers (%)*	*No information (%)*	*Total (%)*
Jhabua	39(54.2)	4(5.6)	3(4.2)	3(4.2)	23(31.8)	72(100)
Ujjain	53(63.9)	4(4.8)	4(4.8)	2(2.4)	20(24.1)	83(100)
Indore	49(63.6)	3(3.9)	3(3.9)	3(3.9)	19(24.7)	77(100)
Total	141(60.8)	11(4.7)	10(4.4)	8(3.4)	62(26.7)	232(100)

Table 4.9
Number of Gram Sabha Meetings Attended: GS Response

District	*0 (%)*	*1 (%)*	*2 (%)*	*3 (%)*	*4 (%)*	*5 (%)*	*Total (%)*
Jhabua	21 (29.2)	14 (19.4)	15 (20.8)	11 (15.3)	7 (9.7)	4 (5.6)	72 (100)
Ujjain	28 (33.7)	17 (20.5)	24 (28.9)	9 (10.8)	5 (6.0)	—	83 (100)
Indore	30 (39.0)	15 (19.5)	19 (24.7)	5 (6.5)	4 (5.2)	4 (5.2)	77 (100)
Total	79 (34.1)	46 (19.8)	58 (25)	25 (10.8)	16 (6.9)	8 (3.4)	232 (100)

Thus, the Gram Sabha members themselves seem to be apathetic towards the supreme body at the grassroots. Neither the leaders nor the followers seem to feel the need to be responsible, a situation not congenial to the use of influence and authority in the pursuit of common objectives. If the members of Gram Sabha are mobilized just to attend the Gram Sabha meetings, this can lead to institutionalizing the basic activity of participation which vitalizes democracy. Gradually, this may lead to planning by the people themselves and to controlling the execution of policies as well, thus preparing a ground for dynamic leadership to emerge at the grassroots.

Existence of Caste Panchayats in villages and their influence on Panchayat work evoke responses in not collaborating with each other.

Table 4.10
Existence of Caste Panchayat: PRR Response

District	*Yes (%)*	*No (%)*	*Don't know (%)*	*Total (%)*
Jhabua	15 (21.4)	44 (62.9)	11 (15.7)	70 (100)
Ujjain	5 (5.9)	69 (81.2)	11 (12.9)	85 (100)
Indore	2 (2.6)	62 (79.5)	14 (17.9)	78 (100)
Total	22 (9.4)	175 (75.1)	36 (15.5)	233 (100)

Table 4.11
Influence of Caste Panchayats on Panchayat Work: PRR Response

District	*Supporting (%)*	*Neutral (%)*	*Negative (%)*	*Don't Know (%)*	*Total (%)*
Jhabua	55 (78.6)	6 (8.6)	2 (2.8)	7 (10.0)	70 (100)
Ujjain	63 (74.1)	14 (16.5)	4 (4.7)	4 (4.7)	85 (100)
Indore	53 (67.9)	17 (21.8)	2 (2.6)	6 (7.7)	78 (100)
Total	171 (73.4)	37 (15.9)	8 (3.4)	17 (7.3)	233 (100)

Caste Panchayats have a strong hold over their village people, but the highest percentage of PRRs in all the three districts deny the existence of such Panchayats in their villages. The field situation, however, reveals that Caste Panchayats do exist not only in rural areas but in urban areas too. Basically, these are active in local dispute settlement, i.e., the dispensation of justice in the community in accordance with their caste traditions.

Constitutional Panchayats are also playing their roles side by side, but the Caste Panchayats seem to be more influential. Even if a dispute is settled in a court of law, the settlement, to be effective, needs the final approval of the Caste Panchayat.

Table 4.11 reveals the existence of Caste Panchayat, though indirectly, as the PRR's highest response is for the supporting the directives of Caste Panchayat in all the three districts, which is 73.4 per cent. The next lower response is 'neutral' and a few PRRs also respond that Caste Panchayat influence is 'negative'. These together constitute a total of 92 per cent vis-à-vis a total of 75 per cent response of non-existence of Caste Panchayat in villages in Table 4.10.

To explore the PRRs awareness of various groups and committees operating in Panchayats, examples of self-help groups and watershed committees were taken as test cases, as self-help groups have economic dimensions and water scarcity being the most crucial problem in villages.

Table 4.12
Groups Working in Panchayat: PRR Response

District	*SHGs in Panchayat*				*Watershed Committee in Panchayat*			
	Yes (%)	*No (%)*	*Don't Know (%)*	*Total (%)*	*Yes (%)*	*No (%)*	*Don't Know (%)*	*Total (%)*
Jhabua	42 (60.0)	19 (27.1)	9 (12.9)	70 (100)	15 (21.4)	43 (61.4)	12 (17.1)	70 (100)
Ujjain	48 (56.5)	27 (31.8)	10 (11.8)	85 (100)	9 (10.6)	63 (74.1)	13 (15.3)	85 (100)
Indore	38 (48.7)	27 (34.6)	13 (16.7)	78 (100)	6 (7.7)	58 (74.4)	14 (17.9)	78 (100)
Total	128 (54.9)	73 (31.3)	32 (13.7)	233 (100)	30 (12.9)	164 (70.4)	39 (16.7)	233 (100)

Table 4.13
Decision Making: PRR Response

District	*Beneficiary Selection*					*Development Plans*					*Panchayat Problems*				
	Sarpanch (%)	*PRRs (%)*	*GS (%)*	*Don't Know (%)*	*Total (%)*	*Sarpanch (%)*	*PRRs (%)*	*GS (%)*	*Don't Know (%)*	*Total (%)*	*Sarpanch (%)*	*PRRs (%)*	*GS (%)*	*Don't Know (%)*	*Total (%)*
Jhabua	17 (24.3)	12 (17.1)	37 (52.9)	4 (5.7)	70 (100)	8 (11.4)	18 (25.7)	39 (55.7)	5 (7.1)	70 (100)	10 (14.3)	21 (30.0)	34 (48.6)	5 (7.1)	70 (100)
Ujjain	32 (37.6)	14 (16.5)	30 (35.3)	9 (10.6)	85 (100)	26 (30.6)	17 (20.0)	34 (40.4)	8 (9.4)	85 (100)	20 (23.5)	22 (25.9)	32 (37.6)	11 (13.0)	85 (100)
Indore	22 (28.2)	11 (14.1)	32 (41.0)	13 (16.7)	78 (100)	18 (23.1)	15 (20.5)	33 (42.3)	11 (14.1)	78 (100)	17 (21.8)	18 (23.1)	33 (42.3)	10 (12.8)	78 (100)
Total	71 (30.5)	37 (15.9)	99 (42.5)	26 (11.1)	233 (100)	52 (22.3)	51 (21.9)	106 (45.5)	24 (10.3)	233 (100)	47 (20.1)	61 (26.2)	99 (42.5)	26 (11.2)	233 (100)

Table 4.14

Discussion in Gram Sabha: GS Response

District	Beneficiary Selection				Development Plans				Panchayat Problems			
	Yes (%)	No (%)	Don't Know (%)	Total (%)	Yes (%)	No (%)	Don't Know (%)	Total (%)	Yes (%)	No (%)	Don't Know (%)	Total (%)
Jhabua	46 (63.9)	14 (19.4)	12 (16.7)	72 (100)	53 (73.6)	7 (9.7)	12 (16.7)	72 (100)	53 (73.6)	7 (9.7)	12 (16.7)	72 (100)
Ujjain	46 (55.4)	35 (42.2)	2 (2.4)	83 (100)	57 (68.7)	23 (27.7)	3 (3.6)	83 (100)	58 (69.9)	23 (27.7)	2 (2.4)	83 (100)
Indore	40 (51.9)	35 (45.5)	2 (2.6)	77 (100)	54 (70.1)	22 (28.6)	1 (1.3)	77 (100)	58 (75.3)	18 (23.4)	1 (1.3)	77 (100)
Total	132 (56.9)	84 (36.2)	16 (6.9)	232 (100)	164 (70.7)	52 (22.4)	16 (6.9)	232 (100)	169 (72.8)	48 (20.7)	15 (6.5)	232 (100)

PRRs of all the three districts respond to the highest count that SHGs are working in their Panchayats. Jhabua records 'Yes' response to the count of 60 per cent, Ujjain 56.5 per cent and Indore 48.7 per cent. 'No' response is also significant in all the three districts. Those who record 'Yes' response could hardly name a few SHGs as these, they agreed were not associated with Panchayats. PRRs 'No' response for watershed committees to the highest count in all the three districts is a matter of great concern as most of the PRRs have not taken steps to get the watershed committee constituted.

An assessment is made of the PRRs awareness about the decision-making agency on crucial issues like beneficiary selection, development plans and Panchayat problems. A cross tally from the members of Gram Sabha is also tried as to whether such issues are put forth before Gram Sabha for discussion prior to making a decision. The tables 4.14 reflect the situation.

Most of the PRRs are aware of the fact that Gram Sabha is entrusted with all the powers devolved on the Panchayats. Their response in all the three districts is accordingly highest for Gram Sabha making decisions related to beneficiary selection, development work and other Panchayat problems. Quite a few in all the three districts name Sarpanch making these decisions and lesser percentage is for PRRs. All the three districts display a similar trend (Table 4.13). Members of Gram Sabha have also responded in a similar manner in all these matters. This exhibits their knowledge of the powers and functions of Gram Sabha, but the field situation differs as the Gram Sabha meetings are rarely held, and when held, these are very often a stage performance. Respondents admit that their signatures are obtained later by the secretary or the PRRs. However, the fact that they know about Gram Sabha as the most powerful institution at the grassroots may make them aware of using the powers devolved for the welfare of their community. PRRs as members of Gram Sabha can also give right direction to Gram Sabha by assuming a constructive and active leadership role.

About dispute/conflict resolution in Panchayats the awareness of PRRs was judged by asking them as to the persons/agency who undertake this activity.

Table 4.15
Dispute/Conflict Resolution: PRR Response

District	*Sarpanch (%)*	*PRRs (%)*	*Gram Sabha (%)*	*Influentials (%)*	*Don't know (%)*	*Total (%)*
Jhabua	13 (18.6)	17 (24.3)	25 (35.7)	4 (5.7)	11 (15.7)	70 (100)
Ujjain	20 (23.5)	13 (15.3)	27 (31.8)	11 (12.9)	14 (16.5)	85 (100)
Indore	18 (23.1)	15 (19.2)	22 (28.2)	7 (9.0)	16 (20.5)	78 (100)
Total	51 (21.9)	45 (19.3)	74 (31.8)	22 (9.4)	41 (17.6)	233 (100)

The highest percentage of PRRs in all the three districts respond that 'Gram Sabha' is the agency which undertakes the activity of dispute resolution, 'Sarpanch' and 'PRRs' working for conflict resolution in Panchayats receive a sizeable response from the PRRs in all the three districts. Quite a few in all the three districts name 'influentials' as solving disputes and the 'don't know' response is also a significant one.

When it was verified from the members of Gram Sabha as to whether the dispute resolution activity is undertaken by the Gram Sabha, the respondents' negative response is nearly three times more to their affirmative response; Jhabua being the only exception.

Table 4.16
Dispute/Conflict Resolution in Gram Sabha: GS Response

District	*Yes (%)*	*No (%)*	*Don't know (%)*	*Total (%)*
Jhabua	31(43.1)	27(37.5)	14(19.4)	72(100)
Ujjain	20(24.1)	61(72.5)	2(2.4)	83(100)
Indore	19(24.7)	55(71.4)	3(3.9)	77(100)
Total	70(30.2)	143(61.6)	19(8.2)	232(100)

Nearly 43.1 per cent respondents (GS members) of Jhabua depict highest 'Yes' response to dispute resolution being done in Gram Sabha, while 37.5 negate it. In Ujjain the affirmative response is just 24.1 per cent, while the negative response is three times more, 72.5 per cent. Similar is the response in Indore district of 24.7 per cent for 'Yes' and 71.4 per cent for 'No'. Jhabua district gives an impression of more disputes being put forth for resolution in Gram Sabha. The stronghold of Jati Panchayat is, however, perspicacious in Table 4.11. The PRRs of Ujjain and Indore districts also respond to the highest count that disputes are resolved by Gram Sabha (Table 4.15) but the response of GS members in these districts do not collaborate with the response of the PRRs.

As regards the disputes in Panchayats their subject/type and whether it could be solved, the PRR response is at variance with their dispute resolution response (Table 4.15).

Table 4.17

Disputes in Panchayats: Subject/Type and Solution: PRR Response

District	*Development disputes solved (%)*	*Personal disputes not solved (%)*	*Don't know (%)*	*No disputes (%)*	*Total (%)*
Jhabua	8 (10.0)	·1 (1.4)	1 (1.4)	61 (87.1)	70 (100)
Ujjain	12 (14.1)	21 (24.7)	8 (9.4)	44 (51.8)	85 (100)
Indore	9 (11.5)	4 (5.2)	6 (7.7)	59 (75.6)	78 (100)
Total	28 (12.0)	26 (11.2)	15 (6.5)	165 (70.4)	233 (100)

The PRRs 'No Disputes' response is the highest in all the three districts. Panchayats seem to be solving 'development disputes' only, that too is very meagre, just 10 per cent in Jhabua, 14.1 per cent in Ujjain and 11.5 per cent in Indore. Personal disputes are placed before Panchayats but they are not solved. The overwhelming 'No disputes' response to the count of 87.1 per cent in Jhabua, 51.8 per cent in Ujjain and 75.6 per cent in Indore is quite astonishing as rural societies are prone to disputes. Personal and group disputes abound in Panchayats but people prefer to refer these either to their Jati Panchayats or to law courts.

The PRR and GS response to the process of decision making in Gram Sabha has some similarity though they do not seem to be aware of the constitutional provisions in this regard.

Table 4.18
Process of Decision-making

District	*PRR response*					*GS response*				
	Sar-panch (%)	*PRRs (%)*	*Common consent (%)*	*Don't know (%)*	*Total (%)*	*Sar-panch (%)*	*PRRs (%)*	*Common consent (%)*	*Don't know (%)*	*Total (%)*
Jhabua	17 (24.3)	14 (20.0)	30 (42.9)	9 (12.9)	70 (100)	22 (30.6)	5 (7.0)	36 (50.0)	9 (12.4)	72 (100)
Ujjain	28 (32.9)	24 (28.2)	23 (27.1)	10 (11.8)	85 (100)	43 (51.8)	16 (19.3)	20 (24.1)	4 (4.8)	83 (100)
Indore	21 (26.9)	18 (23.1)	28 (35.9)	11 (14.1)	78 (100)	38 (49.4)	3 (3.8)	30 (39.0)	6 (7.8)	77 (100)
Total	66 (28.3)	56 (24.0)	81 (34.8)	30 (12.9)	233 (100)	103 (44.4)	24 (10.3)	86 (37.1)	19 (8.2)	232 (100)

The PRRs of Jhabua record the highest count of 42.9 per cent for 'common consent'. Gram Sabha members of Jhabua also exhibit a similar trend to the count of 50 per cent. Likewise PRRs (24.3 %) and Gram Sabha members (30.6 %) of Jhabua respond that it is the Sarpanch who takes final decisions in Gram Sabha.

PRRs of Indore district also record the highest count of 35.9 per cent for decisions by 'common consent' whereas 26.9 per cent of them name Sarpanch as the decision-maker. The response of

Gram Sabha members of Indore records a different opinion. Their highest response of 49.4 per cent is for 'Sarpanch' as a decision-making agency, while 39.0 per cent of them opine that decisions in Gram Sabha are taken by 'common consent'. Ujjain district shows a very different trend of both PRRs and members of Gram Sabha indicating their highest choice of 32.9 per cent (PRRs) and 51.8 per cent (GS) for 'Sarpanch' as a decision-making person in Gram Sabha. PRRs of Ujjain have their next option for decision-making by 'PRRs' to the count of 28.2 per cent and they place decision by 'common consent' as their third choice to the count of 27.1 per cent. The Gram Sabha members of Ujjain, however, record their next lower choice to the count of 24.1 per cent in favour of decision-making by 'common consent' and their third choice is for PRRs making decision to the count of 3.8 per cent only.

A sizeable percentage of PRRs and also the members of Gram Sabha in all the three districts stand for Sarpanch as the decision-making agency. However, this trend is opposed to the very spirit of the 73rd Constitutional Amendment Act, 1993 which regards Gram Sabha as the supreme decision-making institution. Jhabua is the only exception where both PRRs and Gram Sabha members favour decision-making by 'common consent' in Gram Sabha to the highest count. This may be traced to the cultural tradition of Jhabua where 'Tadwi', the traditional leader of the community, used to obtain prior common consent of the whole body of people in his acts of decision-making for the community. Ujjain and Indore districts, though more developed and more urbanized, record a very high percentage in favour of 'Sarpanch' as decision-making person in Gram Sabha. This is a surprising situation. The historical background of powerful dynasties ruling the area still lurks somewhere in the minds of the people. This is indeed a question which needs serious attention in the larger interests of evolution of healthy practices for the Panchayat Raj system.

Table 4.19
Appointment Making Body: PRR Response

District	*Sarpanch (%)*	*PRRs (%)*	*Gram Sabha (%)*	*Don't know (%)*	*Total (%)*
Jhabua	12 (17.1)	16 (22.9)	27 (38.6)	15 (21.4)	70 (100)
Ujjain	25 (29.4)	22 (25.8)	19 (22.4)	19 (22.4)	85 (100)
Indore	20 (25.6)	19 (24.4)	19 (24.4)	20 (25.6)	78 (100)
Total	57 (24.5)	56 (24.0)	66 (28.4)	54 (23.1)	233 (100)

Power of appointments is constitutionally vested with the Gram Sabha. The response of PRRs in Ujjain and Indore districts however, shows that Sarpanch and PRRs make appointments. Again, Jhabua is an exception where the highest count of 38.6 per cent of PRRs mention Gram Sabha as the appointing body. A sizeable percentage of about more than 20 in each of the three districts are not aware of the agency using the power of appointments. They admit that they 'don't know'.

Table 4.20
Work Plan of Gram Sabha: PRR Response

District	*Sarpanch (%)*	*PRRs (%)*	*Secretary (%)*	*Don't know (%)*	*Total (%)*
Jhabua	7 (10.0)	3 (4.3)	22 (31.4)	38 (54.3)	70 (100)
Ujjain	18 (21.2)	6 (7.1)	15 (17.6)	46 (54.1)	85 (100)
Indore	14 (17.9)	4 (5.1)	17 (21.8)	43 (55.1)	78 (100)
Total	39 (16.7)	13 (5.6)	54 (23.2)	127 (54.5)	233 (100)

Preparation of work plan for Gram Sabha has evoked a very astonishing response from PRRs. All the three districts record the highest percentage of 'don't know' response. It is more than 54 per cent in each of the three districts. A 31.4 per cent of the PRRs of Jhabua respond that secretary decides the work plan, 21.8 per cent of Indore PRRs also record their option for secretary deciding the work plan, but the PRRs of Ujjain name Sarpanch deciding the work plan to the count of 21.2 per cent. More than half of the PRRs being unaware of this basic function is a sign contrary to the evolution of active leadership at the grassroots. Those who have named the secretary or Sarpanch deciding the work plan are also not aware of the legal provision which provides for the Village Development Committee with the help of the secretary to decide the work plan.

Table 4.21
Working Process of Panchayat and Gram Sabha: GS Response

District	*Panchayat*					*Gram Sabha*			
	Works unanimously (%)	*PRR do all work (%)*	*Sarpanch and Secre. (%)*	*Don't know (%)*	*Total (%)*	*Works unanimously (%)*	*Just take signature (%)*	*Don't know (%)*	*Total (%)*
Jhabua	21 (29.2)	13 (18.1)	20 (27.8)	18 (25.0)	72 (100)	28 (38.9)	7 (9.7)	37 (51.4)	72 (100)
Ujjain	12 (14.5)	24 (28.9)	16 (19.3)	31 (37.3)	83 (100)	21 (25.3)	18 (21.7)	44 (53.0)	83 (100)
Indore	17 (22.1)	13 (16.9)	14 (18.2)	33 (42.8)	77 (100)	23 (29.9)	19 (24.7)	35 (45.5)	77 (100)
Total	50 (21.5)	50 (21.5)	50 (21.5)	82 (35.5)	232 (100)	72 (31.0)	44 (19.0)	116 (50.0)	232 (100)

Members of Gram Sabha too do not seem to know the working process of both Panchayat and Gram Sabha. 37.3 per cent of Ujjain and 42.8 per cent of Indore GS do not know the working process of Panchayat. In Jhabua the 'don't know' response though lower to the count of 25 per cent, the situation does not seem to be encouraging.

Regarding working process of Gram Sabha itself, the members of Gram Sabha have the highest count of 'don't know' response in all the three districts. The members of Gram Sabha being unaware of the working process of grassroots institutions, are not in a position to ensure responsiveness of the PRRs to the community problems.

The members of Gram Sabha do not seem to be the active participants in the working of Gram Sabha; neither are they sensitive to the problems of their Panchayat as the following table depicts.

Table 4.22
Problem Raised in Gram Sabha and PRRs Attending to it: GS Response

District	*Any problem/issue raised in Gram Sabha by GS*			*PRRs paying attention to these*		
	Yes (%)	*No (%)*	*Total (%)*	*Yes (%)*	*No (%)*	*Total (%)*
Jhabua	19 (26.4)	53 (73.6)	72 (100)	10 (52.6)	9 (47.4)	19 (100)
Ujjain	45 (54.2)	38 (45.8)	83 (100)	12 (26.7)	33 (73.3)	45 (100)
Indore	43 (55.8)	34 (44.2)	77 (100)	12 (27.9)	31 (72.1)	43 (100)
Total	107 (46.1)	125 (53.9)	232 (100)	34 (31.8)	73 (68.2)	107 (100)

Many of the members of Gram Sabha accept that they did not raise any problem/issue in the Gram Sabha. Jhabua has the highest count of 73.6 per cent in negative, while Ujjain and Indore districts have a higher positive response to the count of 54.2 per cent and 55.8 per cent respectively; their negative responses also depict a high count of 45.8 and 44.2 per cent respectively. As regards the PRRs paying attention to the problem/issue raised by Gram Sabha members, a very high percentage of Ujjain and Indore districts reply in negative, that being 73.3 and 72.1 per cent respectively. Though Jhabua records a higher response of 52.6 per cent in positive and 47.4 per cent in negative, its percentage of raising the problem/issue itself is so low—just 26.4 per cent—that it does not mark any significant positive trend. Remembering the golden rule that "eternal vigilance is the price of democracy", it is necessary to inculcate such a habit at grassroots level, specifically among the members of Gram Sabha, in order to ensure that responsive leadership emerges at the grassroots. This points out to the necessity of capability building programmes for the members of Gram Sabha also. In the absence of awareness and active participation of the members of Gram Sabha the entire responsibility of using the devolved powers for community welfare depends on the honesty and commitment of the PRRs.[8] The electors have to keep in mind this situation while electing their representatives.

As regards the work done in Panchayat during their term, the PRR response reflects a limited choice.

Table 4.23
Work Done: PRR Response

District	*Development work (%)*	*Water conservation (%)*	*Education/health (%)*	*Total (%)*
Jhabua	61 (87.1)	5 (7.2)	4 (5.7)	70 (100)
Ujjain	75 (88.2)	5 (5.9)	5 (5.9)	85 (100)
Indore	73 (93.6)	2 (2.6)	3 (3.8)	78 (100)
Total	209 (89.8)	12 (5.1)	12 (5.1)	233 (100)

To an open-ended question of work done by the PRRs, their response is the highest for development work. The coded answers clearly show that their concept of development is limited to some infrastructural facilities for their Panchayats—few kilometres of road/*kharanja*, bridge, water tanks, construction of buildings for schools/primary health centre/Panchayat Bhavan/community hall, digging of lake, houses for the poor and the like. Perhaps these are concrete visible development works which go to support their leadership and also their candidature for the next term. Another choice, though a meagre one, is for water conservation. Most of the Panchayats face acute water problem but water conservation does not seem to be their primary concern. The third and still a scanty trend in all the three districts is for education. Obtaining a school building is the only idea of education that they have in mind. The PRRs are not much bothered about such vital questions as the non-availability of good teachers, large number of youngsters not attending school or disappearing after midday meals, their results or the quality of education they are receiving. Health does not stand anywhere in their priority list of development. Malaria or polio doses, eye camps, HIV check-ups, distribution of iron tablets, etc., are considered less important needs as compared to construction work. Such considerations have a long term negative effect on the health of the community. They consider it a work going to the credit of health visitor. Education and health, the most important indices of development and also of effective democracy, do not find a prominent place in the priority of works undertaken by PRRs.

All this reflects their very narrow and skewed view of development. This is also an indication of PRRs' ignorance about the various other state and central government schemes of rural development/upliftment. Significant issues like sanitation, environment conservation, water harvesting and the like do not find any place in their responses. The deprivation of infrastructural facilities for long, accounts for a great deal of their misjudged sense of rural development.

Table 4.24
Availability of Money: PRR Response

Districts	*Central government (%)*	*State government (%)*	*MP/MLA Fund (%)*	*Don't know (%)*	*Total (%)*
Jhabua	2 (3.4)	42 (72.4)	1 (1.7)	13 (22.4)	58 (100)
Ujjain	2 (3.0)	48 (72.7)	2 (3.0)	14 (21.2)	66 (100)
Indore	1 (1.4)	44 (62.9)	3 (4.3)	22 (31.4)	70 (100)
Total	5 (2.6)	134 (69.1)	6 (3.1)	49 (25.3)	194 (100)

Figure 4.1
Availability of Money: PRR Response

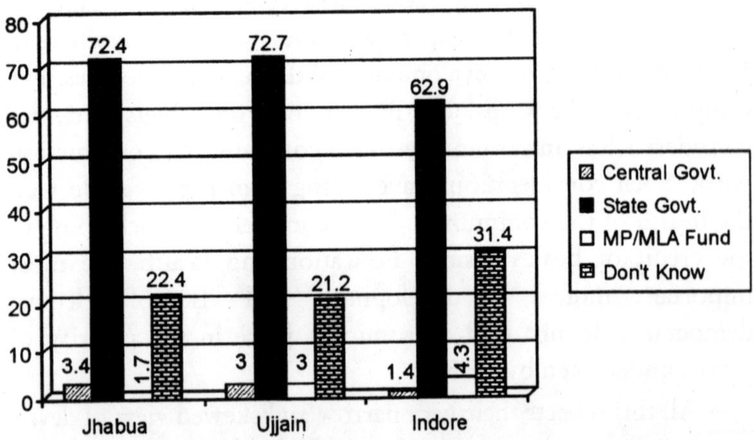

As regards the availability of money for the work the highest count is for state government funds in all the three districts; central government funds for its schemes or MP/MLA funds are meagrely used. The 'don't know' response is also considerable; it is 22.4 per cent in Jhabua, 21.2 per cent in Ujjain and 31.4 per cent in Indore. This again is a sign of their lack of awareness and more

Table 4.25
Types of Gram Kosh: PRR Response

District	*Cash*				*Article*			
	Yes (%)	*No (%)*	*Don't know (%)*	*Total (%)*	*Yes (%)*	*No (%)*	*Don't know (%)*	*Total (%)*
Jhabua	36 (51.4)	9 (12.9)	25 (35.7)	70 (100)	—	36 (51.4)	34 (48.6)	70 (100)
Ujjain	45 (52.9)	3 (3.5)	37 (43.5)	85 (100)	—	42 (49.4)	43 (50.6)	85 (100)
Indore	29 (37.2)	5 (6.4)	44 (56.4)	78 (100)	—	35 (44.9)	43 (55.1)	78 (100)
Total	110 (47.2)	17 (7.3)	106 (45.5)	233 (100)	—	113 (48.5)	120 (51.5)	233 (100)

District	*Grain*				*Labour*			
	Yes (%)	*No (%)*	*Don't know (%)*	*Total (%)*	*Yes (%)*	*No (%)*	*Don't know (%)*	*Total (%)*
Jhabua	1 (1.4)	35 (50.0)	34 (48.6)	70 (100)	1 (1.4)	35 (50.0)	34 (38.6)	70 (100)
Ujjain	—	42 (49.4)	43 (50.6)	85 (100)	—	42(49.4)	43(50.6)	85(100)
Indore	—	35(44.9)	43(55.1)	78(100)	—	35 (44.9)	43 (55.1)	78 (100)
Total	1 (0.4)	112 (48.1)	120 (51.5)	233 (100)	1 (0.4)	112 (48.1)	120 (51.5)	233 (100)

dependence on the state government funds only. Partly this is also due to the fact that getting funds from sources other than the state government requires a lot of information, awareness, contacts and efforts. Some of the PRRs have frankly admitted that getting money from any of these sources requires a 'share percentage' to be parted with along with plenty of time to be spent, hence they avoid even tapping such "other sources". The PRRs of all the three districts avoid generating their own legally granted resources by way of taxation, as they consider that such a measure would antagonize the people. This kind of thinking is not supportive of self-governance, as funds are the main controlling strings of power. Unless the PRRs draw upon their own resources guaranteed to them by the Panchayat Act, they will not be in a position to achieve the goal of self-governance at the grassroots level.

The PRRs response to their knowledge of *Gramkosh* in various forms shows their apathy quite distinctly. Except for the 'cash' variety which they respond in affirmative, their distinct 'no' and 'don't know' responses for 'article', 'grain' and 'labour' appear very curious. PRRs of Indore district depict the highest percentage of 56.4 for 'don't know' for the 'cash kosh' also. For the rest of the three 'kosh' all the three districts have nearly equal counts for 'no' and 'don't know' answers. Only Jhabua PRRs respond positively for 'grain' and 'labour' kosh to a very insignificant count of 1.4 per cent each. PRRs of Ujjain and Indore record nil response to 'article', 'grain' and 'labour' kosh. Jhabua too records nil response to 'article' kosh.

Villagers ready to contribute their share to the *Gramkosh* can hope for development, and PRRs who can persuade the community to come forward for building up Gramkosh can undertake development and other works with confidence. Dependence on funds from state government or any other agency deprives the PRRs of their power of control and authority which in turn hampers their role as people's representatives. As the PRRs are not aware of these funds, the question of procuring or generating one's own resources through the various funds does not arise. Lack of knowledge of the process withholds the PRRs from tapping these resources.

Table 4.26
Committees under Gram Swaraj

Districts	*PRR Response*					*GS Response*				
	Formed and functioning (%)	*On paper only (%)*	*Not formed (%)*	*Don't know (%)*	*Total (%)*	*Formed and function -ing (%)*	*On paper only (%)*	*Not formed (%)*	*Don't know (%)*	*Total (%)*
Jhabua	11 (15.7)	21 (30.0)	2 (2.9)	36 (51.4)	70 (100)	8 (11.1)	13 (18.1)	5 (6.9)	46 (63.9)	72 (100)
Ujjain	7 (8.2)	25 (29.4)	3 (3.5)	50 (58.9)	85 (100)	4 (4.8)	29 (34.9)	10 (12.1)	40 (48.2)	83 (100)
Indore	5 (6.4)	22 (28.2)	5 (6.4)	46 (59.0)	78 (100)	6 (7.8)	23 (29.9)	4 (5.2)	44 (57.1)	77 (100)
Total	23 (9.9)	68 (29.2)	10 (4.3)	132 (56.6)	233 (100)	18 (7.8)	65 (28.1)	19 (8.1)	130 (56)	232 (100)

Concerning the committees to be formed under Gram Swaraj system a total of 9.9 per cent of PRRs and a total of 7.8 per cent of Gram Sabha members respond that these are formed and functioning. Approximately an equal percentage (29.2 PRRs and 28.1 GS) respond that the committees exist on paper only. A total of 4.3 per cent of PRRs and 8.1 per cent of GS respond that these are not formed. The highest percentage of both the PRRs and the GS in all the three districts do not know about the situation. Thusm, it is clear that either the PRRs or the GS do not take cognisance of the committee system as such. Working through committees could be of great help in generating specific information for planning for development and can also prove to be an efficient means for work distribution, thus creating more and more space for participatory democracy.

Table 4.27
Problems before Panchayat: PRR Response

District	*Development (%)*	*Drinking water/ water conservation (%)*	*Health and education (%)*	*Funds (%)*	*Corruption/ bureaucratic arrogance (%)*	*No problem (%)*	*Don't know (%)*	*Total (%)*
Jhabua	36 (51.4)	11 (15.7)	—	6 (8.6)	2 (2.9)	10 (14.3)	5 (7.1)	70 (100)
Ujjain	55 (64.7)	11 (12.9)	3 (3.5)	3 (3.5)	6 (7.1)	3 (3.5)	4 (4.7)	85 (100)
Indore	43 (55.1)	11 (14.1)	1 (1.3)	—	7 (9.0)	13 (16.7)	3 (3.8)	78 (100)
Total	134 (57.5)	33 (14.2)	4 (1.7)	9 (3.9)	15 (6.4)	26 (11.2)	12 (5.2)	233 (100)

The highest number of PRRs in all the three districts identify development as the main problem before the Panchayats, though by development they understand just infrastructural development. Drinking water and water conservation has been identified as problems of next priority. Health and education have been identified as problems at the lowest level in each of the districts. The response of Jhabua PRRs is nil. Ujjain records 3.5 per cent and Indore 1.3 per cent response to health and education as problems before their Panchayats. Looking at the availability of ample infrastructural facilities for health and education in Ujjain and more so in Indore district, their low estimation of available health and education related problems in their Panchayats, is a reflection of the negligence of PRRs towards health and education of the people, specially in view of ill-health and illiteracy prevailing in Gram Panchayats. Jhabua PRRs nil response about these two variables depicts the lowest value they attach to health and education the most significant indices of rural upliftment. Work done during their terms by the PRRs has also evoked a similar response of lower priority towards health and education. This can be attributed to lack of proper education of the PRRs themselves.

Mostly depending on state funds, the PRRs of all the three districts do not consider funds as a great problem. PRRs of Indore district record 'nil' response for funds as a problem for them. If so, this should reflect in Panchayat scenario. Ground realities of Panchayats depict lagging in development and rural upliftment in general. A sizeable percentage of PRRs in all the three districts respond that there is 'no problem' in their Panchayats which again does not seem to be in agreement with the real situation. Again a very low count of PRRs formally record corruption, long delays, lethargy and arrogance of government officials as problems for them. However, in informal discussions they do indirectly agree that they have to part with their fixed shares at Janpad and Zilla Panchayat levels for getting their grants released. They also reveal that they are required to visit the higher level offices and officers a number of times for this and are very often treated demeaningly by the district bureaucracy.

Table 4.28
Initiative for Reforms and Result: PRR Response

District	*Social reforms initiated successful (%)*	*Social reforms initiated not successful (%)*	*SHGs formed (%)*	*No initiative (%)*	*Total (%)*
Jhabua	7(10.0)	17 (24.3)	6 (8.6)	40 (57.1)	70 (100)
Ujjain	8 (9.4)	7 (8.3)	13 (15.3)	57 (67.0)	85 (100)
Indore	4 (5.1)	4 (5.1)	14 (18.0)	56 (71.8)	78 (100)
Total	19 (8.2)	28 (12.0)	33 (14.2)	153 (65.6)	233 (100)

Table 4.29

Panchayat Initiative in Socio-economic Development: GS Response

District	*Against social discrimination*		*Preventing dowry system*		*Preventing child marriage*		*Encouraging family planning*		*Empowering women*		*Generating self-employment*		*Total of each Yes/No columns*
	Yes (%)	*No (%)*	*Yes (%)*	*No (%)*	*Yes (%)*	*No (%)*	*Yes (%)*	*No (%)*	*Yes (%)*	*No (%)*	*Yes (%)*	*No (%)*	
Jhabua	21 (29.1)	51 (70.9)	15 (20.8)	57 (79.2)	13 (18.1)	59 (81.9)	33 (45.8)	39 (54.2)	34 (47.2)	38 (52.8)	13 (18.1)	59 (81.9)	72 (100)
Ujjain	21 (25.3)	62 (74.7)	21 (25.3)	62 (74.7)	20 (24.1)	63 (76.9)	40 (48.2)	43 (51.8)	37 (44.6)	46 (55.4)	10 (12.1)	73 (87.9)	83 (100)
Indore	19 (24.7)	58 (75.3)	16 (20.8)	61 (79.2)	17 (22.1)	60 (77.9)	27 (35.1)	50 (64.9)	28 (36.4)	49 (63.6)	10 (12.9)	67 (87.1)	77 (100)
Total	61 (26.3)	171 (73.7)	52 (23.0)	180 (77.0)	50 (21.6)	182 (78.4)	100 (43.1)	132 (56.9)	99 (42.7)	133 (57.3)	33 (14.2)	199 (85.8)	232 (100)

The highest count of PRRs in all the three districts is for 'no initiative'; the next lower response in Ujjain and Indore districts is for the 'formation of SHGs'—15.3 and 18 per cent respectively. Jhabua PRRs record their next lower response of 'social reforms initiated, but not successful' to the count of 24.3 per cent, much higher than Ujjain and Indore districts on this variable recording 8.2 and 5.1 per cent respectively. Social reforms is an important activity for assuming a dynamic leadership role. Though challenging, an image of a social reformer is deep rooted in society, even more than an economic or politico-legal reformer. However, the PRRs of all the three districts do not seem to accept the challenge of social reforms, most needed in rural and backward communities.

To the question of specific areas of socio-economic reforms, the response of Gram Sabha members also highlight the negative attitude of the Panchayats. The PRR leadership again comes in question for not initiating such reforms.

The highest 'no initiative' response of the members of Gram Sabha in all the three districts against social discrimination, for preventing dowry system and child marriage for encouraging family planning, for empowering women and for generating self-employment depicts a condition of great concern as these are the basic issues which need urgent reforms for the development of Gram Panchayats and the upliftment of the rural masses as per the objectives of 73rd Constitutional Amendment Act, 1993.

Table 4.30
Panchayats Giving Benefits of Government Schemes: GS Response

District	*Yes (%)*	*No (%)*	*Don't know (%)*	*Total (%)*
Jhabua	55 (76.4)	16 (22.2)	1 (1.4)	72 (100)
Ujjain	45 (54.2)	37 (44.6)	1 (1.2)	83 (100)
Indore	50 (64.9)	27 (35.1)	—	77 (100)
Total	150 (64.7)	80 (34.5)	2 (0.8)	232 (100)

The members of Gram Sabha in all the three districts respond in affirmative to the highest count for receiving benefits of government schemes from Panchayats. Field discussions, however, depict that these benefits are related just to housing facilities for the poor and scholarships to the school going children of SC, ST and OBC. They know of none of the other state or central government schemes for rural development which are beneficial to rural masses.

PRRs initiatives for the basic infrastructural facilities of drinking water and school invokes a very high affirmative response from the members of Gram Sabha in all the three districts.

Table 4.31
PRRs Initiatives for Improvement of Drinking Water, School/Education: GS Response

District	*Drinking water*				*School/Education*			
	Yes (%)	*No (%)*	*Don't know (%)*	*Total (%)*	*Yes (%)*	*No (%)*	*Don't know (%)*	*Total (%)*
Jhabua	56 (77.8)	14 (19.4)	2 (2.8)	72 (100)	62 (86.1)	8 (11.1)	2 (2.8)	72 (100)
Ujjain	54 (65.1)	27 (32.5)	2 (2.4)	83 (100)	54 (65.1)	26 (31.3)	3 (3.6)	83 (100)
Indore	53 (68.8)	24 (31.2)	–	77 (100)	56 (72.7)	21 (27.3)	–	77 (100)
Total	163 (70.3)	65 (28.0)	4 (1.7)	232 (100)	172 (74.1)	55 (23.7)	5 (2.2)	232 (100)

The GS of all the three districts depict highest affirmative response for PRRs initiative in the case of improvement of drinking water and schools, but here again their horizon is closed. By improvement of drinking water facilities they mean installation of water tanks in different localities, and by schools they mean a building or its boundary walls. PRRs themselves have given lowest priority to water/school. Water conservation, safe drinking water and quality of education are the basic requirements of rural economy, rural health and rural socio-political awareness. PRRs lower priority to these services and GS's limited horizon do not reflect a constructive developmental scenario.

Decentralization of powers also entrusts responsibilities to those who wield these powers. Madhya Pradesh Panchayat Raj and Gram Swaraj Act, 2001 made Gram Sabha the supreme body at the grassroots, thus making it the ultimate responsible institution for supervision and control of Panchayat activities. Initiatives like periodical supervision/inspection of developmental infrastructure and other services of rural upliftment are vital for their sustainability and progress. Taking care of such activities reflects the vigilance of the community as it is essential to ensure the achievement of objectives of any scheme of reforms and also to keep the leadership on right track. This was tried to be assessed on the basis of PRRs performing the day-to-day visits and inspection of the available infrastructure and of the services for rural upliftment. Gram Sabha members were also contacted on these issues to confirm the responses of the PRRs.

Table 4.32
Inspection of Schools and Anganbadis

District	*Schools*						*Anganbadis*					
	PRR Response			*GS Response*			*PRR Response*			*GS Response*		
	Yes (%)	*No (%)*	*Total (%)*	*Yes (%)*	*No (%)*	*Total (%)*	*Yes (%)*	*No (%)*	*Total (%)*	*Yes (%)*	*No (%)*	*Total (%)*
Jhabua	60 (85.7)	10 (14.3)	70 (100)	54 (75.0)	18 (25.0)	72 (100)	60 (85.7)	10 (14.3)	70 (100)	53 (73.6)	19 (26.4)	72 (100)
Ujjain	56 (65.9)	29 (34.1)	85 (100)	57 (68.7)	26 (31.3)	83 (100)	44 (51.8)	41 (48.2)	85 (100)	53 (63.9)	30 (36.1)	83 (100)
Indore	56 (71.8)	22 (28.2)	78 (100)	62 (80.5)	15 (19.5)	77 (100)	49 (62.8)	29 (37.2)	78 (100)	57 (74.0)	20 (26.0)	77 (100)
Total	172 (73.8)	61 (26.2)	233 (100)	173 (100)	59 (25.4)	232 (100)	153 (65.7)	80 (34.3)	233 (100)	163 (70.3)	69 (29.7)	232 (100)

As regards the inspection of schools and *Anganbadis*, the PRRs and GS of all the three districts depict a higher affirmative response. Ujjain district, however, depicts a considerable negative response as well. It is the highest of the negative responses of all the three districts. It is also noteworthy that both the PRRs and GS of Ujjain district display an identical trend in both the matters.

Table 4.33
Inspection of Ration Shops

District	*PRR Response*			*GS Response*		
	Yes (%)	*No (%)*	*Total (%)*	*Yes (%)*	*No (%)*	*Total (%)*
Jhabua	35 (50.0)	35 (50.0)	70 (100)	36 (50.0)	36 (50.0)	72 (100)
Ujjain	43 (50.6)	42 (49.4)	85 (100)	41 (49.4)	42 (50.6)	83 (100)
Indore	30 (38.5)	48 (61.5)	78 (100)	40 (51.9)	37 (48.1)	77 (100)
Total	108 (46.4)	125 (53.6)	233 (100)	117 (50.4)	115 (49.6)	232 (100)

Inspection of ration shops has evoked a higher negative response in all the three districts, both from the PRRs and the GS. Jhabua PRRs and GS have responded in equal percentage for 'Yes' and 'No' answers, it is fifty per cent in each case. Ujjain PRRs and GS have marginal difference in both the responses; PRRs response is just 0.6 per cent higher in affirmative and GS response is 0.6 per cent higher in negative. Indore PRRs accept in higher percentage of 61.5 that they do not inspect the ration shops, while the GS response is higher in affirmative to the count of 51.9 per cent. The total PRR response is higher towards negation, i.e., 53.6 per cent. The total GS response is just marginally higher towards affirmation just 50.4 per cent. This shows that the basic human need of food is an affair neglected both by the PRRs and the GS. Field discussions evoked complaints of corruption in the public distribution system. Inspection of schools and Anganbadis goes to the credit of PRRs' awareness of their responsibilities but the neglect of rationing system brings their leadership role in question.

Inspection of health centres has evoked a surprisingly higher negative response in all the three districts.

Table 4.34
Inspection of Health Centres

District	*PRR Response*			*GS Response*			
	Yes (%)	*No (%)*	*Total (%)*	*Yes (%)*	*No (%)*	*Not in existence (%)*	*Total (%)*
Jhabua	16 (22.9)	54 (77.1)	70 (100)	12 (16.7)	31 (43.1)	29 (40.2)	72 (100)
Ujjain	19 (22.4)	66 (77.6)	85 (100)	16 (19.3)	43 (51.8)	24 (28.9)	83 (100)
Indore	13 (16.7)	65 (83.3)	78 (100)	20 (26.0)	18 (23.4)	39 (50.6)	77 (100)
Total	48 (20.6)	185 (79.4)	233 (100)	48 (20.6)	92 (39.7)	92 (39.7)	232 (100)

Health is a very significant index of development and PRRs of all the three districts not inspecting health centres of their Panchayats to a very high count of 77.1 per cent in Jhabua, 77.6 per cent in Ujjain and much more 83.3 per cent in Indore is indeed a matter of great concern. Health centre is another field of corruption and PRRs not paying attention towards this vital service to the community is a pitiable situation.

The GS response is also higher towards negative side except Indore district which has a marginal higher count towards affirmation. However, the members of Gram Sabha have displayed a third option 'Not in Existence' to a very high percentage, which is 40.2 per cent in Jhabua, 28.9 per cent in Ujjain and the highest of 50.6 per cent in Indore. Indore, the urban district with best infrastructural facilities for health also giving a response of health centres not existing in its Gram Panchayats is a matter of great negligence on the part of the district administration and the Gram Panchayats themselves.

The infrastructural resources of all the three districts also record the non-existence of health centres in most of the Panchayats. People have to travel 3 to 12 kilometres to avail of this facility, and most of the time they are referred to tehsil and district hospitals for their treatment. The higher negative response of the PRRs in this matter is in tune with the situation.

Looking to the difficulties before the PRRs an attempt was made to find out PRRs views about the type of representatives who could properly implement the Panchayat System.

Table 4.35
Type of Representatives Needed: PRR Response

District	*Educated (%)*	*Honest (%)*	*Conscientious (%)*	*Working in collectivity (%)*	*Working for development (%)*	*Don't know (%)*	*Total (%)*
Jhabua	22(31.4)	12(17.1)	24(34.3)	3(4.3)	2(2.9)	7(10.7)	70(100)
Ujjain	47(55.3)	9(10.6)	17(20.0)	7(8.2)	—	5(5.9)	85(100)
Indore	38(48.7)	14(17.9)	9(11.5)	7(9.1)	5(6.4)	5(6.4)	78(100)
Total	107(45.9)	35(15.0)	50(21.5)	17(7.3)	7(3.0)	17(7.3)	233(100)

Figure 4.2
Type of Representatives Needed: PRR Response

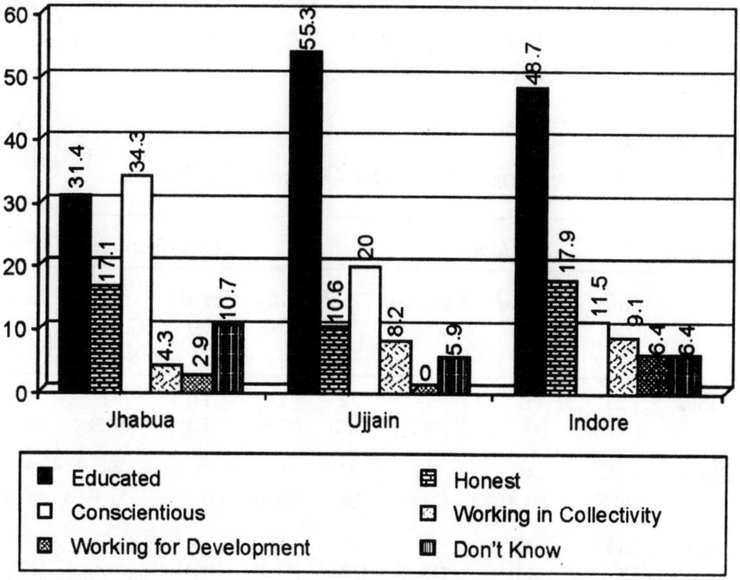

The PRRs of all the three districts give their highest three choices to 'educated', 'honest' and 'conscientious' representatives. 'Working in collectivity' is the next choice in Ujjain and Indore—8.2 and 9.1 per cent respectively. Jhabua PRRs next response of 10.7 per cent is that they 'don't know'. 'Working for development' is the response lowest in Ujjain viz., nil, the next is Jhabua with 2.9 per cent and slightly higher in Indore district, i.e., 6.4. This clearly shows that the PRRs are aware of the qualities that they should possess for proper implementation of the Panchayat Raj system. The point in question is whether they practice these qualities. To cross tally, the members of Gram Sabha were asked as to how many of the PRRs display those qualities in the execution of the Panchayat Raj system and to what extent. As regards education, the highest percentage of illiterates is recorded in Jhabua and Ujjain districts. A sizeable percentage who claim to be literates can just sign. Many of the PRRs have passed primary and middle standards.

Indore has the highest percentage of higher secondary and graduate PRRs (Table 3.3). Thus, on the variable of education PRRs do not exhibit an illustrious record. As regards the other qualities which the PRRs themselves have professed the response of Gram Sabha members is reflected in the table below:

Table 4.36

Panchayat Representatives Having the Qualities: GS Response

District	*Honest*				*Conscientious*			
	Fully (%)	*Partial (%)*	*Dishonest (%)*	*Total (%)*	*Fully (%)*	*Partial (%)*	*Not Conscientious (%)*	*Total (%)*
Jhabua	26 (36.1)	32 (44.4)	14 (19.5)	72 (100)	17 (23.6)	13 (18.1)	42 (58.3)	72 (100)
Ujjain	9 (10.8)	46 (55.4)	28 (33.8)	83 (100)	11 (13.3)	26 (31.3)	46 (55.4)	83 (100)
Indore	16 (20.8)	47 (61)	14 (18.2)	77 (100)	11 (14.2)	38 (49.4)	28 (36.4)	77 (100)
Total	51 (22)	125 (53.9)	56 (24.1)	232 (100)	39 (16.8)	77 (33.2)	116 (50)	232 (100)
District	*Working for development*				*Working in collectivity*			
	Fully (%)	*Partial (%)*	*Not for development (%)*	*Total (%)*	*Fully (%)*	*Partial (%)*	*Not working in collectivity (%)*	*Total (%)*
Jhabua	22 (30.6)	27 (37.5)	23 (31.9)	72 (100)	30 (41.7)	23 (31.9)	19 (26.4)	72 (100)
Ujjain	14 (16.9)	29 (34.9)	40 (48.2)	83 (100)	17 (20.5)	27 (32.5)	39 (47.0)	83 (100)
Indore	17 (22.1)	42 (54.5)	18 (23.4)	77 (100)	25 (32.4)	31 (40.3)	21 (27.3)	77 (100)
Total	53 (22.8)	98 (42.2)	81 (25)	232 (100)	72 (31)	81 (34.9)	79 (34.1)	232 (100)

Gram Sabha members of Jhabua and Indore districts tread a safer path of PRRs being 'partially', 'honest' and 'working for development' as their highest choice. Ujjain district though joins hands with Jhabua and Indore in responding that PRRs are 'partially', 'honest' to the highest count, depicts exception in judging them as 'not conscientious', and not 'working for development', and not 'working in collectivity' to the highest count within the district and among all the three districts. It also records the highest count for 'dishonest' 33.8 per cent, vis-à-vis 19.5 per cent in Jhabua and 18.2 per cent in Indore. Jhabua joins hands with Ujjain in declaring the PRRs as 'not conscientious' to the highest count of 58.3 per cent, but it judges PRRs as 'fully', 'working in collectivity' to the count of 41.7 per cent. Indore depicts the highest count of 40.3 per cent in favour of PRRs 'partially', 'working in collectivity' being the highest within the district and also among all the three districts. Though a sizeable percentage of Gram Sabha members have responded negatively on all the four variables about the qualities expected of PRRs their 'full' and 'partial' assessment of all the variables outnumber the negative responses. This shows that the PRRs do possess the qualities which they have enumerated for proper implementation of the Panchayat Raj system. This is supportive of their constructive leadership role.

Table 4.37
PRRs Involving Villagers in Panchayat Affairs: GS Response

District	*Fully (%)*	*Partial (%)*	*Do not Involve (%)*	*Total (%)*
Jhabua	23(31.9)	28(38.9)	21(29.2)	72(100)
Ujjain	15(18.1)	29(34.9)	39(47)	83(100)
Indore	26(33.8)	30(39)	21(27.3)	77(100)
Total	64(27.6)	87(37.5)	81(34.9)	232(100)

Involving villagers in Panchayat work is significant not only for 'community mobilization' but also for 'participatory democracy'. These are the two basic indices of good governance and PRRs involving villagers in Panchayat affairs can be assessed as a mark of efficient leadership. The Gram Sabha response is significant on this variable as they are the real beneficiaries.

PRRs getting villagers involved to actively take part in Panchayat affairs evokes the highest negative response of Gram Sabha members of Ujjain district but their positive response of 'fully' and 'partially' involving villagers in Panchayat affairs out numbers their negative response. Jhabua and Indore have a higher response for PRRs involving villagers in Panchayat affairs 'fully' vis-à-vis their negative response. PRRs 'partial' involving villagers in Panchayat affairs invokes the highest response in Jhabua and Indore both.

Thus responsibility by way of supervision and responsiveness by involving villagers in the work, are the two hallmarks of participatory democracy. These are well taken care of by the PRRs so far as their awareness is concerned. In practice, however, it seems to be limited as the members of Gram Sabha record a definite negative response in sizeable percentage of 29.2 in Jhabua, 27.3 in Indore and the highest of 47 per cent in Ujjain.

Finance is the crux of any governance but PRRs do not seem to be keen on financial self-sufficiency.

Table 4.38
Procuring Financial Resources: PRRs Response

District	*Government aid (%)*	*Local resources (%)*	*Don't know (%)*	*Total (%)*
Jhabua	36 (51.4)	9 (12.9)	25 (35.7)	70 (100)
Ujjain	44 (51.8)	14 (16.4)	27 (31.8)	85 (100)
Indore	36 (46.2)	12 (15.4)	30 (38.4)	78 (100)
Total	116 (49.8)	35 (15)	82 (35.2)	233 (100)

The PRRs of all the three districts consider the matter of finance as the sole responsibility of the government. The highest percentage of respondents record that procuring 'government aid' is the main concern of their efforts for financial resources. The next lower percentage of the PRRs of all the three districts is that they 'don't know' about procuring financial resources. 'Local resource to be developed' is the response of only 12.9 per cent respondents in Jhabua, 16.4 per cent in Ujjain and 15.4 per cent in Indore. Financial self-sufficiency is of utmost importance for self-governance and the best way is 'contributory effort' which is possible only through local taxation. The PRRs, however, do not like to undertake such efforts for fear of incurring people's wrath, if they are burdened by way of local taxes.[9] A sizeable percentage of 'don't know' response in all three districts is also a matter of great concern.

Exceptions are there when efforts were made to control local resources to generate income for Panchayat, but lack of proper support from district administration thwarted such attempts. Amarsing Dewada, Upsarpanch of Gram Panchayat Bardia of Mahidpur tehsil of Ujjain district, narrated his efforts to generate income from a special variety of stone found in the Panchayat area. Amarsing was Panch for five times before. As the Panchayat was reserved for SC woman he agreed to be Upsarpanch after the elections held in the year 2000. He informed that the stone in the area is a hard stone of special variety used particularly for railway bridges since British times. He tried, applied and pleaded with district administration Ujjain to handover the control of this stone mining to the Gram Panchayat so that the Panchayat could generate its own income by way of taxation but he could not succeed owing to 'administrative-political-commercial' alliance as he puts it.

As regards utilizing the available budget the response of Gram Sabha members clearly reflect a lukewarm attitude of the PRRs as the Table 4.39 shows:

Table 4.39

PRRs Utilizing the Allocated Budget: GS Response

District	*Fully (%)*	*Partial (%)*	*Don't utilize (%)*	*Don't know (%)*	*Total (%)*
Jhabua	31 (43.1)	16 (22.2)	18 (25.0)	7 (9.7)	72 (100)
Ujjain	12 (14.5)	43 (51.8)	27 (32.5)	1 (1.2)	83 (100)
Indore	13 (16.9)	47 (61)	15 (19.5)	2 (2.6)	77 (100)
Total	56 (24.1)	106 (45.7)	60 (25.9)	10 (4.3)	232 (100)

The members of Gram Sabha of only Jhabua district record their response in favour of PRRs 'fully' utilizing the budget. 43.1 per cent is their highest count within the district and among all the three districts. The highest percentage of Gram Sabha members of Ujjain district respond that the PRRs utilize the budget only 'partially' (51.8%). Indore district records the highest of 61 per cent for 'partial' utilization. The next lower response in all the three districts is that the PRRs 'don't fully utilise' the budget; it is 19.5 per cent in Indore, 25 per cent in Jhabua and 32.5 per cent in Ujjain. The 'don't know' response is very meagre in all the three districts. PRRs not fully utilizing the available budget is again a situation of serious concern. Individual discussions with PRRs revealed the obstacles put by higher Panchayats on their way as the budget is not released directly to Gram Panchayats.

Active support of the community and institutionalization of practices can help PRRs in assuming a dynamic leadership role. The Table 4.40 however, portray a dismal picture of the field.

Table 4.40
Capability to Mobilize People: PRR Response

District	*All/Most (%)*	*Very few (%)*	*None (%)*	*Total (%)*
Jhabua	52 (74.3)	18 (25.7)	–	70 (100)
Ujjain	56 (65.9)	20 (23.5)	9 (10.6)	85 (100)
Indore	55 (70.5)	14 (17.9)	9 (11.6)	78 (100)
Total	163 (70)	52 (22.3)	18 (7.7)	233 (100)

The highest percentage of PRRs in all the three districts record that they can mobilize all/most people in the community; but this does not collaborate with the actual situation in the field. Basically this should include at least the maximum presence of people in Gram Sabha meetings. However, Table 4.6 PRRs attending Gram Sabha meetings and Table 4.9 GS attending Gram Sabha meetings both clearly depict the contrary position, a matter hardly congenial to the emergence of self-governance.

Gram Panchayats are constitutionally empowered but PRRs face a number of problems in the field which withhold them from using the powers bestowed. Though most of them are not aware of what is to be done for empowering Panchayats in practice, they do think of various indices which may lead to their practical empowerment.

Table 4.41
Efforts for Panchayat Empowerment in the Field: PRR Response

District	*Training (%)*	*Education (%)*	*More Money (%)*	*Observation of rules (%)*	*Supervision (%)*	*Don't know (%)*	*Total (%)*
Jhabua	23 (32.9)	12 (17.1)	3 (4.3)	4 (5.7)	1 (1.4)	27 (38.6)	70 (100)
Ujjain	11 (12.9)	13 (15.3)	5 (5.9)	18 (21.2)	10 (11.8)	28 (32.9)	85 (100)
Indore	6 (7.6)	7 (9)	4 (5.2)	11 (14.1)	20 (25.6)	30 (38.5)	78 (100)
Total	40 (17.2)	32 (13.7)	12 (5.1)	33 (14.2)	31 (13.3)	85 (36.5)	233 (100)

Though, the highest percentage of PRRs in all the three districts respond that they 'don't know' about the efforts to be made for Panchayat empowerment, they do enumerate various other variables which can lead to Panchayat empowerment. The next lower response of 32.9 per cent of PRRs of Jhabua is for 'Training'. Ujjain PRRs opt for 'observation of rules' to the count of 21.2 per cent while Indore PRRs consider proper 'supervision' to be made for empowerment to the count of 25.6 per cent. 'Education' is the third choice of the PRRs of Jhabua and Ujjain districts. A few respond for more money to Panchayats to the count of 4.3 per cent in Jhabua, 5.9 per cent in Ujjain and 5.2 per cent in Indore. Thus the PRRs of all the three districts seem to be aware of the fact that constitutional empowerment alone is not enough, they need more training, more education, more money, more supervision and observation of rules.

As regards the plans for future development the PRRs response is for more infrastructural facilities rather than for health and education. Response of 'No Plan' is also sizeable.

Table 4.42
Plan for Future Development: PRR Response

District	*Construction Work (%)*	*Health (%)*	*Education (%)*	*Water (%)*	*No Plan (%)*	*Total (%)*
Jhabua	28 (40)	—	3 (4.3)	13 (18.5)	26 (37.2)	70 (100)
Ujjain	50 (58.9)	5 (5.9)	3 (3.5)	4 (4.7)	23 (27)	85 (100)
Indore	53 (67.9)	1 (1.3)	2 (2.6)	13 (16.7)	9 (11.5)	78 (100)
Total	131 (56.2)	6 (2.6)	8 (3.4)	30 (12.9)	58 (24.9)	233 (100)

Planning for future development at the grassroots is the basic objective of 73rd Constitutional Amendment Act, 1993. Various commissions for rural development have stressed time and again that planning should emanate from the grassroots. Rural community should let the higher levels know what their needs are. However, PRRs do not seem to be perceptive about their own development needs. Their concept of development is limited to 'construction work'. The highest response of PRRs of all the three districts is for 'construction' as their plan for future development.

Next lower response of PRRs of Jhabua is 'no plan' with 37.2 per cent. A 18.5 per cent of respondents, though, mark 'water' as their priority in plan for future development; their total neglect of health and meagre attention to 'education' is a matter of great concern. A very high percentage of 27 of Ujjain PRRs admit that they have 'no plan' for future development. They also give a very low priority to 'health', 'education' and 'water'.

An 11.5 per cent of Indore PRRs admitting that they have 'no plan' for future development is quite astonishing. They do give priority to 'water' (16.7%) but are negligent of the importance of health and education.

Thus, 'construction work' acquires the highest priority while 'health' and 'education' are placed at the lowest rung of the ladder by the PRRs of all the three districts.

The overall scenario seems to be quite miserable so far as planning for development at grassroots is concerned. PRRs need to develop a wider vision of development so that they could decide their priorities in proper order and proceed accordingly.

Thus, the PRRs seem to be aware of the powers devolved by the 73rd Constitutional Amendment Act, 1993, to a great extent, but they do not seem capable of exercising these powers to the desired goals. Powers could be used effectively only when the PRRs get ready to shoulder the responsibilities that go with power and here they seem to fall far short of the expectations.

The overall awareness of the PRRs about the state and central government schemes for rural upliftment is also lacking, not to talk of international/world schemes for rural development.

Representatives of enlightened districts like Indore (General) and Ujjain (SC) were expected to exhibit a better trend of awareness and execution vis-à-vis the tribals of Jhabua (ST), but the field study does not show a marked difference. Central and state governments have a number of special schemes of development for Jhabua (ST) district, but the PRRs as also the Members of Gram Sabha of Jhabua being unable to take advantage, creates a very disappointing scenario.

This is partly due to the fact that the central and state governments prefer to operate through the bureaucratic set ups at their disposal. The PRR's capability to be a part of the devolution process is thus hampered to a great extent. This makes them apathetic towards the great experiment of planning for development and self-governance at the grassroots.

The Constitutional Amendment Act, 1993 vitalizes participatory democracy at the grassroots by way of providing reservation to the so far marginalized groups. Reservation for SC, ST apart, the Act undertook a progressive step by constitutionally projecting women on political platform in the hope of ensuring social justice and equity. This has installed a number of women Sarpanch and Panch in 33 per cent seats at Gram Panchayat level also. However, rural women who are still under the yoke of socio-cultural, economic, political, educational and such other limitations find themselves unable to stand up to the opportunities thrown open to them. How are they faring on ground realities in assuming their leadership role will be taken up in the following chapter.

Notes

1. G. Palanithurai has made exhaustive case studies of Gram Panchayat leaders in Tamil Nadu in Path Finders series *Leadership Matters in Grassroots Governance*, Gandhigram Rural Institute, Gandhigram 2003–2006. He specifically highlights the honesty and commitment of the PRRs specially the Sarpanch for attaining

the specified goals. Lack of powers, funds and functionaries do not distract such leaders from achieving their goals.

2. What a conscientious and knowledgeable leader can achieve for his/her community has been vividly recorded by G. Palanithurai in Pathfinders Series.
3. This happens as the villagers still observe caste barriers strongly and their localities in most of the villages are segregated. When a dominant subcaste fields their candidate unanimously he is sure to win and then give priority to the needs of his caste/subcaste people/locality.
4. Rekhabai a woman Panch of Gram Panchayat Baledi of Badnagar tehsil of Ujjain district, disclosed that her elder brother-in-law, who looks after her Panchayat work promised her before filing her nomination papers that she would not even be required to step out of the house if elected. Educated upto standard two she dislikes politics, but as the ward was reserved for women, she had to accept the proposal of the family. She told that in fact it was her condition for putting her signatures on the nomination papers that she would not go out.
5. Third elections to the Constitutional Panchayats in 2005 reflected the national scenario of violence at the grassroots level also which needs to be controlled. In Madhya Pradesh 2,08,657 Panch out of a total of 4,43,229 and 803 Sarpanch out of a total of 30,900 were elected unopposed which is not a healthy sign. Nearly one lakh seats remained uncontested. *Madhya Pradesh Panchayika*, March 2005/23.
6. PRRs of Indore district record a very high percentage of more than 9 meetings held the previous year but none of the Gram Panchayats have a record of all the nine or more meetings. The maximum record found was 7 only.
7. Mr. N. Jagatheesan, President of Grandline Village Panchayat near Chennai city on the basis of his own experience says, "Working with people can achieve anything whether powers are given to the Panchayat or not" quoted by G. Palanithurai, Pathfinders Series–16.
8. Responsiveness of PRRs to people can muster support to Panchayat activities thereby enhancing the status of their

leadership as well. What a leader can achieve with people's support has been aptly presented by G. Palanithurai, with reference to Maravamangalam Gram Panchayat in *Leadership Matters in Grassroots Governance*, Pathfinders Series 13, Gandhigram - 2005.

9. Table 4.24 also reflects a similar trend. Local taxation succeeds only when the community as a whole agrees to pay such taxes. This needs the local community to be convinced about the advantages which the community could reap if it pays the taxes, which again requires the skill of local leadership to undertake such efforts. The PRRs of all the three districts do not seem to be enthusiastic to undertake such efforts.

5

Women in Grassroots Panchayat Raj Leadership

Social justice and equity are the declared objectives of Indian Constitution, the central issue towards its realization is to throw social opportunities open to all women who are ordinarily the victims of most demeaning discrimination in India. Unless equal social opportunities are extended to the female population, no political authority or society can usher in social, political or economic advancement. Indian women constituting nearly the 50 per cent of the entire population have remained the most marginalized one so far as the socio-political power structure is concerned. Hence development has tended to be lop-sided. It was the phase of 18th–19th century social reform movements in India which paved the way for the liberation of Indian women from traditional social customs. Compared to the women of western world, who had to undergo a long struggle for their political rights, Indian women received these rights at a stroke of pen as the constitution provided for adult franchise and freedom from discrimination on the basis of sex. However, this could not make them overnight equal partners in the decision-making process of political and constitutional institutions. A broad cultural value-base of respect for women supported by ancient Indian scriptures could not prevent sex discrimination either at socio-economic or at political levels. They were consistently marginalized from the power structure of Indian society/polity determining structures through ages. A long debate on reservation of seats for women in parliament and state legislatures has proved meaningless for them. Social reform movements talked of restoring status of respect and honour for women by dismantling the discriminatory and exploitative practices against them in different walks of life, but none pleaded for their participation in political processes and decision-making. Gandhiji, for the first time declared that Swaraj in its real sense could not be attained without women's participation and fair equality on a wider scale. Besides the general provisions of equal opportunities for all, the constitution of India too had no specific provisions for ensuring women's participation at various levels of governance.

Efforts in this direction were undertaken from time to time without any substantial results. In 1958 National Development Council, though accepted Balwant Rai Mehta Committee's suggestion of co-opting women at all the three tiers of Panchayats, a very few State Acts provided for this and many did not accept the suggestion; and those who stood for it did not follow it in practice.[1]

Report of the Committee on the Status of Women in India, 1974, pointed out that in order to associate women with the decision-making process, they need to be uplifted from their discriminated social status. A step towards this was to provide them more representation in local bodies. It suggested constituting all women Panchayats within Panchayat Raj system.[2] West Bengal, Maharashtra and Andhra Pradesh undertook some steps on this suggestion but other states did not pay any attention.

Successive Review Committees suggested that serious attention should be paid by government for invigorating the system and giving it a constitutional status. However, there was no mention of ensuring women's participation.[3] West Bengal was the pioneer in providing for a notional women representation in Panchayats including SC and ST women since 1973. During 1985–1990 State Acts of Maharashtra, Gujarat, Karnataka, Kerala and Orissa provided for reservation for women at various levels of Panchayats in varied numbers/percentage by way of co-option/election.

Against this backdrop, the 73rd Constitutional Amendment Act, 1993 is a revolutionary step so far as it ensures woman's empowerment on an expanded scale. This expansion includes not only scheduled castes and scheduled tribes but 33 per cent reservation for women of all categories in all the three tiers of Panchayat Raj and also at Sarpanch and Panch levels in Gram Panchayat.[4] Thus, it was women's entry on the threshold of political power structure though at the grassroots level.

Keeping in view this reservation provision, the sample of the study was framed to study the reality of reservation for women in the field. While selecting Gram Panchayats from the selected tehsils of the three districts two lists were prepared on the basis of sex variable. Three Panchayats with male Sarpanch and two Panchayats with female Sarpanch were randomly selected.[5] Besides these, at least two women panch were interviewed from Gram Panchayats with male sarpanch and at least one more woman panch was interviewed from Gram Panchayats with female sarpanch. Thus the sample includes seventy nine women respondents out of a total of 233 PRRs; this constitutes a 33.9 per cent representation of women PRRs. Besides an analysis on an overall basis, responses of women PRRs are analysed on the basis of a few specific questions addressed to women PRRs only regarding their problems or otherwise due to gender differences. Their performance is assessed with reference to their SES background, level of participation, their development perceptions, their capability to make changes in rural scenario as per the aspirations of rural masses and the challenges they face in the task of overall rural development. Thus, it is an attempt to investigate all such aspects of women PRRs' performance in shaping the grassroots units as units of self government and in attaining sustainable development. In short, attention is focussed on various categories of women PRRs to assess their real position vis-à-vis their constitutional empowerment, i.e., women and ground realities.

Constitutional empowerment apart, socio-cultural limitations still persist on a wider scale for women in general, and SC, ST and poor women in particular.[6] Reservation has ensured their membership in Panchayats, but strings of decision-making are still in the hands of male members. Consequently, women PRRs' responses do not correspond to ground realities so far as their problems and practices are concerned. Field observations have clearly exposed their real position as "proxy representatives". Barring a few exceptions women PRRs admitted that they were PRRs because their seats were reserved for women. Most of them were from the same families whose male members were PRRs in the previous Panchayat. Normally, after a few responses their answer invariably was that some male member of the family, may be husband/father-in-law/son/nephew, etc., looks after their Panchayat affairs and the investigators should address questions to them. It was difficult to reach women PRRs and talk to them without some male member of their families accompanying them. Most of the time these males gave the information sought. As such, their responses were male-oriented responses and quite different from the actual situation observed in the field.

Table 5.1
Age

District	*25–34 (%)*	*35–44 (%)*	*45–54 (%)*	*54 and above (%)*	*Total (%)*
Jhabua	3 (15.0)	7 (35.0)	9 (45.0)	1 (5.0)	20 (100)
Ujjain	4 (14.28)	6 (21.43)	11 (39.29)	7 (25.0)	28 (100)
Indore	3 (9.68)	12 (38.71)	11 (35.48)	5 (16.13)	31 (100)
Total	10 (12.66)	25 (31.65)	31 (39.24)	13 (16.45)	79 (100)

Agewise, women PRRs display the overall age pattern of PRRs. The highest percentage in all the three districts fall within the middle-aged groups of 35–44 and 45–54.[7] However, they lag behind on the variable of education. This creates a wide gap in their awareness as also the knowledge of their position as PRRs, not to talk of practice.

Table 5.2
Education

District	*Primary (%)*	*Middle (%)*	*Hr. Sec. (%)*	*Graduate (%)*	*Illiterate (%)*	*Literate (%)*	*Total % of 5–6*	*Total (%)*
Jhabua	—	1 (5)	—	—	12 (60)	7 (35)	95	20 (100)
Ujjain	1 (3.57)	—	—	1 (3.57)	22 (78.57)	4 (14.29)	92.86	28 (100)
Indore	6 (19.35)	3 (9.68)	—	1 (3.22)	18 (58.7)	3 (9.68)	67.75	31 (100)
Total	7 (8.87)	4 (5.06)	—	2 (2.53)	52 (65.82)	14 (17.72)	83.54	79 (100)

The highest percentage in all the three districts is of illiterates (65.82%) and the next lower percentage in the three districts is of literates (17.72%) which means that they can only sign their names that too with great difficulty. During field visit it was observed that the self-professed literates could neither read nor write anything else, except their names, not even the name of their Gram Panchayat. The total percentage of overall illiterate and literate PRRs is just 45.5 but the percentage of 'illiterate' and 'literate' women PRRs is very high—83.54.[8] Thus woman PRRs lag far behind on the variable of education and this tells upon their awareness and also the practice. Very few have education upto primary level, still few are middle passed and none is higher secondary. Just around 3 per cent each are graduates in Ujjain and Indore districts and none in Jhabua district.

On economic front though women share a larger burden of family so far as inputs of labour and participation in earnings are concerned, they have almost no say in expenditures incurred. None of the women PRRs has land or other assets in her name. They work harder in the fields and household work is their sole responsibility. They are good at bargaining during their out-migration expeditions, but they have no say in decision-making either in the family or in the polity. The field observations were very clear that as most of the women PRRs were found working in the fields or in homes the field investigators had to communicate with them there only, while men PRRs were located in markets, offices or commuting on motorbikes to Janpad and Zilla Panchayats.

Women PRRs of Jhabua record a higher response for having 'no problems' due to 'Purdah system' (65%), due to 'social conventions' (80%), due to 'male domination' and 'male PRRs' (95%) each.

Table 5.3
Socio-Political Problems before Women PRRs

District	*Purdah system*		*Social conventions*		*Male domination*		*Male PRRs*		*Particip-ation in Pancha-yat*	*Total of each Yes-No*
	Yes (%)	*No (%)*	*Yes (%)*	*No (%)*	*Yes (%)*	*No (%)*	*Yes (%)*	*No (%)*	*No (%)*	
Jhabua	7 (35)	13 (65)	4 (20)	16 (80)	1 (5)	19 (95)	1 (5)	19 (95)	–	20 (100)
Ujjain	20 (71.4)	8 (28.6)	18 (64.3)	10 (35.7)	18 (64.3)	10 (35.7)	8 (28.6)	13 (46.4)	7 (25)	28 (100)
Indore	15 (48.4)	16 (51.6)	15 (48.4)	16 (51.6)	13 (41.9)	18 (58.1)	3 (9.7)	7 (22.6)	21 (67.7)	31 (100)
Total	45 (53.2)	37 (46.8)	37 (46.8)	42 (53.2)	32 (40.5)	47 (59.5)	12 (15.2)	39 (49.4)	28 (35.4)	79 (100)

Women PRRs of Indore district also record the highest percentage within district for 'no problems' due to all the above practices but in lower degrees—'purdah' (51.6%), 'social conventions' (51.6%), 'male domination' (58.1%) but their response of no problem from male PRRs is just 22.6 per cent. It can be inferred that women PRRs of Indore do face problems on most of these fronts. However, 67.7 per cent of women PRRs of Indore district admit that they do not attend Panchayat meetings. This shows that they have no problems only because they do not participate in the process.

Ujjain district records a different situation nearer to ground realities observed in the field. For them 'purdah system' is a problem for 71.4 per cent, 'social conventions' and 'male domination' for 64.3 per cent each. Though 46.4 per cent of them respond that they have 'no problem from male PRRs' but their 'no participation' in Panchayat (25%) and problem from male PRRs (28.6%) together constitute 53.6 per cent, higher than their 'no problem from male PRRs'.

Surprisingly, women PRRs were responding with veils worn that 'purdah' is no problem for them; and most of them were communicating to the field investigators through male members of their families that they have 'no problem' either due to social conventions, 'male domination' or 'male PRRs'.

Women PRRs of Jhabua recorded a higher percentage of 'no problem' though their actual position did not seem to be different from the women PRRs of the other two districts.

Tolabai, a tribal woman Sarpanch for two terms of Ban Gram Panchayat of Ranapur tehsil of district Jhabua, endowed with extraordinary qualities like educated upto standard sixth, belonging to a family with sound financial position and having a political background of a panch father-in-law, panch brother-in-law and an MP uncle, was quite frank with the field investigators in admitting that she needed exhaustive training in Panchayat process as she has no idea about groups or SHGs working in Panchayat or about Gramkosh. The only source of fund she knows is state government and MP fund (as her uncle is an MP). She had no idea about issues in her election. Her idea of development is limited to school/road/hand pumps. She thinks that a PRR should be soft spoken, educated and one who can go around and manage the work. She also admitted that her husband and brother-in-law look after the affairs of Gram Panchayat and that she is Sarpanch because the post was reserved for women. Another woman panch informed that due to political connections of the family they managed to get the Ban Panchayat reserved for women for two consecutive terms and Tolabai was Sarpanch for nearly ten years. Her husband had gone to Janpad Panchayat for Panchayat work on her behalf. The moment her husband arrived, she covered her face, picked up her tools and disappeared in her maze fields. Attempts to follow her yielded no result. Her husband replied a few more questions on her behalf and went away in the nearby Panchayat Bhavan to chair a meeting of PRRs—all males which was called on behalf of his Sarpanch wife. The case speaks for itself. Since Tolabai comes from a sound socio-political and economic background she did communicate with field investigators. However, she went away as soon as her husband arrived. In the absence of her husband she admitted that male domination was a problem and it was immediately confirmed. Ground realities in case of other women PRRs is worse as they are illiterates to the count of 60 per cent. Another 35 per cent consider themselves as literates because they can just sign their names. Thus a total of 95 per cent are illiterates.

Women PRRs of Ujjain district also admit that 'purdah', social conventions, male domination and behaviour of male PRRs' are problems for them. Similarly, Indore PRRs also face these problems to some extent but the ground situation in both the districts is not very encouraging. Ujjain being an SC district, women PRRs face these problems in an acute form. Indore is slightly better, being a General category district. In Jhabua (ST) the situation is not so bright as the women PRR's responses indicate.

Similar trend is seen in women PRRs' responses about their 'illiteracy', 'lack of knowledge about Panchayat processes', 'communication skills' and 'household work'; these are common problems for them in the rural and backward areas. The table 5.4 depicts a clear trend of Jhabua (ST) where women PRRs declare in a very high percentage that these are not problems for them. Women PRRs of Indore (General) also declare, though, to a lower percentage, that they do not face problems on these fronts. Responses of women PRRs of Ujjain (SC) depict higher percentage of having problems on all these fronts, which is nearer to ground realities. Except for problems due to household work (57.1%) their responses for having problems on all other counts rise above 70 per cent.

Table 5.4
Personal Problems Before Women PRRs

District	*Illiteracy*		*Lack of knowledge of processes*		*Communication*		*Household work*		*Total of each Yes-No*
	Yes (%)	*No (%)*	*Yes (%)*	*No (%)*	*Yes (%)*	*No (%)*	*Yes (%)*	*No (%)*	
Jhabua	10 (50)	10 (50)	9 (45)	11 (55)	6 (30)	14 (70)	1 (5)	19 (95)	20 (100)
Ujjain	20 (71.4)	8 (28.6)	23 (82.1)	5 (17.9)	20 (71.4)	8 (28.6)	16 (57.1)	12 (42.9)	28 (100)
Indore	15 (48.4)	16 (51.6)	16 (51.6)	15 (48.4)	14 (45.2)	17 (54.8)	12 (38.7)	19 (61.3)	31 (100)
Total	45 (57)	34 (43)	48 (60.8)	31 (39.2)	40 (50.6)	39 (49.4)	29 (36.7)	50 (63.3)	79 (100)

If it is accepted as per the responses of women PRRs of table 5.4 that 'illiteracy', 'lack of knowledge of Panchayat processes', 'communication' or 'household work' are not problems for them, it should reflect in their achievements in the respective Gram Panchayats. This was not observed on ground realities. Almost all the women PRRs were either avoiding communication or directing the field investigators towards the male members of their families who seemed to be the de facto wielders of power/decision-making.

Table 5.5
Help from Others

District	*Family members (%)*	*No participation (%)*	*No help (%)*	*Total (%)*
Jhabua	17 (85)	2 (10)	1 (5)	20 (100)
Ujjain	18 (64.3)	7 (25)	3 (10.7)	28 (100)
Indore	27 (87.1)	1 (3.2)	3 (9.7)	31 (100)
Total	62 (78.5)	10 (12.7)	7 (8.8)	79 (100)

Figure 5.1
Help from Others

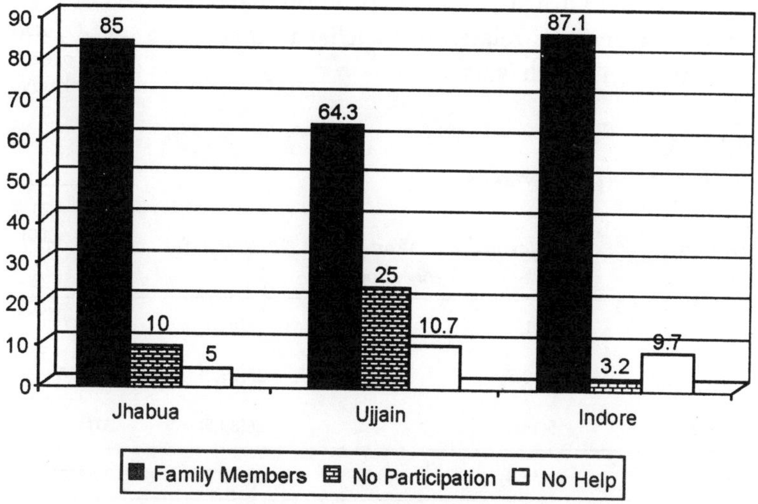

The Table 5.5 clearly depicts the situation on ground realities. Taking help from others is not objectionable but when it is to the extent of dependence it undermines the substance of women empowerment. The case of Rekhabai of Gram Panchayat Baledi of Ujjain district discussed in Chapter 3 is an example of self-withdrawal instead of empowerment. The two child norm has also adversely affected women in general and women PRRs in particular. Male PRRs found scrupulous ways of escape.

Women PRRs of Jhabua (ST) who record in very high percentage that they have no problems—social, economic educational or otherwise—also admit that they do take help from other persons who are invariably their husbands/other male members of their families. Their percentage is 85, another 10 per cent respond that they do not participate in Panchayat activities. Similarly 64.3 per cent of Ujjain (SC) women PRRs take help from others while 25 per cent admit that they do not participate in Panchayat work. Indore (General) is no different as the percentage of those who take help from family members is 87.1, and 3.2 per cent record no participation response which constitutes a total of more than 90 per cent. Thus women PRRs of all the three districts either depend on male members of their families in matters related to Panchayat affairs or they do not participate in Panchayats.

Table 5.6
Women Project Undertaken

District	*SHG formed (%)*	*Women education (%)*	*No project (%)*	*Total (%)*
Jhabua	1(15)	7(35)	12(60)	20(100)
Ujjain	3(10.7)	—	25(89.3)	28(100)
Indore	5(16.1)	—	26(83.9)	31(100)
Total	9(11.4)	7(8.9)	63(79.7)	79(100)

Figure 5.2
Women Project Undertaken

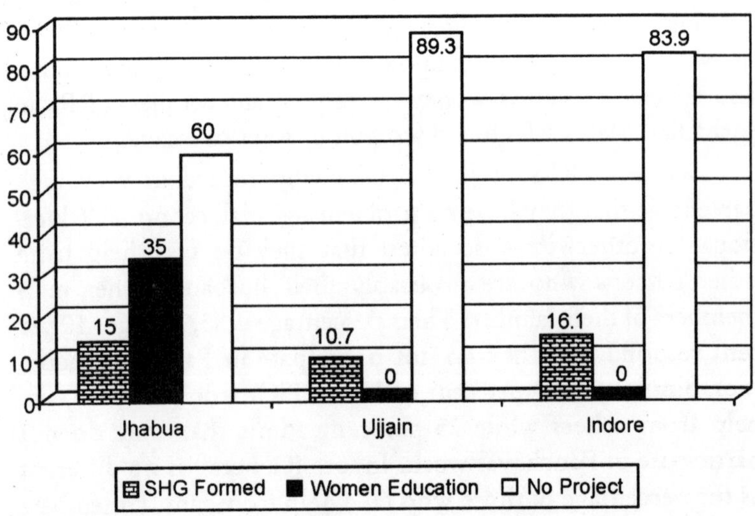

Women PRRs of all the three districts record the highest percentage for 'no women project'. 35 per cent of Jhabua women PRRs respond that they have taken projects for 'women education' but none could name any. Thus, women's education is an ideal for them to be realized but they are unaware about what is to be done for it. The infrastructure facilities of the selected Gram Panchayats indicate the existence of at least a primary or a middle school in each Gram Panchayat. However, no special facilities for women and girls' education were observed in the field. Also adult education facilities for women could not be located in any Gram Panchayat.[9] Women PRRs were not aware of state government programmes of education for female children. The illiteracy percentage is 92.8 in Jhabua district and is between 72.1 and 98.5 in the Gram Panchayats of Jhabua. This is the situation when the ratio of females to males in all the Gram Panchayats of Jhabua district is higher than that of the state and also higher than that of the district in most of the Gram Panchayats. In majority of Gram Panchayats the ratio crosses the thousand mark.[10]

In view of this profile of the overall situation the asymmetry between the responses of women PRRs and ground realities observed leaves one in no doubt.

Table 5.7
Willingness to Contest in Absence of Reservation

District	*Yes (%)*	*No (%)*	*Don't know (%)*	*Total (%)*
Jhabua	9 (45)	9 (45)	2 (10)	20 (100)
Ujjain	5 (17.9)	21 (75.0)	2 (7.1)	28 (100)
Indore	5 (16.1)	26 (83.9)	—	31 (100)
Total	19 (24.1)	56 (70.9)	4 (5.1)	79 (100)

An astonishing response is noticed related to the question regarding their contesting elections in the absence of reservation provisions for women.

A 45 per cent women PRRs of Jhabua record a 'yes' response and an equal percentage of 45 records a clear 'no', 10 per cent of them 'don't know' what they would do under that condition. A 75 per cent of women PRRs of Ujjain (SC) district and 83.9 per cent of Indore (General) district give a categorical 'no', only 17.9 per cent women PRRs of Ujjain district and 16.1 per cent of Indore district record a positive response.

Thus an analysis of field responses of women PRRs of all the three districts reflects different situations. Women PRRs of Jhabua (ST) depict an encouraging picture, Ujjain and Indore portray a gloomy scenario despite having a better developmental infrastructure and urban educational background. However, ground realities portray a very different picture. Women PRRs of Jhabua are in no better position than those of the other districts chosen for the study. Rural areas of urban majority district of Indore were expected to display a better leadership role but the position of women PRRs in Indore district do not depict any significant mark, except that a higher percentage of them could communicate better. However, they also do not seem to have any active participation in the Panchayat processes having almost no say in political decision-making.

Women PRRs of Ujjain (SC) district clearly project the class distinctions prevalent in Indian society. Women PRRs of Ujjain district have the highest percentage of illiteracy (78.5) amongst all the three districts. A 14.29 per cent of them say that they are literates but their literacy is also confined to their ability to sign their names. In most of Gram Panchayats SC localities were situated away from the main village locales. Some of them were quite vocal about the discriminatory treatment meted out to them in villages. They felt easy in residing away from other caste people in society. Women PRRs of Ujjain (SC) are victims on double counts namely, being SC and being women. Shetanbai, a woman Panch of Gram Panchayat Dhanodia informed that her caste people have moved away from the main village to a nearby new settlement called Navakheda because of the frequent insulting and abusive behaviour of the upper caste people specially towards her caste women.

Use of power to 'recall' the elected representatives have some mal-intentioned stories behind the curtain. In majority of cases it is maligning women PRRs on false allegations. It is a sad aspect of the situation.

Exceptions were found in the field, when strong social opposition by villagers and also caste people, weak economic condition and illiteracy could not deter a woman Sarpanch, Kamlabi, of Makdon Gram Panchayat from assuming an active leadership role. She had to face boycott by her Jati Panchayat for the activities of social upliftment of SC women. Vocal and bold in her attempts to solve village problems, she had to face insults from villagers as well. The case is discussed in Chapter 3. Leaving apart a few exceptions, no constructive leadership role by women PRRs in any of the districts could be identified in universe of the study. Equality of sex face an inherent challenge as the socio-psychological set up of Indian society is still invested with the mental makeup of the superiority of the males. Women themselves have not been able to come out of this set-up, hence the discouraging scenario.

The 73rd Constitutional Amendment Act, 1993 vitalizes participatory democracy based on equality at the grassroots level by providing reservation to the so far marginalized groups specially women of all categories. It is a progressive step of projecting women on political platform in the hope of ensuring social justice and equity, the benchmarks for development. However, women still under the yoke of socio-cultural, economic, educational and such other constraints find themselves unable to standup to the opportunities thrown open to them. It was expected that they would act as catalytic agents for peace, honesty, commitment and other civil qualities which would ensure community participation with grace. Ground realities so far do not verify the fulfilment of these expectations. Women marginalized for long from the mainstream of socio-economic-political field cannot be expected to suddenly step forward towards empowerment through a Constitutional Amendment. The basic need of equity and social justice has to be nurtured at social level to ensure the liberal and welfare-oriented goals of the Act. Reservation of seats for women at the grassroots political field may appear as their forced entry into the political arena today, it may, however, lead to their active participation in course of time. Expansive women's education, more liberal attitude towards them at family and social levels, continuous training in view of their real problems, etc., could prove to be some of the important steps to ensure reality of their participation in political field, leading to equality, and in turn prepare solid grounds for development as visualized by Constitutional Amendment Act, 1993.

By and large, women face problems due to gender bias in society, but male PRRs particularly of rural areas with poor socio-economic background also face challenges that keep them away from assuming dynamic leadership roles in the community. The challenges faced by majority of PRRs in general of all the castes will be taken up in the next chapter.

Notes

1. Report of the team for the study of Community Projects and National Extension Service under the chairmanship of Balwant Rai Mehta, 1957.
2. Department of Social Welfare, Government of India, Report of the Committee on the Status of Women in India, New Delhi, 1974.
3. Department of Rural Development, Government of India, Report of Ashok Mehta Committee, 1978, Report of Laxmimal Singhvi Committee, 1986, New Delhi.
4. 73rd Constitutional Amendment Act, 1993, Article 243 G (2) Section (1) and (4).

5. Table 1.3.
6. George Mathew and Ramesh C. Nayak, "Panchayats at work: What it Means for the Oppressed", Institute of Social Sciences, New Delhi, 1996, *Occasional Paper Series, 19.* Focusing on Madhya Pradesh, the paper analyses the violent incidents against women Sarpanch and Panch, like stripping, gang rapes and brutal attacks specially directed toward SC Panch/Sarpanch. The authors conclude that self-government cannot work in a society ridden with caste, feudal attitudes and poverty. A decade has passed since then and these practices are not so common these days; however, the situation cannot be said to have drastically changed.
7. Compare Table 3.4.
8. Compare Table 3.3.
9. See infrastructural facilities of district Jhabua, Table 2.3.
10. See human resource of district Jhabua, Table 2.4.

6

Structural and Implementational Challenges

Democratizing development having been accepted as sine qua non of sustainability, equity, human dignity, social justice and peace, people's participation is the crux of the process and leadership its driving force in concrete situations. In this sense, leadership relates to the influence one has in community decision-making and extracting people's voluntary cooperation in implementing those decisions, thus setting institutions in motion. Faster economic growth alone is neither an indicator of development nor does it necessarily trickle down to the grassroots. It is active participation of people that can lead to development with equity. Decentralization is its major tool allocating added significance to leadership at the grassroots. As powers get devolved at lower and lower levels, those who wield power at each successive level have to assume more and more responsibility.

People also have to be mobilized to help themselves and at the same time be accountable for the results of the use of power. In rural context it is an Herculean task of awakening the docile rural masses which the rural leadership has to perform. The task becomes more difficult as the rural leadership itself, emerging out of the so far marginalized groups of General category, Scheduled Castes, Scheduled Tribes and women, all lacking in experience of power operation. As the 73rd Constitutional Amendment Act, 1993 has sown democratic seeds at the grassroots, Gram Panchayat leadership has a key role in attaining the objectives on ground realities by directing it to the specific goals of need-based planning, local resource mobilization and striving for local peace and social justice.

Implementation of the system at the grassroots is not an easy task. Challenges arise at structural level vertically as also horizontally, and more so at practical levels. The 73rd Constitutional Amendment Act, 1993 provided a structure for the Panchayat Raj system improving upon the experiences of the earlier experiments of Panchayat Raj under Article 40 of Indian Constitution and its practice by states in different forms. Recommendations of various committees constituted from time to time for improvisation of the system were also taken into consideration while deciding upon the structure.

Accordingly, the Gram Sabha, of all the voters of Gram Panchayat, is equipped with the supreme decision-making authority for the development of its community. A Gram Panchayat of elected representatives is constituted to look after the implementation of those decisions. It consists of various categories—General, Scheduled Castes, Scheduled Tribes and women—all are included within the political space provided under the Act. Other significant provisions are: a fixed term of five years of the elected representatives, State Finance Commission to allocate Panchayat share of funds, twenty nine subjects earmarked from the State List for devolution of powers to Panchayats, and the power of Gram Sabha to 'recall' the elected representatives when they misuse the authority.

Madhya Pradesh Panchayat Raj Act, 1994 is amended a number of times between 1994 and 2004 to adjust the structure in view of the difficulties experienced on ground realities.[1] Panchayat and Gram Swaraj Amendment Act, 2001 is a landmark in so far as it transformed the representative democracy into direct democracy at the grassroots. Madhya Pradesh was the first state to take this progressive step.

Structural Challenges

All the structural adjustments, however, have neither been able to make the path smoother to tread for the emerging Gram Panchayat leadership, nor have the liberal pronouncements of decentralization of powers been able to set the system in proper prospective. Instead of emanating at the grassroots, the power is devolved from above, consequently the vertical hold of the units at higher levels has not been loosened. The need based plan of Gram Panchayat has to climb up the ladder through Janpad Panchayat, Zilla Panchayat, State Legislature to Parliament and the bureaucratic set-up at each level. Survey and observations in the field indicate that the grassroots leaders on an average reach up to the chairperson Janpad Panchayat, CEO Janpad Panchayat and occasionally the local MLA. These are the levels immediately higher to the grassroots leaders. The rest of the higher level political and administrative persons are rarely contacted by the grassroots leaders, thus vertically limiting their exposure which can enrich them for better fulfilment of their responsibilities. The object of PRRs' contacts is invariably for getting the funds released for their Gram Panchayat. They admit that they do not feel the need to contact the other persons.

Horizontally, the Caste Panchayats, the traditional leaders, the Self-Help Groups (SHGs), Watershed Committees, the influential persons in the community, the money lenders, the priests, etc., operate in parallel with Gram Panchayats. Various programmes of rural upliftment and poverty eradication, education, etc., are also run simultaneously by the state and central governments in Gram Panchayat space, but Gram Panchayats are allocated neither the functions and functionaries nor the funds for operating those schemes. Even when the co-option of PRRs and members of Gram Sabha is provided for in the schemes, the central/state government officials observe it in a very casual and formal way. Thus many horizontal structures and activities operate within Gram Panchayats by totally evading the Panchayat Raj system. District Poverty Eradication Programme of World Bank, operating through the state bureaucratic machinery has recently exhibited a curious trend in some areas. The rural people after being elevated from their positions of extreme poverty are slowly capturing the Panchayat seats through elections, but these are a few exceptions. SHGs do cooperate with Gram Panchayats depending on their sweet will. PRRs in many Gram Panchayats are not aware of SHGs working in their Gram Panchayats and where they are aware of these, they are not enthusiastic about actively involving the SHGs in Gram Panchayat work.

Structural linkages within the three-tier Panchayat system also pose a challenge to Gram Panchayat leaders. The decentralized power could be activated only when the three tiers of the Panchayat Raj system act in coordination. Gram Panchayat being the lowest unit in the ladder, it is able to reap the fruits of this activization in the last resort. Hence, the Gram Panchayat leadership has to ensure the intra-Panchayat linkages as well in order to obtain the desired results.

During the first two terms of the Constitutional Panchayats, the Madhya Pradesh government experimented with an overpowering institution of 'Zilla Sarkar'. It was headed by a cabinet minister of the state. Members of Parliament, Members of the Legislative Assembly, chairpersons of all the Janpads of the district and chairperson of Zilla Panchayat were its members. Gram Panchayats had no representation in it and the chairpersons of the other two tiers were to play decorative roles, relegated to the background in the matter of decision-making and evaluation of work processes. Amidst shouts and noises the Janpad and Zilla Panchayat representatives used to boycott the 'Sarkar' meetings on many occasions. It was finally abolished in the year 2004. Parallel structures for various state and central government schemes still operate side by side in all Gram Panchayats in the name of Rural Upliftment/Village Development/Poverty Eradication/Malaria or Polio Eradication/Education for all/Gokul Grams/Ayodhya Bastis and many more. International agencies have their own schemes and their own infrastructures for the 'welfare of the rural poor'.[2] Thus, the emerging Gram Panchayat leadership is deprived of an active role in important field activities. Not only that the community develops a low-profile view of the constitutionally empowered Panchayat Raj representatives but it also causes an erosion of the decentralized powers posing a great challenge to the capability building process of Gram Panchayat leadership.

Proximity of Constituents

Besides these structural challenges Gram Panchayat leadership faces numerous challenges at operational level. The 73rd Constitutional Amendment Act, 1993 transformed the nature of Panchayat Raj system from service institution to decision-making and enforcement agency. This has converted the PRIs into the base of the democratic pyramid of the country. This has raised the demands and aspirations of the rural masses which the grassroots leadership is called upon to fulfil. The performance of the grassroots leaders is under constant social audit of the village community. The proximity of Panchayat Raj representatives to their constituencies tells upon their capabilities to meet the constant demands and aspirations of the community. The grassroots leaders have to directly encounter the rural masses, anticipate their aspirations, assess these vis-à-vis the constraints of the politico-legal power structure of the system and on the operational level, try to bridge the gaps and divert them towards the achievement of the desired goals. This requires great acumen and dynamism to face such challenges. The case of Sarpanch Sohanlal of Gram Panchayat Ringnodia of Sanwer tehsil of district Indore (General) well illustrates the point. He told that he does not go to the interior localities of his Gram Panchayat, as the people hurl abuses for his inactivity considering him as the most corrupt Sarpanch. People are unable to understand the politico-legal constraints and the decision of the court about the financial ban on his Gram Panchayat. Thus, the proximity of the constituency becomes a source of nuisance for PRRs on many occasions.

Traditional Centres of Power

The traditional epicentres of power in villages—the landlords, the moneylenders, the priests, the males in the family—pose constant challenges to the emerging Gram Panchayat leadership by way of exercising such direct and subtle controls that the seat of power occupied by emerging leaders finds itself devoid of the real source of power. Resisting these traditional centres of power is itself very challenging, and succumbing to their pressures strains the system, eroding the substance of the expanded democratic base. The Scheduled Castes (SCs) and Scheduled Tribes (STs) are mostly the economically weaker sections of society, almost landless or very small landholders, strongly tied to socio-cultural traditions, requiring financial resources every now and then for observance of their traditions and even for their daily needs. This throws them in the clutches of the landlords and moneylenders who cater to their smallest need for their own selfish purposes of either holding them as bonded labour or earning a very high rate of interest on the money lent.

Economic backwardness of the tribals of Jhabua also forces them to seasonally migrate out for earning their livelihood. This keeps them away for longer periods from people and localities whom they are supposed either to represent or to control and supervise as members of Gram Sabha.

Reservation

The 73rd Constitutional Amendment Act, 1993 has sought to bring the weaker sections, the socially and economically backward groups—the SCs, the STs and Women of all stratas into the mainstream of the power structure to ensure their active participation for their own development. Thus, the provision of reservations has compulsorily brought a generation of leaders with a backward socio-economic background and varied cultural settings. They still lack equal opportunities for education—general and political—and operate within the cultural limitations of their groups which hampers the assumption of dynamic leadership roles by them.

Socially, the tribals have not been able to integrate themselves to the general community as a whole. Panchayat Extension to Scheduled Areas Act, 1996 has bestowed special status on Panchayats of tribal areas in view of their distinct socio-cultural traditions and transferred the control of their local economic resources traditionally belonging to them. This was an effort to safeguard their distinct identity and assuring them equality within the community at large. However, field observations clearly exhibit demarcation of even localities between the tribals and the very few non-tribals residing in Jhabua.

Similar is the situation of SCs in Gram Panchayats of Ujjain (SC) and Indore (General) districts, though, however, Scheduled Caste population is fast assuming the ways of General category people in these areas. The SCs have their separate localities in Gram Panchayats of both these districts and the SC PRRs—even Sarpanch—in some Gram Panchayats sit at a level lower to the upper caste representatives. Untouchability though not openly observed, is practiced in such subtle forms that it is not detectable by an outsider. In Gram Panchayat Dhanodia of Mahidpur tehsil of Ujjain (SC) district, an SC Panch—Shetanbai informed that her caste people have moved away from the main village and developed a new settlement called Navakheda.

Women PRRs are the victims of male domination. Even the General category urban district of Indore does not exhibit a distinct mark. Women PRRs of Indore record the highest percentage of 87.1 for taking help from male members of their families. It is also the highest in all the three districts.

Thus, a high percentage of male PRRs are representatives for name-sake and a very meagre percentage of women PRRs are worth the name of their position.[3] All efforts by government and non-government organizations by way of training and encouragement for active participation of the PRRs of general and of reserved categories in particular have not been able to achieve the desired results on an expanded scale. A few exceptions are of course found as silver lining. On an average, however, dynamic leadership could not emerge on the basis of equity out of the policy of reservations. Theoretical training apart, leadership skills need to be consistently developed in the field so that the PRRs could assume active leadership roles free from all the constraints of caste, tribe, sex, economic status and the like, so that they can become the actual agents of transformation for self-governance.

Paradox of Decentralization

The emerging leadership of Gram Panchayats have also to encounter the dilemma of decision-making by village community in its final operational phase. Village Development Committee has to evolve the need based plan for Gram Panchayat. This plan has to pass through, Janpad Panchayat, Zilla Panchayat and State plan finally to become part of the national plan. The National Planning Commission has wider horizon of overall national development where exigencies of national interests receive top priority. The village plan articulating the demands and aspirations of village community almost looses its identity in the final shapes to come. Thus arises the paradox of decentralized decision-making and ultimate centralized plan. The Gram Panchayat leadership has to explore the process of resolving this paradox and inculcate a sense of participation and fulfilment in the village community. Thus the need based plan by Gram Panchayat, the first step towards self-governance, is nipped in the bud before it reaches the operational stage.

The committee system declared as the means of further expanding the democratic base by way of more decentralization did not yield the expected results. Two terms of Panchayat Raj could not ensure the formation, not to talk of operation of these committees in Panchayats. Madhya Pradesh Panchayat Raj Act, 1994 initially provided for three permanent committees of the villagers to be formed and empowered by Gram Panchayat to work under its general guidance. These committees were to be the agencies to assist the Gram Panchayat in the implementation of its various development schemes. Explaining their importance the Act specifically mentioned that this was a step to further vitalize the concept of decentralization of powers and responsibilities.[4] On 26 January 2001 the state government empowered Gram Sabha as the supreme body at the grassroots, thus establishing direct participatory democracy in Madhya Pradesh.[5] Accordingly committees were to be formed by Gram Sabha to work under its supervision. Eight permanent committees were provided for with the Village Development Committee to be the apex body for formulation of need based plan for Panchayat. The PRRs and the members of Gram Sabha were neither aware of the need based plan nor of the committees that were formed or were operational in their Panchayats. The two major responses from the field were that they 'don't know' about the committees and the 'committees exist only on paper'. Madhya Pradesh still continues to experiment with the committee system. The State Amendment Act, 2004 dissolved the eight committees that were neither constituted nor operational. The Act now provides for two committees only—the Village Development Committee and the Village Construction Committee. The VDC was still to be the apex body, funds were to be allocated by the State government directly to the Village Development Committee over the head of Gram Panchayat. No member of the Gram Panchayat was to be its member. After strong protests by elected representatives of Gram Panchayats the provision was withdrawn and the Sarpanch were included as chairpersons of the two committees.[6] However, this has in no way encouraged the committees to work for the benefit of Gram Panchayats. The committee system intended to vitalize decentralization has defeated the very objective of the provision. Gram Panchayats consider the formation of committees as a challenge to their leadership role.[7]

Finance

Finance poses a still greater constraint on the capability of the PRRs. Since independence the central and state governments were entrusted with resources, powers and responsibilities for the development and welfare of the masses, rural and urban. The 73rd Constitutional Amendment Act, 1993 devolved some of these powers and responsibilities on grassroots, i.e., the village level. The Act also made financial arrangements for this third tier of governance thus devolving the resources as well. The State Finance Commission along with the financial support of state and central governments for their respective rural development schemes constitute the infrastructure for financial devolution. The delay in the formation of State Finance Commission and routing of the state and central government grants for their sanctioned schemes through the state power structure strip off the actual decentralized governance and the operative capability of the grassroots leaders. The only source of fund that the PRRs and the members of Gram Sabha know is the state grant. Even this grant is routed through Zilla and Janpad Panchayats. The PRRs have to undertake great efforts to get this grant released. As most of them disclosed in group discussions in the field that they have to part with 'percentage share' even for the sanctioned grants. This has trickled down corruption at the grassroots level also. Besides this the Sarpanch and the Upsarpanch have to spend most of their time at Janpad office instead of the Gram Panchayat locale, causing negligence of their supervisory activity as well.

The thrust of the 73rd Constitutional Amendment Act, 1993 is on their own resource mobilization by the Gram Panchayats. The resource mobilization in the kind of cash, grain, labour and things do not have a hopeful record. Many a PRRs and members of Gram Sabha is not aware of these resources. Their 'don't know' response about these funds is the highest in all the three districts. The Panchayats are expected to generate their cash funds by levying taxes on activities relating to subjects devolved on Panchayats in accordance with the 11th Schedule.[8] The Panchayat Raj leadership is unwilling to exploit these resources as it entails people's resistance and wrath which may cost them their political posts. Some PRRs complained that when they try to control/develop their resources for financial gains for Gram Panchayat they face the challenge from the current users and the negligence of district bureaucracy. The situation, thus, imposes further financial constraints on Panchayat leaders as functionaries of village development activities.

To mobilize community opinion for development with 'self-financing' is the most critical issue for which the entire Gram Sabha has to be mobilized in the desired direction. Local self-governance, the pivot of Panchayat Raj system, can effectively operate only with a sound financial base of its own. This is all the more difficult as rural populace was used to view its own development and welfare as the sole responsibility of the state and central governments. Finance being the crux of the entire game, the challenge to the Gram Panchayat leadership is to find out the ways and means of financially self-supporting Gram Panchayat. Experiments undertaken by Panchayat Raj leaders in some other states to generate their own financial resources by levying taxes had to face strong resistance from the community at initial stages. They had to convince the community that the funds thus collected would be for better services to the community and its welfare. The leaders had to prove their intentions at operational level, it is only then that the community was ready to pay the taxes and financially evolve a self-supporting Panchayat. This later fetched funds from state/central governments also. The emerging Gram Panchayat leadership in the three sample districts of Madhya Pradesh have still to undertake such bold steps with courage honesty and commitment.[9]

Globalization

On the other hand, globalization is forcing the national government to evolve New Economic Policy to integrate the national economy with the global one. Village economies had to undergo drastic transformation in this perspective. The centrality of globalization and decentralization of powers require immense acumen on the part of Gram Panchayat leadership to effectively resolve the issue to the best advantage of village development schemes. The technicalities of these financial processes pose a great challenge to emerging Gram Panchayat leadership—the novice in the game. Gram Panchayat leadership mostly emerging from agricultural background face the dilemma more acutely. Rural areas of Madhya Pradesh are facing the problem of suicides by village farmers who come under mental stress due to excessive loans and bankruptcy because of the complications of these economic processes which they are unable to understand. The first burnt of the situation has to be borne by the Gram Panchayat leadership, itself not very skilful or trained to deal with the negative impact of the entire activity.[10]

Bureaucracy

Bureaucracy, the traditional operative centre of all the earlier rural development schemes poses yet another challenge to Panchayat Raj leadership. The 73rd Constitutional Amendment Act, 1993 and the conformity State Act, though marginalize the role of bureaucracy, it still wields overwhelming power in Panchayat Raj system. All the key power points for final appeal and decisions at various levels of the three tier Panchayat Raj system are controlled by state bureaucracy from Divisional Commissioner, Collector,

Chief Executive Officers of Janpad and Zilla Panchayats, Tehsildars to Secretary Panchayat Department and so on. They are all highly educated, trained and well-versed in administrative procedures. The Gram Panchayat leadership feels diffident when it is required to deal with these officials. The highest percentage of PRRs have responded that they contact the officers only up to Janpad level and that too for the release of their sanctioned grants. This keeps the PRRs aloof from wider exposures and hence, better awareness. Gram Panchayat leaders do feel the need of constant intensive training for a better understanding and effective operation of the system.

Moreover, the 73rd Constitutional Amendment Act, 1993 has provided for transfer of subjects from the 'State List' but that is not much appreciated at the political and bureaucratic levels within the state. For political persons, bureaucracy proves a handy instrument in putting the Panchayat Raj Institutions in reverse gear. Lack of awareness, education, proper training and experience of PRRs stand to the strengthening of bureaucracy vis-à-vis the PRRs. Thus the bureaucracy though supposed to train PRRs in efficient handling of the powers devolved, pose instead a crucial hindrance to PRRs who are expected to generate need based plan for the development of Panchayat and execute it. The plans framed at Gram Panchayat level have to pass through various ascending political and bureaucratic levels and descend back through the same strata. In the process the original plan is reshaped and deshaped at almost all levels making its ultimate execution at grassroots level a challenging activity for the PRRs. Bureaucrats lending a helping hand to Gram Panchayat leaders are exceptions, not generally found in the field. Group discussions with PRRs and with members of Gram Sabha revealed that not only the political persons but bureaucrats also expect 'percentage share' without which they would not move the papers. Sohanlal, Sarpanch of Gram Panchayat Rignodia of Sanwer tehsil of Indore district and Bhagirath Dewada Upsarpanch of Gram Panchayat Bardiya of Badnagar tehsil of

Ujjain district were very bitter about their experiences with bureaucracy, which, they felt, almost paralysed their Gram Panchayats by their misleading/delaying tactics.

Unit of Non-violence

Mahatma Gandhi visualized Gram Panchayat as a basic unit of non-violence. He envisaged Indian villages to be self-sufficient, self-contained, self-reliant socio-economic political structures so as to ensure real freedom to the people thereby generating a non-violent psyche. The Constitutional Gram Panchayats are expected to emerge as smaller 'Zones of Peace' and PRRs to assume 'Peace Messengers' role.[11] Social justice and Peace are the declared objectives of 73rd Constitutional Amendment Act, 1993. The newly acquired power positions along with the accompanying financial empowerment are generating violence in the territorial space of Gram Panchayats. The elections to Panchayats in early 2005 were full of violence and ill will. Two major political parties, Congress and the Bhartiya Janata Party—have indirectly entered the scene, though the Act provides for partyless system at the grassroots level. This has added fuel to the fire as it has spread factionalism, indiscipline and ill-will among the groups in villages. The PRRs openly profess their party affiliations. Some Gram Panchayats were obviously seen being divided on party lines to the extent that the PRRs of one party did not join even the informal discussions with field investigators, if the PRRs of the other party were present. The BJP PRRs of Chander Gram Panchayat of Depalpur tehsil of Indore (General) district and of Baledi Gram Panchayat of Badnagar tehsil of Ujjain (SC) district were quite vocal in admitting that they boycott the Panchayat meetings when Congress PRRs are in majority, and vice versa, the Congress PRRs boycott Panchayat meetings when BJP PRRs are in majority.

Palwa Gram Panchayat of Mahidpur tehsil of Ujjain (SC) district has a pitiable scenario as a member of Gram Sabha—a former Sarpanch and retired teacher—expressed with grief that the parties have divided the Gram Panchayat and created bitterness among the various groups which was not the situation earlier. The result, he said, is that many efficient youngsters have shifted to nearby villages and are working with great enthusiasm there. He was also unhappy that due to the party divide in Palwa, the Palwa Gram Panchayat is just a Gram Panchayat for namesake and all the development activities like road, bridge, school, water conservation, etc., are undertaken in the nearby village of Belakheda which is a part of Palwa Panchayat. Palwa village has just a dilapidated Panchayat Bhawan where Panchayat meetings are never held and the Bhawan is a haven for animals and thieves. All this, he confessed, has left the village backward, unclean and devoid of development activity. A group of women members of Gram Sabha including a women Panch were quite upset as they informed that the new Gram Panchayat has 'awarded' the village with more fights and no development.

Bhuribai, a Panch of Gram Panchayat Ban of Ranapur tehsil of Jhabua (ST) district belonged to the minority group of Gram Panchayat. When she saw the field investigators talking to the Sarpanch of Congress family she was hesitant to join the discussion and left the place shortly. When the field investigator followed to interview her she frankly told that she would not talk anything about the Panchayat work because conveying the real situation would incur the wrath of the Sarpanch who is also a woman, and her family who would hurl abuses at her and may commit even violence. It was after great persuasion and assurance of confidentiality that she answered a few questions. Thus, all the ills of party system like factionalism, corruption, violence, etc., prevalent on the state and national scenes have trickled down to the grassroots level.

It is said that the 73rd Constitutional Amendment Act, 1993 has decentralized more of corruption than the powers. Corruption generates violence more frequently in villages than at the state or national levels. Villagers, the proximate constituents of PRRs are in constant knowledge of the activities of PRRs.

Candidates mustering more muscle power spread an atmosphere of fear among villagers and instead of being messengers of non-violence they are looked upon as messengers of corruption and violence.[12] The third term elections to Panchayats in 2005 witnessed widespread corruption, violence and even murders. The aspiring candidates took resort to various methods of appeasing or frightening the village voters which included distribution of sweets for months together, distribution of clothes, bedsheets, household goods, liquor, etc. Elected Gram Panchayat PRRs were taken into custody by party politicians for favourable voting for the next higher level posts. At Gram Panchayat level many seats were left vacant, and on many more only a single nomination paper was filed as none else was ready to contest a candidate with more muscle power. A few villages randomly surveyed highlighted the fear of disputes and violence in the minds of the villagers. Women PRRs of the universe of this study, with rare exceptions, confided that they would not contest elections in future.

Gram Panchayat representatives, thus, face a subtle challenge to their role of 'Propogators of non-violence' and of 'clean administrators'. Equality of sex also face an inherent challenge as the socio-psychological set up of Indian society is still invested with the mental make up of priority to males. Thus, the dynamics of grassroots leadership in the power structure of Panchayat Institutions throws multiple challenges to emerging leadership to assume the role of initiators and administrators of decentralized democracy at the grassroots.

The scenario, however, is not altogether gloomy. The main task of rural reconstruction, of creating self-reliant, self-governing rural communities on vast expanse of Indian territory is not an easy endeavour, specially when the rural masses were marginalized from the entire power structure for long. Exceptions of Kerala, Karnataka, West Bengal, Tamil Nadu, Maharashtra and parts of Gujarat and few others can be viewed as trendsetters, where Panchayat leadership undergoing exhaustive training and backing of a sound infrastructural and financial base have built up capabilities to successfully face the various challenges.[13] Welfare activities, like running schools, supervising dispensaries, harvesting rainwater, setting up of small power plants with village resources have been undertaken by a few Gram Panchayats. Even matured political activities of referendum and recall have also been performed by many Gram Panchayats in Madhya Pradesh. Use of the power to 'recall' the elected representatives have some mal-intentioned stories behind the curtain. In many cases its use against women PRRs is a sad side of the situation. The very fact of its awareness in rural scenario might be taken to be the step towards actualization of 'Swaraj' where masses seem to have developed "a sense of their capacity to regulate and control authority when it is misused". The emerging leadership, thus, can be placed on track. Need based planning, local resource mobilization and striving for equity and social justice may still be far away. The success of participatory democracy also depends on its practice where leadership is the pivot of the community activity. Examples positive and negative could be multiplied. These, however, are the clear signals of growing awareness among the rural populace. The positive exceptions need expansion and the negative ones need positive channelization and that is where the emerging grassroots leadership has to steer clear the multiple challenges to their role play as navigators of the vast experiment of democratic decentralization.

Notes

1. For Amendments of the State Act see Madhya Pradesh Gazetteer (Extra Ordinary) dated 27.7.94, 23.12.94, 19.12.95, 07.01.97, 24.4.97, 05.12.97, 04.09.98, 05.04.99, 24.8.2001. The one in 2004 reduced the number of committees from eight to two. The last one in June 2005 authorized State Election Commission to conduct elections of Upsarpanch of Gram Panchayats and Presidents and Vice Presidents of Janpad and Zila Panchayats. Sarpanch is made

ex-officio chairman of both the committees and the quorum for Gram Sabha is reduced to 10 per cent without any binding of the presence of reserved categories.

2. An example of World Bank Scheme on District Poverty Eradication Programme is a case in point. Operating in village space, it has its own infrastructure, functionaries and funds totally apart from the Panchayat Raj System. Similarly Sarva Shiksha Abhiyan and the rural health schemes have their own paraphernalia in which Gram Panchayat leadership has no role at decision-making level. Cooption at implementation level depends on the sweet will of the otherwise authorized functionaries.
3. Experiments of all Women Panchayats in some states are exceptions. Though initially these worked well with the support from outside the system, they could neither be sustained for long nor replicated with the same results.
4. Madhya Pradesh Panchayat Raj and Gram Swaraj Act, 1993, came into force in January 1994, Madhya Pradesh Gazetteer (Extra Ordinary) 25 January 1994, Article 46(2), (3) and (5).
5. Madhya Pradesh Panchayat Raj and Gram Swaraj Act, 2001, *Madhya Pradesh Gazetteer*, 25 January 2001.
6. Madhya Pradesh Panchayat Raj and Gram Swaraj Amendment Act, 2001 and 2004. Madhya Pradesh Gazetteer (Extra Ordinary) 25 January 2001 and 2004, further amended in June 2005.
7. Prabhat Datta, *Decentralisation Participation and Governance*, Delhi, 2006, contains a chapter on "Democratic Decentralisation in India: The Emerging Challenges". pp. 27–61.
8. For financial dynamics of Panchayat Raj Institutions see Sandeep Joshi, *Panchayaton ka Vitta Poshan: Madhya Pradesh Sandharbha*, Ujjain, 1998. The situation has slightly improved, though not remarkably during the last ten years.
9. Tamil Nadu success stories invariably display honesty, sincerity and commitment of leaders and also their struggle in reaching the current situation. G. Palanithurai's Path Finders' Series 1 to 24. Gandhigram, 2003–05.
10. Even the people of most developed countries like USA are bearing the brunt of globalization process.

11. S. Narayan Swami, 'Village Panchayat as Primary Zone of Peace', in G. Palanithurai et al. (ed.), *Major Issues in New Panchayat Raj System*, New Delhi, 1997, pp. 71–108.
12. The 'Dabri' episode of Gram Panchayat Lutia Junarda of Ujjain district (not a sample unit) where the Sarpanch procured wheat for small water conservation units by individuals which were not there at all. Bureaucratic units of Janpad and Zilla Panchayat were also parties to this corruption on a very wide scale.
13. Many success stories raise the question of their sustainability. The much talked about Kerala experiment is slowly receding in reverse direction has been exposed by R. Krishnakumar, "Derailing decentralisation: Kerala Experiment", *Frontline*, December, 31, 2004, pp. 41–44. Sustaining achievements needs greater attention than just one time achievement.

7

Conclusion

In concluding the study an effort will be made to explain the major findings about the various issues/objectives with which the study had been undertaken. The major themes addressed are the core theoretical concepts of the study, the plan, its objectives, perceptions of the respondents regarding management and governance of PRIs, gender equity, the challenges faced and an overall assessment of the emerging leadership of SC, ST and General category Gram Panchayat representatives.

A word may be added here about the purpose of the study. While there were attempts to involve local people in the management of Panchayat affairs, rural social structure was predominantly hierarchical, based on caste, class, religion, economic status and sex disparities; the creamy layer people of society—public leaders, civil servants and men of wealth and social status ruled the social-political roost. Various experiments for the improvement of Panchayat system brought home the wisdom to the advocates of democratic decentralization that power to the people and the marginalized sections of rural society, the dalits and women in particular, need to be drawn into the process of decision-making at the grassroots level. The enactment and thereafter implementation of 73rd Constitutional Amendment Act, 1993 opened the doors for the involvement of such sections of society that had remained excluded from self-governance at local levels. The result of the implementation of the 73rd Constitutional Amendment Act, 1993 was the emergence of new local leaders through the reservation policy, an essential ingredient of the said Act. Thus ended the sway and rule of the former wielders of power of the villages viz., the landlords, moneylenders and the socially influential people; power now passed on into the hands of the newly emerging leadership of the so far neglected backward classes and women. This was a silent and peaceful revolution, paving way for local democracy with the goals of liberty, equality and social justice.

The provisions of the Act were further fortified by the Panchayat Extension of Schedule Areas Act, 1996, by providing special status to the tribal area people that each Panchayat in their area would be headed only by a tribal Sarpanch.

In sum, the study was intended as an attempt to evaluate the quality of new leadership that had emerged in Scheduled Tribe, Scheduled Caste and General category areas in Madhya Pradesh. Three districts, a predominantly tribal area of Jhabua district with tribal population (86.8%), a predominantly Scheduled Caste area of Ujjain district with SC population (24.7%) and a General category area of Indore district with General category population (77.6%) were selected for study.

The purpose behind this kind of choice of districts for the study was to examine as to how the respondents of the three categories of population thought about the various aspects of Panchayat Raj. Secondly, two specific categories of respondents selected have been (a) the Panchayat Raj representatives (PRRs)—Sarpanch/Upsarpanch and panch and (b) Members of Gram Sabha (GS); and the total number of such respondents was 465, PRRs 233 and GS 232. Thirdly, another object of the study was to investigate the quality of leadership at the grassroots strata of the PR system, i.e., at the Gram Panchayat level particularly keeping in view their perceptions about making each Gram Panchayat a focal institution of self-government, democratic decentralisation, women's empowerment, rural development—in a word their understanding of the objectives of the 73rd Constitutional Amendment Act, 1993 and their own capabilities to put in practice the objectives cherished by the Act.

In a nutshell, the study had the following objectives in view:

- to investigate the types of grassroots leadership that have emerged in Madhya Pradesh Panchayat Raj Institutions keeping in view their socio-economic characteristics (SES);
- to investigate the development perspectives of the emerging grassroots leaders; and
- to examine the capabilities of such leadership whether they are competent enough to realize the objectives enshrined in the Act.

Panchayat Leadership

As the central theme was to assess the quality of Gram Panchayat leadership, we reviewed here some of the characteristics of Gram Panchayat leaders based on the facts gathered by the field study. Almost all the Gram Panchayats portray poor standard of leadership: leaders lack education; they have limited vision of the future, are ignorant of the roles that the Act expects them to play so far as the development of the Gram Panchayats is concerned, and hence incapable to achieve the liberal goal of converting Gram Panchayats as units of self-governance. These are the major drawbacks of Gram Panchayat leadership, be that a tribal, Scheduled Caste or General category Panchayat. In case of women Sarpanch and Panch of any category it is clear that the guiding power behind the office is some male relative of women holding the office, be it the husband, father-in-law, brother-in-law, nephew or some such male person.

What is most surprising is the common response from almost all the Panchayat Raj representatives and the members of Gram Sabha which points out that the local leaders have a very limited idea of rural development. Rural development for them means construction of a primary school building or laying a pucca road in the village or nearby town, handpumps dug or water tanks installed, a ration shop or a health centre started. Even PRRs, not to say of the common villagers, are ignorant of the concept of planned development of the village, social mapping, empowerment of women, searching out newer ways of job opportunities for the poor people who may earn livelihood for all the twelve months of a year. The end result of this situation is that most of the areas reveal a dismal picture of the Panchayats.

While opinions about questions related to the essential positive qualities of the local leaders may differ, there is a thread of uniformity about them that they do share kickbacks with higher level of local leaders and even with government servants posted in their areas from construction activities. Thus, there exists a cancerous cell of corrupt practice of bribery in tandem with developmental activities both in the rural and urban areas. This problem calls for urgent administrative attention of the powers that be. This step can also be supplemented with more of value education imparted to the common people who elect their leaders.

For the evaluation of the quality of emerging rural leadership in Panchayats, we took note of educational standard of leaders of the three districts, Jhabua, Ujjain and Indore, their standard of education at Higher Secondary level is 10 per cent, 10.6 per cent and 29.5 per cent respectively. This indicates that the level of education of SC and ST PRRs is regrettably low. There are no graduate leaders in Jhabua ST district, while only 4.7 per cent of Ujjain SC district and 6.4 per cent of Indore General district have education up to graduate level. The overall illiteracy percentage of PRRs in the districts is 38.6 per cent in Jhabua, 32.9 per cent in Ujjain and 25.6 per cent in Indore. Certainly, this illiteracy rate of PRRs is very high. Added to these are the so-called literates who can just sign; with this the percentage of illiterates rises much higher. It should be inferred then that the emerging leaders of Gram Panchayats and their vision of socio-economic development and empowerment of people, specially women, would be a narrow one.

A look at the economic status of the PRRs shows that the urban General category district of Indore has the highest percentage of yearly income of Rs 60,000 and above; Jhabua, the rural ST district has the lowest percentage in this slab. Yearly income of Rs 10,000 and below has the reverse trend. Ujjain SC district has middle position in both the slabs. Similar is the situation in case of assets. The PRRs of Indore district have more assets vis-à-vis the PRRs of Ujjain and Jhabua. More income and more assets were expected to generate more confidence in the PRRs of Indore district but the ground realities did not exhibit that. PRRs of all the three districts were found lacking in confidence in making decision for development for their Gram Panchayats.

General Awareness of Panchayat Leaders

An assessment of awareness of PRRs about the Panchayat system and its goal of need based planning from below, for rural development culminating in participatory democracy and self-governance does not depict an encouraging picture either. PRRs firmly declare that they were elected on the basis of villagers' support and not on caste or wealth or party affiliation. They emphasize their personal identity/public image as leaders. However, their overall awareness of the provisions of the 73rd Constitutional Amendment Act, 1993 as regards the working of the system, the various 'kosh' (funds), the committees, the Gram Sabha its working process and functions, the responsibilities bestowed and the ultimate goals to be achieved do not evoke enthusiastic response from them. They visualize their role in Gram Sabha to the extent of giving 'suggestion for development, and 'participating in discussions', quite unaware of their leadership role of taking decisions for development and directing the system to self-governance for equity, social justice and peace. Caste Panchayats do influence their activities significantly in the area of conflict resolution. Though the PRRs deny the existence of Caste Panchayats, they accept the supportive influence of such Panchayats. Beneficiary selection is the main activity which attracts village community at large and the PRRs in particular.

Thus the level of such poor awareness calls for the need of intensive, exhaustive and continued training not only of the PRRs but also of the members of Gram Sabha which is constitutionally the supreme body in Gram Panchayats.

Political Background of the PRRs

We tried to assess whether PRRs had any political background before they entered Panchayat politics, and also, whether they were ever elected to the positions of Sarpanch, Upsarpanch or Panch. For personal political background, 'yes' response of Jhabua, Ujjain and Indore district PRRs was 21.4 per cent, 27.1 per cent and 23.1 per cent respectively and the negative response was 78.6 per cent in Jhabua, 72.9 per cent in Ujjain and 76.9 per cent in Indore. This scenario indicates that most of the emerging new Panchayat leaders were raw, beginners in the arena of politics/public life. Those who held Panchayat posts before the implementation of the 1993 Act in the earlier regimes were, Sarpanch 17.9 per cent, Upsarpanch 10.7 per cent and Panch 71.4 per cent respectively.

They endorse that their previous political experience has helped them in better understanding of the legal processes and the political dynamics at the grassroots and thus assuming a more fruitful leadership role than the one in their previous terms, but their total count is about just one-third.

Manifestation of political party affiliations of a person is related to political actions he/she undertakes. Such actions are participation in political activities, rallies or acquaintances with higher up leaders like Janpad and Zilla Panchayat. chairpersons, local MLAs, MPs and Ministers. Such relationships have been denied by most of the PRRs; only the committed party loyalists look for the party bosses while taking decisions in line with the party they belong to.

The positive side of contacts with party leaders is that such contacts, particularly of the illiterates, may help PRRs in raising their political awareness which may be useful for the local community. But as ground realities indicate, PRRs of all the three districts view their political contacts with men of influence or party leaders only from the point of view of financial support which they can procure for development work of their Gram Panchayats.

The aforesaid account has to be understood in the context of the political party affiliations of PRRs. Madhya Pradesh has two party system, consisting of Indian National Congress and Bhartiya Janata Party (BJP), and the loyalties of most of the PRRs are attached either to Congress or BJP. As such the political background of PRRs is cast in the ideological framework of either of the two parties which colours their world view of Panchayat system also. Jhabua has 51.4 per cent, Ujjain 31.8 per cent and Indore 39.7 per cent PRRs with Congress party affiliations and 28.6 per cent, 27.1 per cent and 14.9 per cent with BJP affiliations respectively. This depicts that the tribal district of Jhabua has the highest percentage of Congress affiliation and the General category urban district of Indore is dominated by BJP affiliation. Quite surprising it is to note that 41.2 per cent PRRs of Ujjain district respond that they have no political affiliations with either of the two parties. Thus it is quite clear that the two major national political parties have entered the portals of grassroots political institutions and, their ideologies determine their decisions about the issues related to the local Panchayat/s.

In short, sharp party differences between Congress and BJP was found in the field and this has hampered the realization of the goals and ambitions of the 73rd Constitutional Amendment Act, 1993. During the third Panchayat elections in 2005, 1,36134 Panch were elected unopposed out of 4,43,229, and 291 Sarpanch were elected unopposed out of a total of 517. The curse of party affiliations and muscle power are to be considered as the reasons of this political malady.

Not only in elections but also in day-to-day management of Panchayat affairs the political parties have penetrated at the grassroots level. This has greatly hampered the emergence of grassroots leadership on its own. Village level communities were expected to rise above the ideological perspectives of political parties so far as the ground level local issues of welfare are concerned. Mahatma

Gandhi, the great proponent of Gram Swaraj also admonished this view. An important point to note is that the Act visualizes party less democracy at the grassroots.

The political contacts of PRRs is a significant issue in this connection. PRRs mostly maintain contacts with local MLAs because they have an MLA fund which they easily sanction for development works in Gram Panchayats and thus nurture their constituencies. MPs and Ministers too have such funds but the PRRs inform that it is very difficult to contact them and much more difficult to get a share from their funds as their constituencies cover a larger area of the three-tier system of Panchayat Raj. The PRRs prefer to be in touch with the chairperson of Janpad Panchayat rather than with chairperson of Zilla Panchayat. This again has financial dimensions as the Janpad Panchayat is the body which finally releases the sanctioned funds of all types to Gram Panchayats. Other social or political leaders are considered as traditional power rivals of the PRRs, and PRRs like to keep a safe distance from them. During the field investigations it was found that the PRRs, particularly Sarpanch and Upsarpanch could be easily contacted at Janpad Panchayat office rather than in their own Gram Panchayats. Most of them have their own motorcycles which facilitate their mobility for this purpose.

The PRRs agree that the political persons with whom they have contacts have supporting influence on their work. However, the total count of such contacts is so low that the PRRs drawing benefit of their contacts for their Panchayats remains insignificant. This also obstructs PRRs in receiving the benefit of experience of contact with political persons/representatives, which would otherwise support their activity in a practical way.

A majority of the PRRs, in all the three districts do not contact even the government officials, including the district collector, the CEO of Janpad or the BDOs for issues related to Panchayat affairs. This shows that PRRs lack the culture of public/official relationships which are otherwise useful in getting help in Panchayat matters and in promoting their image and influence in public life. Thus, the emerging leadership of the

Gram Panchayats is unaware of the utility and possible benefits of the practice of maintaining social-political contacts with district authorities in matters related to the Panchayats. Of course, they do keep contacts with officials/political persons like Janapd CEO, Janpad chairperson or MLA of the area as these are the persons who hold the strings of purse; they have the power of releasing funds for Gram Panchayats. Such a behaviour is indicative of the fact that their vision is confined to short-term immediate financial benefits. This is to reiterate that the 73rd Constitutional Amendment Act, 1993 has opened wider vistas of genuine development of the villages but the short-sighted leadership has failed to take full advantage of the constructive ventures.

Panchayat Leaders and Rural Development

The 73rd Constitutional Amendment Act, 1993 and the conformity State Act of 1994 envisage emergence of such rural leadership which should be capable of ushering the process of rural development. In the light of high expectations of the Acts the ground realities at the grassroots level, the abilities and visions of the emerging rural leadership seem quite frustrating. Theoretically speaking, leadership is the quality of a person who has capacity of influencing people who can willingly come forward through group activities to achieve common goals of the community. However, realization of developmental goals depends on knowledge, skills, attitudes and personal relations of a leader, because ultimately it is the leader who is supposed to plan and execute development works, procure necessary funds for such projects and coordinate a variety of community programmes to ensure general welfare of the people. Madhya Pradesh, along with Bihar and Rajasthan, is generally regarded as a 'BIMARU' state, and the general welfare of the community is rendered much harder a task to achieve.

What is needed of the people's representatives is their awareness/knowledge of the constitutional structure of Panchayat and its objectives, and their willingness to proceed toward these objectives whole-heartedly. This includes overall rural development so far as Panchayat Raj is concerned. When the PRRs of the three chosen districts were asked about the issues of development, a majority of PRRs—78.7 per cent—responded that in meetings of Gram Sabha they did make 'suggestions for development' and 'participated in discussions' for the welfare of local communities, but they could not assume an active constructive role either in the field or in deciding the area, subject, process, agency, etc., for development of their Gram Panchayats. Summarizing PRRs responses regarding 'development', we may say that their concept of development is limited to some infrastructural facilities for the Panchayat, few kilometres of construction or repair of rural roads, 'kharanjas'/minor bridges or culverts, water tanks, construction of school building, establishment of primary health centre, Panchayat Bhavan building, community hall for the villagers' meetings, construction of houses for the poor of the village. An estimate of such so-called developmental activities also shows that education for them is just erecting a one or two room building for the school, without bothering about such issues and necessities as non-availability and recruitment of committed and efficient teaching staff; irregular and inadequate attendance of school children; even midday meals not drawing more students to schools; and the quality of their results. Similar is the scenario on other issues of development.

Health-related hazards like polio, malaria, HIV are simply ignored by the PRRs. Just a room for health centre and biweekly visit of health visitor constitute their view of catering to the health of the community. One of he significant indices of development, better quality of health and education, find little or no place in their scheme of development.

It may be stated with some emphasis that the idea of emerging leadership about rural 'development' is misplaced, narrow and distorted. The leadership is unaware of a plethora of central and state government schemes and projects of rural development, human resource development and of all round human environmental development, it reflects a gloomy scenario. However, all such shortcomings of their view of development is the end result of their age old social, economic and cultural deprivations. The rural generation that has entered the arena of local governance does not have any experience of either self-rule or self-management. Above all, lack of funds is the most critical issue which the PRRs avoid. MP and MLA funds or state government grant is insufficient in the absence of indigenous financial resources which the PRRs are not ready to generate.

However, this is not to say that no development schemes have been implemented in the Panchayats, but most of these are planned and implemented by funds, functionaries and even infrastructure other than the Panchayat system. This creates great hurdles in the emergence of Gram Panchayat leadership and also people's participation in development activities.

Women PRRs and Ground Realities

Indian Constitution aims at providing social justice and equity to the citizens of India. The focus is on the marginalized ones in respect of caste, class and sex. Women being the most discriminated against, have had no social, political or economic opportunities and rights. They live under the bondage of traditional social customs. Mahatma Gandhi was the great proponent of women's rights, he boldly declared that 'Swaraj' could not be attained without the participation of women in social-political life of the community. Great efforts of social-political reformers did create a space for women but could not ensure their entry into political life either as active participants or as decision-makers. The 73rd Constitutional Amendment Act, 1993 was a revolutionary step in this direction as it provided 33 per cent reservation of seats for women of all categories in Panchayats. Thirty three per cent seats of Sarpanch and Panch in Gram Panchayats were also reserved for women, thus involving them in political life at key positions of grassroots level. How women PRRs of ST, SC and General category operate can be viewed on the basis of their performance in the operationalization of Gram Panchayat.

Field observations make it very clear that though women have been constitutionally empowered, yet socio-cultural limitations still persist, which thwarts their genuine empowerment and advancement. Such limitations are more prominent in ST, SC, poor and socially backward women PRRs. Reservation has provided positions to women in Panchayats, but in practice they have no real share in decision-making as the males still hold the strings of power. Women PRRs are 'proxy representatives'. Most women PRRs honestly believe and frankly express that de facto wielders of their political powers in Panchayats are their male relatives—husband, father-in-law, brother-in-law, son, nephew or some dominant caste leader. In majority of instances women PRRs responded in right earnest that questions about Panchayat affairs be addressed to male members, the real runners of the show. Violent atrocities against women Panch/Sarpanch include their stripping, brutal attacks on them, heaps of insults and the like. Thus the fruits of Panchayat Raj system cannot be attained as long as women's position in Panchayat System is not improved and genuine power of decision-making is not bestowed on them.

Challenges

It is quite clear that the implementation of the system at the grass-roots is far from smooth, challenges arise at structural level vertically as also horizontally and as well at practical levels. The 73rd Constitutional Amendment Act, 1993 though provided a structure improving upon the earlier experiences and the suggestion of the various review committees, the path is hazardous to tread for the emerging Gram Panchayat leadership and also for the rural masses. Power devolved from above keeps tight the vertical hold of higher level units. Horizontally, Caste Panchayats, traditional leaders, influential persons, self-help groups, watershed committees (where operational), money lenders, priests operate parallel to Gram Panchayat. State and central government plans and even international schemes for rural upliftment work simultaneously in Gram Panchayat space with their own infrastructure and funds.

Gram Panchayats being the lowest level unit in the Panchayat Raj system can only reap the fruits in the residual resort.

Within the Panchayat the proximity of Panchayat Raj representatives to their constituents tells upon their capabilities to meet the constant demands and aspirations of the community. The masses being unaware of politico-legal difficulties hold PRRs responsible for all the deprivations they face.

Reservation provisions, though intended to bring the marginalized ones in the mainstream, they operate within the socio-cultural limitations of their groups. SC and ST people have not been able to become the integral parts of the general community. Women PRRs are still the victims of male domination in such subtle ways that it cannot be noticed on the surface. They remain proxy representatives despite their constitutional empowerment.

The need based plan that emanates at Gram Panchayat level has to be routed through Janapad and Zilla Panchayats to reach the state plan and ultimately the national plan. In the process the plan of Gram Panchayat looses its identity in the final shape to come. This exposes the paradox of decentralized decision-making and centralized plan.

Gram Sabha visualized as the supreme body to plan and control Panchayat development, and all other activities, falls much short of its conceptualized role. Finance poses a still greater constraint as the Gram Panchayats rely on state funds only. They avoid generating their indigenous financial resources as these involve taxation for which community at large is resistant. Again the centrality of globalization and decentralization of powers require immense acumen on the part of PRRs to turn it to the best advantage of village development schemes. The PRRs—novice in the game—are unable to face the challenge which has a negative impact in the form of excessive loans, bankruptcy and mental strain. Bureaucracy is not very congenial towards the Panchayat system and poses many technical problems before the PRRs. State and national politics infested with violence and corruption has percolated to Gram Panchayats also. Though visualized as party-less democracy at the grassroots, the evils of party politics have affected the Gram Panchayats adversely.

Training

Whichever way we look the study sends an important message that PRRs should be given adequate training to handle with efficiency and integrity the affairs of Gram Panchayats. The primary need is to make them aware of the main provisions of the Act and the process of its operationalization. The high percentage of illiteracy of PRRs calls for the translation of the provisions of the Act in local dialects and their oral presentations. This would give them a fair idea of what they are expected to do. The formal training imparted to them by government agencies and NGOs is insufficient. Training has to be intensive, exhaustive, goal-oriented and in small groups.

Again, imparting training to a few elected Panchayat leaders is not enough. Timely meetings of the Gram Sabha should be held to acquaint them with the do's and don'ts of public responsibilities related to the governance of the Panchayats. The idea behind this is to build a sound infrastructure of public life with civic education of the people, in this way the superstructure is bound to be viable and people-friendly. Public education of this kind at the grassroots would be a boon to the larger interests and training of women, the poor and the dalits. This would be a right step in drawing in a group of people who have so far remained outside the frame of socio-political structure. An overwhelming majority of PRRs admit that they have received short-term training in Panchayat processes only. Training in agriculture, environmental protection, water conservation, etc., have not been imparted, the most needed ones at grassroots level.

Training is required for raising PRRs' educational and information levels making them more knowledgeable about the Panchayat system in a holistic manner with a view to inculcating in them the values and norms of the new socio-political order. This would give them training in wise decision-making about developmental problems of the community that they represent. Thus training on issues like agriculture, water management, forest and environmental conservation and resource mobilization of men and material, if imparted properly, can make PRRs capable of taking care of ground level problems of the community. This would make them the true representative leaders of the communities as there is a symbiotic relationship between abilities of PRRs and their training needs.

Thus, the kind of training delineated here would take care of (a) the elected PRRs, and (b) the members of Gram Sabha.

The scenario, however, is not altogether gloomy. The main task of rural reconstruction of creating self-reliant, self-governing rural communities on the vast expanse of Indian territory is not an easy undertaking, specially when the rural masses were marginalized from the entire power structure for long. Moreover, the rural areas located far away from the mainstream developed areas are still to get the required exposure. The Panchayat System passing through its nascent stage requires some more time to improve. More of training programmes, political education, economic advancement can bring the rural people to centre stage. Besides, more of social awakening can prepare the ground to strengthen the roots of Panchayat Raj system in Malwa and in Madhya Pradesh at large, paving the way for the emergence of dynamic leadership. A significant point to be noted is that Gram Panchayats have unique problems as per their categorywise profile and also as an individual unit. Accordingly, they face different challenges along with some common ones and these differences need to be catered for individually.

Formal education of quality from time to time to tone up PRRs awareness and understanding of Panchayat management, wardwise meetings, direct approach to PRRs by government for policy matters and funds with information disseminated to community at large could be of immense help to PRRs. Panchayat Raj system would greatly benefit if the practices of Panchayat working are institutionalized to enable the community at large to participate in the development process and thus strive to achieve the declared objectives of 73rd Constitutional Amendment Act 1993.

Bibliography

Primary Sources

Census of India, 2001.

District Statistical Book, 2003, District Statistical Office, Indore, 2004.

District Statistical Book, 2003, District Statistical Office, Jhabua, 2004.

District Statistical Book, 2003, District Statistical Office, Ujjain, 2004.

Food and Agriculture Organisation of UN, Decentralisation: The Indian Experience, Rome, 1997.

Government of India: Report of the Task Force on Devolution of Powers and Functions upon PRIs, 2001, New Delhi, Ministry of Rural Development.

Government of Karnataka, *Panchayati Raj in Karnataka*, Bangalore, Department of Rural Development and Panchayati Raj, 1997.

Madhya Pradesh Panchayat Raj Act, 1993, Gazetteer of Madhya Pradesh (Extra Ordinary) Part 2, Section 3(two) dated January 25, 1994.

Official Records of Gram Panchayats chosen for study.

Participatory Research in Asia, Strengthening Local Self Governance in India, Finances of Panchayats in Madhya Pradesh, Madhya Pradesh: Study sponsored by UNICEF, PRIA, Delhi, July 2000.

Seventy Third Constitutional Amendment Act, 1993, Gazetteer of India (Extra Ordinary) Part 2, Section 3(two) dated April 24, 93.

Books

Alagh, Y. and Buch, D., *Sustainable Development: India 2020*, United Nations University/IAS, Tokyo, 2000. www.fao.org/docnep/005/ac623e/ac623e07.htm

Ambedkar, S.N. and Nagendra, Shailaja, *Women Empowerment and Panchayati Raj*, ABD Publisher, Jaipur, 2005.

Aziz, Abdul, *Decentralised Planning: The Karnataka Experiment*, Sage, New Delhi, 1993.

Barik, Bishnu C. and Sahoo, Umesh C. (eds.), *Panchayati Raj Institutions and Rural Development: Narratives on Inclusion of Excluded*, Rawat Publications, Jaipur, 2008.

Begin, Monique, Towards a Critical Mass: Women in Politics, J.P. Naik Memorial Lecture, Centre for Women's Development Studies, New Delhi, 1998.

Bhargava, B.S., *Grassroots Leadership: A Study of Leadership in Panchayati Raj Institution*, Ashish, New Delhi, 1979.

Bhatt, Ashish, *Loktantric Vikendrikaran Evam Janjatiya Neturtva*, (Hindi), Rawat Publications, Jaipur/Delhi, 2002.

Bhatt, G.D., *Emerging Leadership Pattern in Rural India*, MD Publications, New Delhi, 1994.

Buch, N., *From Oppression to Assertion: A Study of Panchayats and Women in Madhya Pradesh, Rajasthan and Uttar Pradesh*, CWDS, New Delhi, 1999.

Cartwright, D. et al., *Group Dynamics: Research and Theory*, Harper and Row, New York, 1968.

Chakravarty, K. and Bhattacharya, S.K., *Leadership Factions and Panchayati Raj*, Rawat, Jaipur, 1993.

Chaudhari, D.S., *Emerging Rural Leadership in Indian States*, Manthan, New Delhi, 1981.

Chaudhary, S.N., *Dalit and Tribal Leadership in Panchayats*, Concept, New Delhi, 2004.

Cheema, G.S. and Rondinelli, D.A. (eds.), *Decentralisation and Development: Policy Implementation in Developing Countries*, Sage, London, 1993.

Collins, Larry and Lapierre, Dominique, *Freedom at Midnight*, Vikas, New Delhi, 1976.

Dahl, Robert A., *Democracy and Its Critics*, Yale, New Haven, 1988.

—, *The Ambiguity of Leadership*, New Haven and London, 1966. http://home.uchicago:edu/abtm1-03-04/dahl.doc

Darshankar, Arjun Rao, *Leadership in Panchayati Raj: A Study of Beed District*, Panchsheel, Jaipur, 1979.

Das, Pravakar, *Emerging Pattern of Leadership in Tribal India*, Manak, New Delhi, 1994.

DePree, Max, *Leadership is an Art*, Dell Trade Paperback, New York, 1989.

Dreze, Jean and Sen, Amartya, *India: Development and Participation*, Oxford, New Delhi, 2002.

Dubey, M.P. and Padalia, Munni, *Democratic Decentralisation and Panchayati Raj in India*, Anamika, New Delhi, 2002.

Dubin, Robert (ed.), *Human Relation in Administration: The Sociology of Organisation with Reading and Cases*, Harper Collins, New York, 1951.

Dwivedi, R.S., *Madhya Pradesh Panchayat Raj Adhiniyam*, Suvidha Law House, Bhopal, 2000.

Elwell, E.A. and Malik, L.G., *Leadership: A New Perspective*, R&K Publishing House, New Delhi, 1974.

Fisher, Julie, *Non-Governments: NGOs and the Political Development of the Third World*, Jaipur, Rawat, 2003.

Prabu, R.K., Compiler, *India of My Dreams: Mahatma Gandhi* Navjivan Trust, Ahmedabad, 1947.

Gangrade, K.D., *Emerging Patterns of Leadership*, Rachna, Delhi, 1974.

Garth, H.H. and Mills, C.W. (eds.), *Essays in Sociology*, Oxford University Press, London, 1946.

Gaud, K.K., *Bharat mein Gramin Netritva ka Udayeemaan Swaroop*, Manak, New Delhi, 1997.

George, Homans, *The Human Group*, Harcourt, Brace and Company, New York, 1950.

Ghosh, B.N. and Maity, *Creativity of the People at the Grassroot*, Mimeo, India Statistical Institute, Calcutta, 1993.

Ghosh, B.N., *Rural Leadership and Development*, Mohit, New Delhi, 1996.

Gouldner, Alvin W. (ed.), *Studies in Leadership*, Harper and Row, New York, 1950.

Gupta, A.K., *Emerging Pattern of Political Leadership*, Mittal, Delhi, 1991.

Hemphill, J.K., *Leadership Acts*, Columbus: Ohio State University, Research Foundation, 1954.

Hunter, Floyed, *Community Power Structure*, Chapel Hill, University of North Carolina Press, 1953.

Hust, Evelin, *Women's Political Representation and Empowerment in India*, Manohar, New Delhi, 2004.

Isaac, Thomas T.M. et al., *Local Democracy and Development: People's Campaign for Decentralised Planning in Kerala*, Left Word Books, New Delhi, 2000.

Jain, S.C., *Grass Without Roots: Rural Development Under Government Auspices*, Sage, New Delhi, 1999.

Jennings, H.H., *Leadership and Isolation*, Longmans, London, 1950.

Jha, S.N. and Mathur, P.C. (eds.), *Decentralisation and Local Politics*, Sage, New Delhi, 1999.

Joshi, R.P. and Narwani, G.S., *Panchayat Raj in India: Emerging Trends Across States*, Rawat, Jaipur, 2002.

Joshi, S., *Panchayaton Ka Vitta Poshan*, (in Hindi) MPISSR, Ujjain, 1998.

Kashyap, Subhash, *Blue Print of Political Reform*, Shipra, Delhi, 2003.

Kaushik, Sushila, *Women and Panchayati Raj*, Har Anand, New Delhi, 1996.

Lasswell, Harold D. and Kaplan, Abraham, *Power and Society: A Framework of Political Enquiry*, Yale University Press, New Haven, 1950.

Lasswell, Harold D., Lerner, Daniel and Rothwell, C. Easten, *The Comparative Study of Elites*, Stanford University Press, Stanford, 1952.

Mandal, Amal, *Women in Panchayati Raj Institutions*, Kanishka, New Delhi, 2003.

Mathew, George, *Panchayati Raj*, Concept, New Delhi, 1994.

Meenakshi, J. (ed.), *Women and Panchayati Raj*, Omega, New Delhi, 2007.

Meenakshisundaram, S.S., *Decentralisation in Developing Countries*, Concept, New Delhi, 1994.

Mehta, R.S., *Rural Leadership and Panchayat: A Behavioural Approach*, Bahri, Delhi, 1978.

Mehta, Shibrathan, *Emerging Pattern of Rural Leadership*, Indian Institute of Advanced Study, Simla, 1972.

Mishra, S.N., Kumar, Lokesh and Pal, Chaitali (eds.), *New Panchayati Raj in Action*, Mittal, New Delhi, 1996.

Mishra, S.N., *Pattern of Emerging Leadership in India*, Associated Book Agency, Patna, 1977.

Moore, Jr. Barrington, *Social Origins of Dictatorship and Democracy*, Beacon Press, Boston, 1993.

Mukarji, Nirmal et al. (eds.), *Peoples Representatives and Bureaucracy: The Interface in Panchayati Raj*, Concept, New Delhi, 1995.

Murthy, Rajani K. (ed.), *Building Women's Capacities: Interventions in Gender Transformations*, Sage, New Delhi, 2001.

Nehru, B.K., *Nice Guys Finish Second*, Vikas, New Delhi, 1997.

Palanithurai, G., *Dynamics of New Panchayat Raj System in India*, Vols. I and II, Concept, New Delhi, 2002.

—, *Grassroots Democracy in Indian Society*, Concept, New Delhi, 2000.

—, *Leadership Matters in Grassroots Governance*, Pathfinders Series, 1 to 24, Gandhigram, 2004–2006.

—, "Status of Women Leaders in Local Bodies: Experience from Tamilnadu", paper presented at the Seminar on Women in Local Governance, ISST, Bangalore, 1995.

Purohit, B.R., "Panchayat Raj System in Scheduled Areas of Madhya Pradesh" in Palanithurai, G. (ed.), *Dynamics of New Panchayat Raj System in India*, Vol. I, Concept, New Delhi, 2002.

Rani, Neelam, *New Panchayati Raj Institution: A Sociological Study*, Sunrise, New Delhi, 2008.

Raphael, Jos C., *Decentralised Planning in India*, Anmol, New Delhi, 2000.

Rose, Kalima, *Where Women are Leaders: The Sewa Movement in India*, Zed Books, London, 1992.

Ross, M. and Hendry, C.E., *New Understanding of Leadership: A Survey and Application of Research*, Harper and Row, New York, 1957.

Sathi, K., *Empowerment of Women*, Anmol, New Delhi, 1998.

Satpathy, N., *Sustainable Development: An Alternative Paradigm*, Karnavati, Ahmedabad.

Seth, Pravin, *Women Empowerment and Politics in India*, Karnavati, Ahmedabad, 1998.

Sharma, K.C., *Leadership in Panchayati Raj*, Printwell, Jaipur, 1996.

Shiva, Vandana, *Staying Alive: Women, Ecology and Survival in India*, Zed Press, London, 1988.

Singh, Avtar, *Leadership Pattern and Village Structures*, Sterling, New Delhi, 1973.

Singh, Harjinder, *Village Leadership*, Sterling, New Delhi, 1968.

Singh, J.L., *Women and Panchayati Raj*, Sunrise, Delhi, 2005.

Singh, K.K. and Ali, S., *Role of Panchayati Raj Institutions for Rural Development*, Sarup & Sons, New Delhi, 2001.

Singhal, C.S., *Perception of Rural Problem: A Study of Panchayat Leadership in Haryana*, Haryana Institute of Rural Development, 1996.

Singla, Pamela, *Women's Participation in Panchayati Raj: Nature and Effectiveness*, Rawat Publications, Jaipur, 2007.

Sinha, A.K., *Panchayati Raj and Empowerment of Women*, Northern Book Centre, New Delhi, 2004.

Stogdill, Ralph, *Handbook of Leadership: A Survey of Theory and Research*, Free Press, New York, 1990.

Sudhakar, V., *New Panchayati Raj System: Local Self Government in Community Development*, Mangaldeep, Jaipur, 2002.

Tead, O., *The Art of Leadership*, Inc., McGraw Hill, New York, 1956.

Thapar, Romila (ed.), *India: Another Millennium*, Penguin India, Delhi, 2000.

Trivedi, B.R., *Women and Panchayati Raj*, Cyber Tech Publishers, New Delhi, 2008.

Varma, B.M., *Rural Leadership in a Welfare Society*, Mittal, New Delhi, 1996.

Varma, R.K., *Political Leadership*, Amar, New Delhi, 1991.

Vidya, K.C., *Political Empowerment of Women at the Grassroots*, Kanishka, New Delhi, 1997.

Vidyarthi, L.P. (ed.), *Leadership in India*, Asia, New Delhi, 1967.

Vohra, Gautam, *The New Leadership from Panchayat to Parliament*, Indian Publisher, New Delhi, 2004.

Vyasulu, Vinod, *Panchayats, Democracy and Development*, Rawat, Jaipur, 2003.

Weiner, Myron, "Some Hypotheses on the Politics of Modernisation in India", in Park, R.L. and Tinkers, I. (eds.), *Leadership and Political Institutions in India*, Oxford University Press, London, 1957.

Wriston, Walter, *The Twilight of Sovereignty*, Sribners, New York, 1992.

Journals

Agnihotri, Harendra, "Panchayat Leadership", *Radical Humanist*, Vol. 37, No. 8, Nov. 1973.

Bandyopadhyay, D., "People's Participation in Planning: Kerala Experiment", *Economic and Political Weekly*, Sept. 27, 1999.

Chathukulam, Jos and John, M.S., "Empowerment of Women Panchayat Members: Learning from Kerala (India)", *Asia Journal of Women Studies*, Vol. 6, No. 4, 2000.

Chatterji, Biswas, "Leadership in Panchayat Raj", *Modern Review*, Vol. 117, No. 3, March 1965.

Conyers, D., "Decentralisation: The Latest Fashion in Development Administration", *Public Administration and Development*, Vol. 3, 1993.

Drucker, Peter F., "Beware Charisma: The Changing Demands on Political Leadership", in *The New Realities*, Routledge, London, 1989.

Dube, Leela, "Leadership in Community Development and Decentralised Democracy", *Kurukshetra*, Vol. 14, No. 9, June 1966.

George, Mathew, "Institutions of Self Government in India: Towards Multilevel Federalism", *Review of Development and Change*, Vol. II, No. 2, July–December 1997.

Ghosh, Bholanath and De, Utpalkumar, "Leadership and the Performance of Panchayat in Rural Development: An Experience from Tripura", *Man and Development*, Vol. XXV, No. 4, Dec. 2003.

Gibb, Cecil A., "The Principles and Traits of Leadership", *Journal of Abnormal Social Psychology*, 1947.

Harris, John, "Renewing Development and Deepening Democracy", *Frontline*, Sept. 1, 2001.

Isaac, Thomas T.M. and Harilal, K.N. "Planning for Empowerment: People's Campaign for Decentralised Planning in Kerala", *Economic and Political Weekly*, Jan. 4–11, 1997.

Kashyap, Subhash, "Institutionalisation of Grassroots Governance", *Grassroots Governance Journal*, Published by Academy of Grassroots Studies and Research, India, Tirupati, Vol. 1, No. 1, January–June, 2003.

Klibanoff, P. and Morduch, J., "Decentralisation, Externalities and Efficiency", *Review of Economic Studies*, Vol. 62, 1995.

Krishnakumar, R., "Derailing Decentralisation: Kerala Experiment", *Frontline* (Chennai), Dec. 31, 2004.

Lieten, G.K., "Panchayat in Uttar Pradesh: Namesake Members", *Economic and Political Weekly*, Vol. 31, No. 39, 1996.

Lieten, G.K., "Panchayat Leaders in a West Bengal District", *Economic and Political Weekly*, Vol. 23, No. 40, Oct. 1, 1988.

Manor, James, "Madhya Pradesh Experiments with Direct Democracy", *Economic and Political Weekly*, March 3, 2001.

Mathur, Kuldeep, "Challenges of Decentralisation: The Politics of Panchayati Raj", *Social Action*, Vol. 47, January–March 1997.

Nambiar, Malini, "Making the Gram Sabha Work", *Economic and Political Weekly*, August 18, 2001.

Mukhopadhyay, Asim, "Kultikri: West Bengal's Only All Women Gram Panchayat", *Economic and Political Weekly*, June 3, 1995.

Narayan, Iqbal, "Democratic Decentralisation and Rural Leadership: The Rajasthan Experiment", *Asian Survey*, Vol. IV, No. 8, August 1964.

Narayan, Iqbal, "Necessary Evil or Mixed Blessings? Politics in Panchayat Raj", *Kurukshetra*, Vol. 16, No. 3, December 1967.

Pai, Sudha, "Pradhans in the New Panchayats: Field Notes from Meerut", *Economic and Political Weekly*, Vol. 33, No. 18, 1998.

Pant, S., "The Role of Panchayat Leadership", *Quarterly Journal of Local Self-Government Institute*, Vol. 50, No. 2, October–December 1979.

Roy, Aruna, "From Bureaucracy to Peoples' Movement", *Lokayan Bulletin*, Vol. 13, No. 1, 1997.

Sharma, Kumud, "Transformative Politics: Dimensions of Women's Participation in Panchayati Raj", *Indian Journal of Gender Studies*, Delhi, Vol. 5, No.1, 1998.

Shamim, Ishrat and Kumari Ranjana, "Gender and Local Governance: A New Discourse in Development", South Asian Network of Economic Research Institute, Dhaka and New Delhi, 2002. http://unpan1.un.org/intradoc/groups/public/documents/apcit/unpan

Singh, R.N.P. and Singh, B.P., "Panchayat Raj in Bhagalpur District: Study of Social Participation of Elected Leaders", *Quarterly Journal of the Local Self-Government Institute*, Vol. 43, No. 3, January–March 1973.

Suri, K.C., "Telugu Desham Party: Rise and Prospects for Future", *Economic and Political Weekly*, April 3–9/10–16, Vol. XXXIX, Nos. 14 and 15, 2004.

Tarkunde, V.M., "Partyless Politics and Peoples' State: A Picture for Public Discussion", *The Radical Humanist*, Vol. 66, No. 10, 2002.

Varma, B.M., "Socio-Economic Status of Panchayat Raj Leaders", *Interdiscipline*, Vol. 8, No. 2, Summer 1971.

Vyasulu, P. and Vyasulu, V., "Women in Panchayati Raj: Grassroots Democracy in Malgudi", *Economic and Political Weekly*, December 25, 1999.

Index